THE **TWINS PLATOON**

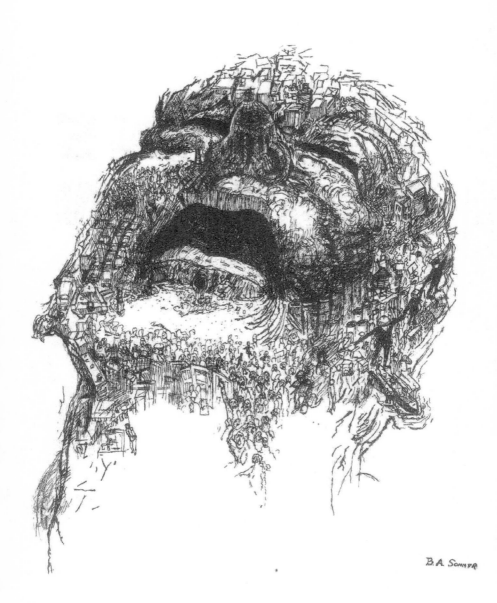

B. A. Sommer

THE **TWINS PLATOON**

AN EPIC STORY OF
YOUNG MARINES AT WAR IN VIETNAM

CHRISTY W. SAURO JR.

ZENITH
PRESS

This edition published by Zenith Press, an imprint
of MBI Publishing Company, Galtier Plaza, Suite 200,
380 Jackson Street, St. Paul, MN, 55101-3885 USA.

MBI Publishing Company Books are also available
at discounts for in bulk quantities for industrial
or sale-promotional use. For details write to Special
Sales Manager at MBI Publishing Company,
Galtier Plaza, Suite 200, 380 Jackson Street, St. Paul,
MN, 55101-3885 USA

Cover and Layout by Rochelle Schultz Brancato

Cover photograph: As incoming North Vietnamese
artillery targets the Khe Sanh medical-evacuation
staging area, Robert Cusick leans over a stretcher and
shields a wounded Marine awaiting evacuation.
—*Robert Ellison/Black Star*

Frontispiece: *Anguish* by Bruce Sommer
—*Author's collection*

ISBN: 0-7603- 2387-9
ISBN-13: 978-0-7603- 2387-8

Printed in the United States

CONTENTS

FOREWORD

I served thirty-one years on active duty as a Marine and led infantry units in close combat in Korea. I also went through boot camp as a private in 1951 during the height of the Korean War. Christy W. Sauro's *The Twins Platoon* tells a story that every Marine—past, present, and future—can relate to. It's a story that every American should read. If they are like me they'll read it with tears in their eyes and pride mixed with sadness in their hearts. It tells the individual stories of a group of young men (the best America had to offer, although that was not recognized at the time) who answered their country's call, fought bravely and well, survived the revilement of the antiwar activists, and quietly rebuilt their lives—most of them succeeded. Nonetheless, the scars remain and Sauro powerfully tells their stories.

Skip Schmidt, one of the members of the Minnesota Twins Platoon, served in my battalion, "The Magnificent Bastards." Skip was medically discharged as the result of wounds received at the Battle of Dai Do in May 1968. He committed suicide in 1972. Skip was a victim of post traumatic stress disorder, a condition that was not recognized at that time by the Veterans Administration. He was posthumously awarded the Silver Star for courageously risking his life to save other Marines.

As we continue to send our best young men and now young women, our sons and daughters, into harm's way to protect our freedom and secure freedom for others, America must know and recognize the human cost. Reading Christy Sauro's *The Twins Platoon* will help our countrymen and women learn this from the sacrifice of this valorous group of Marines.

Semper Fi,
William Weise
Brigadier General, USMC (ret.)

[Publisher's note: Brigadier General Weise served as a mortar section leader and rifle platoon commander in Company G, 3rd Battalion, 5th Marine Regiment, in Korea and in Vietnam as battalion commander of the 2nd Battalion, 4th Marines. While in Vietnam General Weise earned the Navy Cross "for extraordinary heroism" during the Battle of Dai Do.]

Telling a personal story of service is always inspiring, but telling a story about a group of young Americans and their willingness to serve their country in time of war is exceptionally telling. This is particularly true of the stories of those who volunteered to serve as Marines during the particularly trying times of the Vietnam War.

As a retired Marine Corps major general and recipient of the Medal of Honor, I know something about men in combat. I was truly moved by the ability of author Christy Sauro Jr. to tell the stories of his buddies and himself in such an affective manner. Author Sauro has demonstrated exceptional empathy in weaving together the stories of so many young Americans, all of whom were sworn in together on June 28, 1967, in pre-game ceremonies at a Minnesota Twins baseball game.

I encourage all Americans to read *The Twins Platoon*. It has human interest, integrity, and a reminder of what is the true cost of freedom. None of the Marines who graduated from boot camp as members of the Twins Platoon were Audi Murphy, but all were in the prime of life and gave it their best.

Semper Fi,
James E. Livingston
Major General, USMC (Ret.)

[Publisher's note: Major General Livingston was awarded the Medal of Honor "for conspicuous gallantry and intrepidity at the risk of his life above and beyond the call of duty" during the Battle of Dai Do while serving as commanding officer of Company E, 2nd Battalion, 4th Marine Regiment in May 1968.]

PREFACE

On June 28, 1967, a group of over one hundred young men, as well as four young women, were sworn into the Marine Corps at a Minnesota Twins baseball game. I was one of those young men. We were dubbed the "Twins Platoon." This book tells the story of what happened to us after we were cheered off the ball field. It tells of our Marine Corps training, our Vietnam experiences, and what happened to us when we returned home.

In late 1984, more than a decade after I had left the Marine Corps, the thought came to me to write a book about what happened to the Twins Platoon. At that time I knew very little about the fates of the others, because we were so widely dispersed following our boot camp graduation. My knowledge of the Vietnam War—of how our military actions fit into the larger picture—did not extend much beyond my own personal experience. Thinking about it I concluded that it would take years, maybe a lifetime, to gather the information and piece it together. Deciding that it was just too massive an undertaking, I dismissed the idea. Still, as the years passed, I found myself becoming increasingly inspired to take on the challenge. What started as an idea became a calling, and in the summer of 1990 I began to work in earnest on a written account of the Twins Platoon.

My boot camp graduation book contained the names of all my fellow recruits and served as the staring point for locating the others. I conducted my first interview on July 27, 1990. By the end of the year I had completed a total of twenty interviews. An additional twenty-two interviews took place over the next twelve years, with the last interview occurring on August 31, 2002. I prepared and used a questionnaire that contained a list of some twenty-eight open-ended questions. Some of the questions I asked were: "Why did you enlist in the Marine Corps?"; "What was your most memorable experience in training?"; "Were you sent to Vietnam?"; "Were you wounded in action?"; and "Give a chronology of your Vietnam service." I tape recorded the interviews and kept to myself any comments or information that I had until after the interview was completed. This way I avoided biasing the individual's responses. To further verify and accurately detail past events, I obtained, with their consent, each person's military and medical records. In only two cases were the records not complete. Important facts were also obtained from eyewitness accounts, testimonials, and the expanding body of knowledge being assembled by historians and authors. A number of published military histories were used as references. The *Battle for Hue TET 1968* and *The Magnificent Bastards* by Keith William Nolan, and *Khe Sanh: Siege in the Clouds* by Eric Hammel, were especially helpful in piecing together what happened to a number of my fellow recruits. The United States Marine Corps History and Museums Division provided useful information in the form of monthly unit command chronologies, after action reports, and various historical publications. Others resources included newspapers, magazines, periodicals, video tapes, personal letters, photos, and documents from the Minnesota State Department of Health.

By 1998 I had devoted some seventeen thousand hours toward the completion of the manuscript. Researching and writing the book consumed most of my spare time, vacations days, and weekends. At times I worked on it from early morning to late night. On average I worked some forty hours a week on it, while still working my regular full time job as an insurance agent.

I recently came across a high school paper written by my youngest daughter Sharon six years ago when she was fifteen years old. In her assignment paper she wrote about her father: "He wrote his book from when I was 6 to when I was age 15. So I have lived my life hearing about Vietnam. I have talked to and seen what an impact his book had on the families of the ones he wrote about. The book brought closure to part of their lives they did not know about. From a terrible war I have seen good come out of it."

I extensively interviewed twenty-seven recruits and fifteen of their loved ones. Along with the other information that I complied from various sources, this became too voluminous to fit into any one book. I decided not to look for the remaining recruits, because I was confident their experiences would closely mirror those already interviewed.

During the fifteen-year period that I worked to complete the manuscript, I never tired or lost interest in it. I was continually motivated by how things always seemed to fall into place. From finding lost documents to tracking down unknown witnesses, the results were always the same. I always ended up with whatever I needed. On December 11, 2002, I wrote in a Christmas letter to a number of people, "I have always felt very strongly that this manuscript will one day be published. At times it seems to have a life of its own." By the year 2000, I became so convinced that the publication of the book was inevitable that I went public, expressing this view to more than a hundred people over the next three years.

The final version of the manuscript attempts to reflect the breadth of the Marine Corps experience in Vietnam during 1968 to 1969. To do this I had to omit some very intense combat situations. The combat experiences of Jeffrey Barnes, Robert Barrette, Robert Carter, Edward Cirkl, Charles Rice, and Steve Thorkelson were no less compelling than those that follow. Each of these Marines served with distinction, saw many of their brothers-in-arms fall in battle, and lived to grieve over them. Other members of the Twins Platoon, such as James Bain, David Knutson, Terry Marlowe, Michael Ries, and John Gregor, served honorably while seeing little or no combat. It is important for the reader to know that for every Marine I have written about, there are many others whose experiences were similar but go unreported.

I am especially thankful to Cliff Bucan, Diane Finneman, Russ Mansmith, Ed Schryver, and William Weise for their strong words of encouragement on numerous occasions.

I am extremely grateful to the long list of people who unselfishly shared their deeply personal experiences with me so that I might have the privilege of sharing them with others. I strongly believe publication of their experiences will benefit and touch the lives of other people in more positive ways than I can imagine.

I am especially grateful to the following people for their professional help and guidance, most notably Keith Nolan, a leading author of Vietnam books, who out of the goodness of his heart took the time to read my manuscript and ultimately referred me to the literary agent E. J. McCarthy. The truth is he did this for an unpublished book writer he did not know, and he did it at a time when he was faced with a deadline on the publication of his eleventh book *House to House: Playing the Enemy's Game in Saigon, May 1968*. This speaks volumes about this individual. I am indebted to literary agent E. J. McCarthy, for taking on the manuscript and finding the best publisher for it. I am thankful for the editorial help provided by the acclaimed military author Eric Hammel and for his many valuable suggestions, which ultimately made the book more desirable for publication. I am very appreciative of the help provided by the editorial staff at MBI Publishing Company and, above all, that of editor Richard Kane. His attention to detail and knowledge of military history helped root out several small errors that would have detracted from the text.

In the realm of military books, one has only to go to the internet to see that these professionals are literary giants within their field. To have them involved in the publication of this book furthers my conviction that the story of the Twins Platoon was meant to be told.

Lastly, I am indebted to my wife JoAnn and my three children Chris III, Angela, and Sharon for their many years of understanding and support.

PART ONE:

BEFORE VIETNAM

1

THE MINNESOTA TWINS PLATOON

The fighting in Vietnam had been going on before most members of the Minnesota Twins Platoon were born. In 1965 the first American combat troops arrived in South Vietnam to help stop the spread of communism. By 1967 the fighting had escalated to the point where every able-bodied young male not enrolled in college was being called upon to fulfill his military obligation.

Dear Future Marine:
    This letter is being sent at this time to inform you that we plan to send all men scheduled for active duty in the month of June in one platoon. This platoon will go on active duty on the 28 of June, this is your new active duty date. On 28 June 1967, 150 future Marine applicants will be shipped in two platoons, to San Diego, California, recruit training depot. The Minnesota Twins Baseball Team is sponsoring this unit. They will be sworn in on TV at pre-game ceremonies that night, and be guests of the Twins at the game.

Gerald Baltes invited Candi Dupre to the game. She was good-looking and had a lot of spark. Conversations with her were always interesting and often intense. She wasn't afraid to speak her mind. Baltes liked her more than he cared to admit.

He wanted to be with her one last time before leaving for Marine boot camp.

Larry Buske came from the rural town of Hutchinson. He didn't always abide by the law. He never doubted that he could drive safely at speeds considerably higher than the posted limit, especially after he had been drinking.

When it came time to fulfill his military obligation, he already had his mind made up. He wanted to join the Marine Corps. Marine training was said to be the longest and hardest, which suited Buske just fine. He considered himself a hard guy and he liked the challenge. Another reason he favored the Marines was because several of his older buddies had joined the Marines a year earlier. They had left for boot camp right after graduating from high school in 1966. Now with his own graduation approaching, Buske could follow in their footsteps.

In March 1967 Buske walked into the Marine recruiter's office. There was no doubt in his mind that he was tough enough to be a Marine. In high school he had a reputation for being somebody people should not pick a fight with. After some small talk, the recruiter started asking questions. Buske answered each question carefully, fearing that for some unknown reason the Marine Corps wouldn't take him—a horrible thought that up until then had never entered his mind.

"Do you have a criminal record?"

"No," Buske fibbed. He was not certain what might be on his record.

"Why do you want to join the Marines?" the recruiter asked.

Buske made it clear that he knew all about the reputation of the Marine Corps. He told the recruiter he knew Marines had to be tough and that their training was the hardest of all. "In fact, some of the older guys I hung around with in high school joined the Marines. Joe Seller, Tom Healy, and Buck Defreeze went in after they graduated."

"In 1966?" the recruiter asked.

"Right!" Buske felt confident he was on a roll.

The recruiter leaned forward in his chair and stated flatly, "If you are accepted by the Marine Corps, and if you make it through training, you will probably be sent to Vietnam."

Buske wasn't sure if the recruiter was making a statement or asking a question. To be safe, Buske replied, "Yes, sir."

On March 22, 1967, Buske signed his first legal and binding contract as an adult. Just three months after he turned eighteen, he signed his name to the most important document of his life. The document enlisted him into the U.S. Marine Corps for four years under the 120-day delayed entry program. When June arrived, Buske graduated from high school. He had three weeks left before departing for boot camp when he got the telephone call at home. What happened next was a sign of the times.

"Hello," Buske said nonchalantly into the receiver. He could barely recognize Barb's voice on the other end. She had dated his high school friend, Tom Healy, who had joined the Marines a year earlier. She was crying into the receiver.

"What's the matter? Buske asked, wondering why she was so distraught. She just continued to sob and sniffle. "What the hell is the matter?" Buske repeated.

She stopped crying just long enough to say one sentence: "Tom was killed in Vietnam today!"

Buske was not prepared for such shocking news. The next day it was in the local newspaper, as was the shocking news that another former classmate had been killed in Vietnam.

PFC THOMAS HEALY IS 3rd AREA
VICTIM OF VIETNAM WAR

The Vietnam War has claimed the life of a third

Hutchinson area serviceman within a two-week period. PFC Thomas M. Healy of Hutchinson died Wednesday, June 7, of multiple fragmentation wounds to the head from a grenade while on patrol during an operation in the vicinity of Khe Sanh. The 19-year-old Marine had been in Vietnam since December 22, 1966. He was a machine gunner with the 1st Battalion, 26th Marines, Company B.

Funeral services for PFC Healy are pending at Dobratz Funeral Chapel in Hutchinson.

Funeral services for PFC Joseph J. Seller of Hutchinson, who was killed in Vietnam on June 2, are still pending at Zachow Funeral Home in Hutchinson. Services for a third area casualty, Sgt. Gary Rathbun, of Corvuso area, were held Monday, June 5.

In the days that followed, Buske's sadness over the death of Healy and Seller turned to anger. Maybe he could go over there and get some revenge! An eye for an eye and a tooth for a tooth! For Buske, the war had become intensely personal.

Robert Gates could not tell you how old he was when he first heard about the Vietnam conflict, as it had been going on for as long as he could remember. He could recall hearing that it was a nagging problem in a remote distant place, requiring some military advisors and a few combat troops to keep the peace. He expected one day to hear that the trouble was over, but as graduation day drew near, so did his realization that the Vietnam conflict was not coming to an end.

Gates convinced his good friend Timothy Sather to join the Marines with him under the buddy system. Gates and Sather lived in Minneapolis, where they had grown up together, chasing girls and having a good time. For Sather, it was an easy decision. Enlisting in the Marine Corps was a family tradition. His grandfather, Iver Sather, saw combat in World War I, and Tim's father, Allen Sather, continued the tradition by fighting in the Philippines during World War II.

Mark Mulvihill wanted to be a Marine like his older brother. At age twelve he was influenced by what President John F. Kennedy had said in his inaugural address to the American people, "Pay any price, bear any burden, meet any hardship, support any friend, oppose any foe, to assure the survival and the success of liberty. . . . Ask not what your country can do for you—ask what you can do for your country."

Mulvihill, and all young Americans his age, had grown up under the threat of a nuclear attack by the USSR. Classroom activities included civil defense drills that started with the sounding of an air-raid siren and ended with them crawling out from under their desks when the all-clear was given. That wasn't much of a problem for Mulvihill in grade school, but in junior high, Mulvihill wore his desk like a saddle as he neared his adult height of six feet five inches and weight of 265 pounds. He enlisted in the Marines at age eighteen, vowing to defend the world against communist aggression.

The letter mailed to the future members of the Minnesota Twins Platoon included a listing of the other members by name, address, and phone number. More enlistees were needed and current members were encouraged to recruit their friends. Robert Cusick thought it would be a good idea to use the list to get everyone together for a party. He called Christy W. Sauro Jr., who in turn called Larry Jones. The three met at the local burger stand and hit it off. Cusick was slightly older than the other two, who were seventeen. He said he was surprised the Corps accepted him because he had accidentally cut off his big toe while mowing the lawn.

Larry Jones kept to himself that his dad lacked confidence in his ability to succeed in life. "You'll never make it! You'll never amount anything!" his father had yelled at him during a recent argument.

Jones shouted back at his dad, "Well I won't have to! I am going off to war!" Jones had seen the war on the nightly news but never really paid a lot of attention to it, other than knowing he had his military obligation to fulfill. Jones was determined to prove his father wrong by joining the toughest branch of service—the Marines.

Cusick, Jones, and Sauro decided that more than one pre–boot camp beer party was a good idea. By the time they had to leave for boot camp, the three had become good friends.

Wallace R. "Skip" Schmidt was one of five children born to Eugene and Monica Schmidt. Skip had not done well academically and had dropped out of school in the eleventh grade. He had another uphill battle to fight. As a teenager, he painfully discovered that a lot of value was placed on the height of a male; taller was considered better. There were no pictures of short men on the covers of romance novels. Teenage girls described the ideal man as being tall, dark, and handsome— never short. So when Skip Schmidt stopped growing at five feet two inches, he found he continually had to prove himself.

When Skip should have been a senior in high school, he worked as a truck driver delivering flour, and he was at odds with his parents over what he should do with his life. Fortunately, he had four sisters who treated him as someone special. Colleen was the oldest at nineteen. Jackie was sixteen years old, and Shannon, the youngest, was just nine.

Skip had an especially close relationship with his sister Diane, who was eighteen years old. Her sisters jokingly called her Mom because she was so maternal. People who met Diane were quick to place their trust in her. She was politely assertive and in social gatherings she was always sought out, for she could find common ground with anyone and had a real flare for conversation that made people feel comfortable and welcome. Her presence always brought the "shy boys" and "wallflowers" out of hiding, and they went to her like bugs to light.

When Skip walked into the house and proudly announced, "I enlisted in the Marines today," he knew his dad would approve, because he and his brother were former Marines and they both spoke highly of the Corps. His dad's permanent limp was the result of a wound he received in World War II.

Skip did not take the challenge of Marine boot camp lightly. To get in shape he began to run, lift weights, and exercise. The physical part of boot camp didn't worry Skip; it was the educational lessons that really had him concerned.

It was no surprise that Kenneth "Kenny" Goodman joined the Marines. His father, Virgil, always talked about his days in the Marine Corps with pride. When the Marines landed at Iwo Jima during World War II, "Virg" was there. When Virgil returned home from fighting in the Pacific with a bullet-scarred leg and wearing a Purple Heart, he was a local hero. Over the years his military service became a big part of the Goodman family's story. In Ken's eyes his dad was a real hero. Whenever he saw the film footage of the Marines raising the flag on Mount Suribachi, he swelled with pride knowing that his dad was one of the Marines who helped make that historic victory possible.

Over the years, Virgil's reputation expanded from a war hero to that of a hard-working family man and successful businessman who had the best laugh. He and his wife, Bernice, owned and operated an egg produce business in Stewart, Minnesota.

The day before Ken left for boot camp, he tried on his dad's old Marine Corps uniform. He sucked in his stomach and, with some helpful tugging from Eileen McGraw, his girlfriend, was barely able to button up Virgil's World War II service coat. It was so tight around the middle that it made Kenny look like a pork sausage. When Eileen stepped back for a good look she burst out laughing, but it didn't matter to her that Kenny was a little pudgy.

2

THE CEREMONY

The weather was perfect for the Wednesday night baseball game on June 28, 1967, at Metropolitan Stadium. The home team was in a heated race for first place. Up in the bleachers, Gerald Baltes sat with his folks and Candi Dupre. He had made arrangements to have eighteen yellow roses delivered to her after his departure for boot camp. He said his good-byes and joined the other recruits as they assembled near home plate for the pre-game swearing-in ceremony.

The ceremony started with the Marine color guard marching onto the field. The Twins Platoon amateurishly marched behind, all dressed in civilian clothes. Flanked by recruiters wearing dress blues, the first platoon took a position between home plate and first base, while the other platoon lined up between home plate and third base. The two platoons faced the 11,940 fans in attendance.

The ball game announcer said with enthusiasm, "Ladies and gentlemen, I would like to call your attention to the young men assembled on the ball field. These fine young men, and four lassies, will be sworn into the Marine Corps as the Minnesota Twins Platoon."

After the Marine color guard posted the colors, the announcer prepared the crowd by saying, "Ladies and gentlemen. Please rise for the playing of our country's national anthem." As the band played, the unsung lyrics could be heard in the minds of those present: "And the rockets' red glare, the bombs bursting in air, / Gave proof through the night that our flag was still there. / O say, does that star-spangled banner yet wave, / O'er the land of the free and the home of the brave."

Following the national anthem the recruits took the oath:

> I do solemnly swear that I will support and defend the Constitution of the United States against all enemies foreign and domestic; that I will bear true faith and allegiance to the same; that I will obey the orders of the president of the United States and the orders of the officers appointed over me, according to regulations and the Uniform Code of Military Justice. So help me God.

At its completion the announcer shouted enthusiastically, "Let's hear it for the Minnesota Twins Platoon!" Applause erupted from the stands and the band played the Marine Corps' hymn as the new recruits returned to the stands to watch some of the game.

At the end of the sixth inning, the recruits were quietly directed to board the buses that waited to transport them to World-Chamberlain Field Airport. At 11:30 p.m. an American Flyers charter flight carrying some 150 Marine recruits lifted off the Minneapolis runway and flew into the black of night.

3

THE DAY FROM HELL

The charter plane landed at the San Diego International Airport, Lindberg Field, at 2:30 a.m. on a Thursday morning. The airport and recruit depot were side by side, making the bus ride to the training facility a short one. It started with civilian bus drivers shouting, "Hurry up! Hurry up! Get in!" At the base entrance, military police (MP) boarded the bus, did a security check, and then waved the bus through.

In the glow of streetlights, the recruits could see buildings of Spanish design surrounded by tropical plants and shrubs; everything was immaculate. At the receiving barracks stood three drill instructors dressed in tropical brown uniforms and wearing Smokey the Bear–type hats. The sign on the lawn sent a chilling message: "Restricted Area / Receiving Barracks / Keep Out."

The drill instructors used harsh language and physical force to get the recruits to do things quickly and correctly. Once the recruits were properly positioned on yellow footprints, Staff Sergeant Jenkins walked to the front of the platoon and announced that he was the platoon commander.

Standing nearby was Sergeant Lewis, the biggest black man many had ever seen. He looked six feet six inches tall and was built like a wedge. Sergeant Lewis, who was obviously from a highly educated background, spoke in a very articulate manner except when he was upset, which was often. The sight of the

Twins Platoon left him looking like he had tasted a lemon. Frowning, he stated, "I hate privates!" The third drill instructor, Sergeant Taylor, was noticeably hot-tempered and manhandled a number of the recruits.

The platoon was moved a short distance beyond the yellow footprints to the receiving barracks. From the building entrance hung a large sign, which the drill instructors made them read out loud: "To Be a Marine You Have to Believe in: Yourself . . . Your Fellow Marine . . . Your Corps . . . Your Country . . . Your God . . . *Semper Fidelis.*"

Barbers waited on the other side of the door. Sergeant Lewis positioned himself outside the barbershop and waited for the shaven recruits to exit. Every few seconds another shocked skinhead emerged from the building. Gates overheard Sergeant Lewis say something sarcastic to one recruit with an irregular head. The remark was humorous to Gates, so his lips parted ever so slightly into a smile. Unfortunately, he was looking at Sergeant Lewis at the time, and their eyes met. Within seconds the enormous drill sergeant was in front of Gates shouting, "I better never see your teeth again. If I see your teeth that means you is smiling. Smiling leads to liking. Liking leads to fucking. And you ain't ever going to fuck me."

At Marine Corps Recruit Depot (MCRD) San Diego, there was no such thing as the Minnesota Twins Platoon. There were two platoons of about seventy-five men in each; Sauro's was simply Platoon 3011. Everything the recruits brought into the recruit depot from the civilian world, except for their naked bodies, was put into a box and mailed back to their next of kin. It was common for the drill instructors to use a swift kick or punch to make their point. The recruits were not permitted to speak, but they communicated with each other by way of facial expressions and eye movements. Their expressions indicated that MCRD was worse than expected.

The billet area consisted of row after row of drab, unpainted Quonset huts made of gray corrugated steel. The anonymity of the place was overpowering and somewhat depressing. Reminding the tired recruits the day was far from over was the crackling sound of a trumpet playing morning reveille over the loudspeaker. Within two minutes, thousands of recruits poured out of the surrounding billets and formed into platoons that began marching from all directions to the mess halls. Every platoon was flanked by drill instructors calling cadence. With great creativity and surprisingly wide variation, they gave the same harsh verbal commands, "Left! Right! Left!"

The trip to the mess hall provided a good diversion, and the food was great. The entire process was regimented, following a strict protocol. Recruits are not allowed to talk—not even at breakfast.

After breakfast they got a closer look at their new home, which was two side-by-side Quonset huts that looked identical to the hundreds of others surrounding them. The recruit depot was like a house of mirrors, a superb job in duplication. Identical unpainted steel Quonset huts spaced equally apart lined both sides of the streets. The only thing that set their assigned huts apart from the others was a large rock that had "3011" stenciled in white on it.

The inside of the billet hut was not cheerful; the smell of Listerine filled the air and interior decorating was nonexistent. There were no pictures on the walls, no decorations, no televisions, no radios, no lounge chairs, no refrigerators, and no snack machines—just row after row of identical steel bunk beds on a concrete floor. "This is your new home," Sergeant Jenkins told them. The recruits looked around at their new surroundings with depression written on each of their faces.

The world did not revolve around any individual at MCRD. Being in the Marine Corps meant starting life all over as a person undeserving of any special favors or treatment. The recruits thought about each of the things they had taken for granted. They fondly recalled how great it was to get their own way. The expression "all the comforts of home" had new meaning. Boot camp was a rude awakening. As far as the eye could see were recruits dressed in the same dark green utilities and shiny black boots. There were thousands of them, and from a short distance away they all looked alike.

Platoon 3011's lack of marching ability triggered what was becoming a characteristic mood swing for Sergeant Lewis. The sight of the platoon trying to march in step left him sporting a sour face and a bad temperament. For punishment he made them exercise. Just as they were about to finish, he made them start over because someone was not doing the exercises correctly. The actual number of exercises they did for punishment usually tripled the original order. The drill instructors faulted them for something at every opportunity.

Going to the bathroom, or "head" as the Marine Corps calls it, was an unforgettable experience. The entire platoon was given five minutes to go relieve themselves and be back out on the road, standing at attention in platoon formation. Sixty recruits raced inside the one-story brick building to find there were not enough urinals to go around, so lines quickly formed. Many frantically coaxed those ahead to hurry up, which only added to the problem. The degree of relaxation required to urinate was lacking. Many simply gave up and left so the next guy in line could have a crack at it. The toilet stools were in a row with no walls or stanchions in between for privacy. The idea of sitting on the toilet facing a line of waiting recruits left the stools unused. Time always ran out before everyone had a chance to go.

Smokers often thought about how good it would feel to take a long drag, imagining the satisfaction and stimulating rush that would follow the clouds of smoke into their lungs. They needed a fix, but there was no smoking permitted on the airplane, buses, or anywhere else that they had been since being sworn into the Marines. One private shocked everyone when he requested permission to speak. Sergeant Lewis looked extremely irritated at the prospect of having to converse with a private. His facial expression made it clear he was displeased. "Speak, bitch," Lewis said with a frown.

"Sir! The private smokes, sir."

Sergeant Lewis stormed back and forth in front of the platoon berating the private, "The soft life is over for you! You are in the Marine Corps. Nobody here is going to powder your ass and pat your behind. Is this clear?" Sergeant Lewis snarled.

Sergeant Jenkins was a smoker and was a bit more understanding: "If you're good, I might light the smoking lamp for you later." He gave no indication when that might be. The conversation was over.

After evening mess the recruits were marched back to the billet area. Sergeant Jenkins ordered the platoon to stand at attention. A sleepy Sather looked at Sergeant Taylor as he walked past, and he saw Sather's lingering stare. Outraged, he spun around, made a run at Sather, and had Sather by the throat seconds later. As Taylor squeezed off both carotid arteries, Sather's eyes bulged and he gasped for air. Sergeant Taylor screamed, "Are you eyeball-fucking me?"

Sather tried hard to answer, but his words couldn't get through the clenched hands. Sergeant Taylor shouted obscenities as he shook and choked him. Sather started to pass out from lack of oxygen. His first and last words as he crumpled to the ground gasping for air were "Sir! No, sir."

Sergeant Jenkins and Sergeant Lewis both witnessed the incident but had different reactions. It was as if Sergeant Lewis had been expecting it to happen. He stared suspiciously at the entire platoon as though looking for perverts and degenerates. "I best not catch any of you eyeball-fucking me!" he warned.

In an accusatory manner Platoon Commander Jenkins questioned Sather, "You puke. I saw you looking at Sergeant Taylor. You got some kind of crush on him?" "Sir! No, sir." Sather's reply was hoarse and raspy.

"Get up off the ground, sweet pea. I'm going to be keeping a close on eye you," Jenkins snarled as he waved a clenched fist in front of Sather's face.

The whole platoon was silently abuzz over the incident. When the drill instructors weren't looking, the recruits used eye language to send visual messages back and forth among themselves. Gates used a miniscule facial expression to silently communicate to nearby recruits that Sather, the guy he had enlisted with under the buddy program, was not a homosexual.

Sergeant Jenkins gave the order for the platoon to stand at attention, then he and the other two drill instructors disappeared into the duty hut. It was a test; to stand for an extended period of time without moving was extremely difficult and boring, and the urge to move or fidget became overwhelming. The only way to pass the time was to think. And they thought, *All this exercising is killing me. I hate not being able to speak. A can of pop or a candy bar sure would taste good. I miss listening to rock music on the radio and watching TV. I don't like not being able to come and go as I please. I miss going out with my friends. I'm sick of being treated like dirt. I hate boot camp. I hate being here.*

Finally, the sun reached a low spot on the horizon signaling the day was nearing an end. Sergeant Lewis emerged from the duty hut and saw the sour faces. He immediately diagnosed the problem. "Look at all the sad faces. I think you miss your mommies. I think you is homesick. I have the cure. Some exercises will help you to forget."

The sun was all but gone when they completed their exercises. The time to bed down for the night had to be near, or so they thought. The drill instructors laid out the routine. "Go into the billet hut and strip down to your skivvies," Sergeant Lewis ordered.

"Put your dirty clothes in the white laundry bags hanging from your rack," chimed in Sergeant Jenkins.

Physically exhausted and aching from lack of sleep, the recruits were looking forward to climbing into the ugly-looking metal bunk beds with the green wool blankets. The order was given to go into the billet and return wearing white skivvies and shower shoes. They had two minutes to be back on the road with their shaving kits in hand and the white towels hanging around their necks. Then they marched to the head with orders to "shit, shower, and shave" in five minutes. No one was surprised that the toilet stools remained unoccupied. It seemed as if no one was interested in taking a crap in public.

The recruits quickly finished and returned to the formation. The head call went without a glitch, apparently pleasing Sergeant Jenkins, because he walked to the front of the platoon, cocked his head, and gave the order many wanted to hear. "The smoking lamp is lit. You may take out your cigarettes and have a smoke. When I tell you the smoking lamp is out, you must put out your cigarettes immediately. Don't take one extra drag. Then field-strip what's left of your cigarette."

Sergeant Taylor stepped forward and demonstrated how to field-strip a cigarette properly. "Whatever is left of the cigarette is to be torn into tiny little pieces so small that when tossed away, no evidence of them can be found. Filter tips are not to be discarded. They leave traces for the enemy to find. They are to be put into trouser pockets and disposed of later in a trash receptacle," he instructed.

What followed were the hurried sounds of crackling cellophane followed by the fizz of sulfur matches. While the first inhaled smoke was still in their lungs, Jenkins cocked his head and hollered, "The smoking lamp is out!" The order to put out the cigarettes was followed by the sounds of rapid puffing. Cigarette coals burned bright as the chemically dependent made a frantic effort to draw in enough nicotine to feed their addiction. Sparks flew and fingers got burned as everyone hurried to field-strip their cigarette ahead of the next guy.

Sergeant Taylor rushed toward the formation. The look on his face indicated he was going to make an example of someone. He grabbed a recruit to rough up. While he was punching the recruit, Sergeant Jenkins yelled out in anger, "You slimy turds! How dare you take advantage of my good nature. It'll be a damn long time before I light the smoking lamp again."

Sergeant Lewis was fuming; he could hardly wait to speak. When his turn came he said, "You have an excuse for being stupid! You are privates! But you've got no excuse for disobeying a direct order. We should court martial your asses!" He eyed the platoon knowingly and, basing his next warning on his years of experience, added, "There are at least twelve of you thinking right now that a court martial will get you out of the Marine Corps. You can forget that shit! Hard labor is what a court martial will get you." He intentionally paused, so his remarks could sink in, and then continued, "The time spent in the brig does not count toward your training. It gets you set back. The Marine Corps don't pay you to be bad. You forfeit your pay." He added with smiling displeasure, "You might not even have enough money to go home on leave."

There was another penalty for disobeying a direct order that did not apply to them, but Sergeant Lewis enjoyed telling them about it anyway. "The Marine Corps can also demote. They can take away your stripes. Except this don't apply to you. You are privates. You have no stripes to take away. You too low on the pole! You can't go any lower than you already are."

In the background Sergeant Taylor gathered tiny morsels of tobacco and white bits of paper off the ground. It was like watching someone pick up nails for a coffin. When he finished he tossed all the cigarette bits up into the air. Sergeant Lewis gave the platoon a nasty frown as the flurry of white paper came fluttering down. It was an open-and-shut case; the recruits had failed to field-strip their cigarettes into undetectable scraps.

"They need a trip to the sand pits," Sergeant Jenkins hollered vengefully.

Still wearing their white skivvies and shower shoes, the platoon marched to a sandy place near the billet and had to exercise until the sweat dripped from their bodies. As further punishment, Sergeant Jenkins ordered everyone to drop to their bellies. Then he ordered them to swim in the sand and fling it at each other. To make sure they got well covered with sand, he ordered the recruits to roll over a few times.

Sergeant Lewis picked up on some of the facial expressions and appropriately commented, "I see some nonsmokers who think they shouldn't be punished." Lewis said it with a phony sadness. "It's like this: You all in it together. One of you fuck up, you all fucked up. Is this clear?" To appease him they loudly responded, "Sir! Yes, sir!"

Twenty minutes later and right on time for "Taps," Platoon 3011 stood at attention in front of their billets, covered with brown sand and looking like gingerbread men.

"It will be some time before I light the smoking lamp again for you maggots," Jenkins reminded them with mocking bitterness.

"He might never light it again," Sergeant Taylor remarked snidely.

"And I couldn't care less," Sergeant Lewis said. Then he made an about face and disappeared into the duty hut.

Finally, the first day was nearly over. Everyone was ordered to climb into their racks. Before Sergeant Taylor switched off the light, he told them no one was allowed to leave the billet and there would be no talking.

The recruits climbed into their racks covered with sand but too tired to care. At precisely the same time, the lights in every Quonset hut at the recruit depot went out. A trumpet played "Taps" over the base loudspeaker. Within seconds they were asleep, letting their dreams take them away from their real-life nightmare: Marine Corps boot camp.

4

INSIDE MARINE BOOT CAMP

James Bain had two younger brothers and one older brother who was in the Marine Corps. James wore thick glasses and weighed 135 pounds. He grew up in South Minneapolis, where he graduated from Roosevelt High School in June 1967. Right after graduation he tried to enlist in the army to get into printing school but was told there were no openings. Then he visited the local Marine recruiter and learned that they needed a few people to fill the ranks of the Minnesota Twins Platoon. If he could get one of his buddies to join with him, they would both get a special two-year enlistment period instead of the standard four years. Bain jumped at the chance. He obtained permission from his mother and talked his buddy Michael Sorensen into enlisting with him.

Sergeant Lewis was pissed off when he said, "Private Bain! I say *left*! You turn *right*! You *best* get your shit together!"

"Sir! Yes, sir," squeaked Bain.

That same day Bain did a left shoulder arms when he should have been doing a right shoulder arms. To see Bain marching with his rifle on the wrong shoulder incensed Sergeant Lewis. He took the rifle away from the recruit marching directly behind Bain. The last thing Bain remembered was hearing the voice of Sergeant Lewis saying something that started with, "You ignorant . . . ," and then Bain felt the blow of a rifle butt to the back of his head. His glasses went flying off his face and he saw stars. The incident really bothered Bain, who kept thinking, *I didn't join in the Marine Corps to get beat on.*

Later on, when the platoon was practicing close order drill, Bain dropped his rifle. He was knocked around by one of the drill instructors for being clumsy. Bain stewed over the assault, for he didn't feel they had the right to put their hands on him. He wanted to protest, but he didn't dare. Fresh in his memory was how, on the first day of boot camp, Sergeant Taylor had kicked the crap out of the biggest member of the platoon.

When they came back to the barracks, Sergeant Taylor had everyone in the billet put his M14 rifle on Bain's bunk. As further punishment for dropping a Marine's most vital piece of equipment, Bain had to sleep on top of the rifles. Bain could handle that; what he couldn't handle was being beaten up.

It seemed every time Bain turned around he saw a recruit being punched or kicked by the drill instructors. He saw one private get kicked in the stomach for complaining about having a stomach cramp. He saw another recruit get hit in the head so hard that afterward he didn't know where he was.

At periodic intervals the drill instructors ordered the recruits to write letters home to their loved ones. It was a brief mandatory event that gave Bain the opportunity to inform his mother about the physical abuses. He instructed her to contact his recruiter and tell him about the mistreatment before someone got seriously hurt. When she did, the recruiter assured her that her son's initial reaction to boot camp was not that unusual. He explained that for most young men it was the first time away from home and it would take a while for Bain to adjust.

Later the platoon was practicing close order drill on an immense, hard-surfaced parade field known as "the grinder." Sergeant Lewis saw Bain screw up again by not executing a marching command properly. Extremely upset, he growled,

"Private Bain, when we get back to the billet area, you report to the duty hut."

After evening mess hall, while the recruits stood at attention, Bain left the ranks and went to the duty hut just a few feet away and knocked at the door.

"Sir! Private Bain reporting as ordered, sir!"

"Enter, bitch!" Lewis said in a loud enough voice for all to hear. Bain entered the duty hut. Some of the recruits standing in formation could see into the duty hut through the screen door. Whatever it was that Sergeant Lewis asked Bain, he gave the wrong answer. The huge drill instructor jumped up and slammed Bain against the metal locker. His large hands slipped around the recruit's throat and he squeezed off the flow of blood to Bain's head.

The small recruit created a racket inside the duty hut; he thrashed about with his arms and legs, which were hitting against the metal wall locker as he unsuccessfully gasped for air. The one-sided altercation moved to the floor without Lewis letting go of his chokehold until Bain was unconscious. After some time passed without any movement from Bain, Sergeant Lewis slapped Bain across the face in an effort to revive him. When that failed, he pounded on Bain's chest. Bain twitched and opened his eyes.

"You all right?" Sergeant Lewis asked Bain without remorse. When Bain didn't respond, Sergeant Lewis yelled, "Get up!" With some unfriendly help from the drill instructor, Bain got up and was ordered back into the formation.

That was the last straw for Bain. He decided he wasn't going to put up with the abuse anymore. The following morning at roll call when his name was read off, there was no response. A check of the area revealed he was gone.

"Private Bain is absent without leave. That is a serious crime. He is in big trouble," Sergeant Jenkins told the platoon.

Sergeant Lewis summed it up. "He is AWOL. They will find him. You don't want to be in his shoes."

Bain thought the best thing he could do was leave just before sunup. He ran the whole length of the obstacle course, and then climbed the fence that separated the recruit depot from the naval base. He didn't know where he was going; he just wanted to find someone who could get him out of there. Basically, all he wanted was to get away from the drill instructors, who he thought were crazy and sadistic.

Bain got over the base fence, crossed Lindberg Field, and went by the navy recruit depot. The sun was just starting to come up and he didn't want anyone to recognize him, so he pulled off his green shirt. That left him wearing a white T-shirt, green trousers, and boots. He crossed a road bordering the airport and came upon a guy and a gal fishing. The guy said to Bain, "You're a recruit, aren't you."

"Yeah, I was in the Marine Corps."

"I was in the Marine Corps, too," the guy told Bain. They started to talk to each other. He told the man what the drill instructors were doing to the recruits and about how he had been choked unconscious. "They can exercise me. They can swear at me. But they have no right to put their hands on me," Bain complained.

"You're right. They got no business doing that to you," the former Marine empathized. The man's wife really felt sorry for Bain and suggested, "Let's take him to our house."

"No! We can't take him home," the former Marine told his wife.

"I'm not trying to get out of the Marines," Bain said. "I'm not trying to get out of serving my country. I didn't get drafted. I enlisted for Christ sakes! I just want to get away from those three crazy drill instructors."

"You can do one of two things," the man said. "You can

just take off, but you won't get far. Somebody will see you with your short hair and green pants. Or I can take you back to the main gate and you can talk to them there. And maybe you can get things straightened out."

Bain decided to give it another try. At the main gate, he thanked the man for the help and advice before surrendering himself to the MPs. The MPs took Bain inside and put him up against a wall. "Do you got to go to the bathroom?" the MP asked Bain.

"No," Bain answered. Every few minutes the same corporal came back over and asked Bain if he had to go to the bathroom. His answered remained the same: no.

Finally the corporal came over and said to Bain, "Private Bain you have to go to the bathroom." The MP escorted Bain to the head. As Bain stood at the urinal, with the MP standing behind him, he heard the door open and another MP stepped in. When Bain turned around, it happened: the two MPs proceeded to kick the shit out of him, making sure never to hit his face. Having resigned himself to the beating, as it was happening, Bain thought, *This is just unbelievable. What's going on here? Why? For what purpose? I enlisted. I wasn't drafted. Am I in the wrong country? This can't be America.*

Afterward, Bain was put back up against the wall. One MP guarded Bain while the other went into an adjacent room and watched TV.

All they do is beat on you in this place. Am I going to get beat up for the rest of my life, or what? Bain wondered. He was as scared as he had ever been.

At the first opportunity, Bain sent a letter off to his recruiter, telling him about his most recent experience with the MPs. He had no idea what that would lead to.

Shortly thereafter a Marine with many stripes on his sleeve approached Bain. *He might be an officer?* Bain thought. To be safe, he saluted.

The much older Marine told Bain, "When you go before the commanding officer just plead guilty. Don't open your mouth. Everything is pretty much settled. Just go in there and plead guilty and take your punishment. If you fight it, you're going to be in jail for two or three months. And you'll have to start your boot camp all over. So you're better off to plead guilty. I already know what you are going to get. Just five days in correctional custody and everything will be fine. We'll even put you in another platoon."

Bain pleaded guilty and was sentenced to five days in correctional custody.

Drill instructors constantly scrutinize recruits to determine if they have what it takes to become Marines. For a variety of reasons, some recruits are let go. The drill instructors had already cut one physical weakling and two overweight recruits from the platoon.

The physical weakling was singled out for his inability to do even one push-up. He was harshly ordered to pack his sea bag and was escorted out of the area by Sergeant Jenkins. The two remaining drill instructors made it very clear that the weakling was not fit to be in the Marine Corps and was getting disgracefully booted out. "He will not get an honorable discharge, and he will not be coming back." The fate of the two overweight recruits was less clear, as their evaluation and departure had not occurred in front of the entire platoon.

The culling of Platoon 3011 was not over when Mark Mulvihill, Kenneth Goodman, and Robert Gates were called front and center. What the three had in common was that they looked plump, thus their fate seemed questionable. The three drill instructors walked around the pudgy recruits, looking at their sizes and shapes, while Sergeant Jenkins poked his finger into the sides of each one. Then the three drill instructors walked far enough away so their conversation could only be heard in whispers. At one point Sergeant Lewis looked over and pointed right at Gates.

Sergeant Taylor then returned to the front of the formation and asked the three recruits if they had ever heard of the fat farm, which they had not. Sergeant Taylor joyfully explained that the Corps had a special platoon just for fat people to help them lose weight. Sergeant Lewis was concerned the three privates might misinterpret what Sergeant Taylor was telling them and that it might sound too much like a good thing. So he clarified it by saying, "You stay in the fat platoon until you the right weight. The time you do at the fat farm does not count toward training."

Sergeant Jenkins added, "Boot camp is still eight weeks long. If you go to the fat farm, another platoon will have to pick you up when you get out."

Thinking the explanation still too complicated for the privates, Lewis frowned and for their benefit stated it in the simplest terms possible. "If you in a hurry to get out of boot camp, you do not want to go to the fat farm." Lewis tipped his head down and stared at Gates, Goodman, and Mulvihill, as if he was viewing them over the top of imaginary eyeglasses. Seeing that the three recruits looked visibly shaken, he figured he had gotten through to them. Just to be sure he asked, "Do Privates Gates, Goodman, and Mulvihill want to go to the fat farm?"

"Sir! No, sir!" shouted the three in unison.

Jenkins motioned for another huddle. After the second huddle, Jenkins ordered, "Privates Gates, Goodman, and Mulvihill, give me ten push-ups. Ready! Begin!"

The three were being put to a test. With their loved ones expecting them to graduate from boot camp in eight weeks, the prospect of going to the fat farm was horrifying. No one wanted to write home to say he had been set back for being too fat. The entire platoon stood quietly at attention. Gates did his ten push-ups quickly; that did the trick. Jenkins ordered Gates to get back in formation. The other two weren't as fast and Jenkins informed them, "You're fat bodies. We could try just putting you on the diet tables."

Jenkins was interrupted by the sound of an approaching platoon. He stepped back out of the way, allowing the recruits to see the approaching platoon. The other platoon's ranks were filled with chubby recruits nearing exhaustion. They stumbled as they ran and were barely able to keep from falling down. Each of them had a pasty gray complexion and looked like death warmed over. Their salt-stained utilities looked oversized and baggy, suggesting that the recruits inside had, at one time, been much heavier. Their bulging eyes sent a distressing message easy to decipher.

After the platoon passed by, Sergeant Lewis turned to Sergeant Jenkins and asked in a loud voice, "Is that the platoon from the fat farm?"

"Why, yes it is," Sergeant Jenkins confirmed.

"What a coincidence," Sergeant Lewis said as he rolled his eyes with mock surprise, making it clear that what they had just witnessed was not a random event.

Sergeant Taylor added, "They're on the way to the sand pits to lose a few pounds."

Sergeant Jenkins made Goodman and Mulvihill an offer they couldn't refuse. "We could try putting you on the diet tables and still keep you in the platoon." The two recruits vigorously accepted by shouting, "Sir! Yes, sir!"

Goodman and Mulvihill were put on the diet tables. While everyone else ate plenty of good food, they got one small scoop of cottage cheese, a leaf of lettuce, and a fruit slice at every meal.

In their quest to be Marines, Goodman and Mulvihill lost one of the three pleasures of boot camp. The other two were sleeping and using the toilet.

The Platoon 3011 recruits received a series of shots intended to protect them against the diseases of the world. Afterward, a navy doctor addressed the platoon: "Some of you may not be fit for military service. Some of you may have lied about your medical history to get into the Marine Corps. Some of you may have signed medical waivers in order to enlist. If this applies to you, step forward." Not one recruit stepped forward. One week in MCRD San Diego was enough to make the recruits understand who was in charge, and it wasn't the high-ranking naval officer.

The officer continued, "There is nothing dishonorable about getting a medical discharge. If for any reason you think you might not be fit for military service I want you to go over to the west wall and line up." When no one moved, the officer's face reddened. "Sergeant!" he barked, not hiding his displeasure that he had to funnel his orders through the lower-ranking drill instructors in order to see them carried out.

Sergeant Lewis, who had been leaning against the far wall, straightened up, unfolded his large brawny arms, and stepped smartly to the front of his platoon. He pretended to look displeased, but the recruits knew it was just a guise. From the twinkle in his eye, they knew they had done the right thing. "If you think for some reason you should not be in the Marine Corps, step over to the wall," Sergeant Lewis ordered.

This was an unexpected window of opportunity. A few weeks earlier, most of the recruits would have done almost anything to get into the Marine Corps, but not anymore. If the Marine Corps saw fit to send them home, so be it. The rush was on! The line of recruits against the west wall became comically long. The sight was more than Lewis could stand. He looked up at the ceiling and said loudly with disgust, "Privates!"

The naval doctor left the gymnasium and went to the examination room down the hall. Sergeant Lewis remained behind to run interference. Cusick was first in line to reveal why they might not be fit for military service.

"What's your problem?" Sergeant Lewis asked skeptically.

"Sir! The private is missing his big toe."

"If that's all you missing when you come back from 'Nam, you be lucky," Lewis snarled pointing toward the platoon. Cusick got the message and hurried back to his place in the formation.

"What's your problem?" Lewis asked Buske, who was ready to come clean. He remembered how his recruiter had asked him about having a criminal record and how he had fibbed to the recruiter. Truth be known, he thought maybe he shouldn't be in the Marines.

"Sir, when I was a teenager I was involved in some stolen cars," Buske confessed.

"Ain't good enough!" Lewis said flatly. He motioned for Buske to get back to his spot in the platoon. Sauro was next in line.

"Speak," Sergeant Lewis said with a tone of skepticism.

"Sir, the private has flat feet," Sauro answered.

"Do they bother you?"

"Sir. Sometimes, sir."

"When?" Sergeant Lewis probed.

"Sir. Toward the end of the day, sir."

Sergeant Lewis opened his eyes wide with mock surprise and said, "No shit!"

"Sir. We were told to step up, sir." Sauro's voice trailed off apologetically.

And so it went: one recruit after another stepped forward

to make his pitch. The Twins Platoon marched back to its billeting area with its ranks fully intact. The only sound came from boot heels striking the deck in near perfect unison. Many were troubled by their most recent experience. How quickly they had jumped at the chance to get out of the Marine Corps. What did that mean? Maybe it meant they did not have the stuff it takes to be a Marine. Maybe they didn't have enough guts? Maybe they were cowards?

As usual, Lewis was on top of his game. He knew why many of them looked so troubled and puzzled. "I know what the privates are suffering from," he said in a manner that implied he would have to explain it to them. Then he stopped talking to quickly brush off a piece of lint to restore his uniform to its perfect state. He continued, "I have seen it time and time again. Many of you have got what is called cold feet. It's caused by having too much idle time. When privates have idle time, they start to think. Privates are not supposed to think. They are supposed to follow orders."

Sergeant Lewis stopped talking as if he were waiting for the privates to catch up. He scanned the platoon in silence, making eye contact with all sixty-eight recruits. Satisfied that most of the recruits were still with him, he announced with rising jubilation, "I have the cure for cold feet. It's called exercise! Give me twenty push-ups. Ready. Begin."

Weekends were of no significance in the Marine Corps, and for the recruits, they were sheer misery. Friday and Saturday nights had always been the time to go out and have fun. They kept thinking about their civilian counterparts, who were out having a good time. They missed the fun of dating and the suspense of going to the hot spots, looking for the girls of their dreams. Some recruits missed their sweethearts. Goodman missed being with his fiancée, Eileen McGraw. Baltes thought about Candi

Dupre. Cusick thought about his steady girlfriend, Darlene. And so it went.

The drill instructors seemed to know the recruits were thinking about their girls back home. Because it was only their second weekend at MCRD, the drill instructors decided to set the recruits straight about a few things. First of all, more Marines were needed in Vietnam, and therefore it was a near certainty that those who made it through training would receive orders for Vietnam. That meant the girls back home would not see much of them for a *very* long time. If they were lucky, it might be just once or twice, for only a few days, over the next two to three years.

Sergeant Jenkins began the unpleasant task of "waking the recruits to smell the coffee." He began by telling the privates, "You are property of the Marine Corps. You will go where the Marine Corps wants you to go. You will do what the Marine Corps wants you to do. From now on you should think of the Marine Corps as your mother and father. It will feed and clothe you. It will give you everything you need to exist. You can forget about the girl back home. She will not wait for you. She will be gone by the time you get out. She will have gotten married and will have had children."

Sergeant Lewis watched their reactions. Privates never ceased to amaze him. Shaking his head in disbelief, he addressed the platoon, "I can tell some of you out there don't think this is true. You are having silly fantasies that your girl is going to sit home and miss you. You're thinking you're the greatest lover in the world. You're thinking she can't live without you. Go ahead. Think that if it makes you feel better, if you're stupid!"

Sergeant Taylor could hardly wait to tell them more about the girls they had left behind. He looked down at his watch to make his point; with the time nearing 2100 hours, what he had to say would take the beauty out of the sunset. "You know who is going to try and poke her tonight? Your best friend! That's right! Your best friend! As soon as you left, he started making his moves."

Sergeant Taylor was not content to just stick in the knife in; he had to twist it a few turns. "Right now, he is probably pulling off on some side road, some lovers' lane. By midnight they'll be getting it on." Sergeant Taylor wasn't finished. "If you get a letter from your sweet pea telling you she thinks it's better if you both start to date other people, watch out. That means she's screwing *everybody*."

Sergeant Lewis added, "Not *if* you get the letter, but *when* you get the letter."

It was about 2130 when Sergeant Taylor ordered the recruits to prepare for lights out. Inside the Quonset huts, the recruits stood at attention next to their bunks, all thinking pretty much the same thing. Without a word, they looked around the inside of the Quonset hut taking in the drab surroundings. They thought about all the physical exercise they were doing and the way the drill instructors were treating them. They wondered what had happened to Bain. They missed the comforts of home and realized how much they loved and missed their parents, families, and friends. And some with steady girlfriends were thinking, *What's my best friend up to? How long will it take before some guy seduces her?* Other disturbing thoughts were: *Will I get orders for Vietnam? Will I be wounded? Will I be killed in the war?*

Most members of the Twins Platoon had enlisted for four years of active duty. They had been in the Marine Corps for only slightly more than a week and already they were counting the days until discharge, which was 1,453 days left to serve for most. Prior to arriving at MCRD they could not remember staying in on the weekends. Reality set in with a thud; their days of wine and roses were over.

The drill instructors departed while giving the order "Lights out." For the first time since they arrived at boot camp, the recruits were about to defy the order of no speaking without permission. They glanced around the billet making sure no drill instructors were in sight. No matter what their upbringing, nationality, religion, or level of intelligence, they were all thinking the same thing. It was both shocking and impressive to hear so many recruits turn to each other, and all say at the exact same time, "What the fuck have I done?"

5

WHAT'S T-1?

uske waited in line for his turn on a stool. He was worried about the fact that he had been in boot camp for more than a week without having a bowel movement. It was time to give it another try. The stools were covered with red-faced recruits trying to take a crap. Buske was a fighter, a tough guy, one of the few recruits for whom shaving served a purpose. The platoon was given five minutes to make a head call and time was running out. Buske gave the recruit in front of him a menacing stare. The recruit quickly vacated the stool. Buske had no more than settled down on the warm seat when Sergeant Lewis hollered, "Platoon 3011! On the road!"

In a flash the head was empty. Buske wiped and stood up. Before he could reach down for the trousers around his ankles, Sergeant Taylor was in his face. He slammed his fist into Buske's stomach, causing him to double over. Before Buske could recover from the punch to the breadbasket, Sergeant Taylor slammed him back against the wall. After he had punched Buske a few more times, Sergeant Taylor shoved him toward the door.

The recruits outside could hear the commotion in the head. The slamming of human flesh against a masonry wall makes a distinct thud. If Taylor was beating up Buske, nobody was safe! Buske was not the kind of guy you slap upside the head, but crazy Taylor was doing just that.

While the ruckus in the head continued, Sergeant Lewis stood quietly at the front of the platoon using his thumbnail to push the cuticles back on his fingernails. He was fanatical about his appearance; everything had to be perfect. He pretended he didn't hear a thing. Suddenly there was a loud bang, followed by the sound of a trashcan bouncing end over end. The noise was loud enough to make Lewis pause and smile.

Sergeant Taylor came out the door with Buske in tow. Like a bouncer throwing out a drunk, he tossed Buske out onto the road. Buske got up, stumbling and tripping over his trousers, which were still bunched up around his ankles. With one hand he reached down, pulled them up, and hustled over to his spot in the formation.

To the recruits it seemed like they had been at MCRD forever, but when Sergeant Lewis addressed the platoon, he referred to the next day as "T-1." One of the recruits asked for permission to speak, then asked him, "What is T-1?" At first Sergeant Lewis looked surprised, but then his facial expression changed to one of delight. Jones, a skeptic, became suspicious and sensed they were about to get the shaft. The platoon braced itself for some bad news.

Sergeant Lewis could not contain himself any longer and blurted out, "T-1 is short for training day one!" Seeing the puzzled looks on their faces, he continued, "Tomorrow, you officially start your first day of training. You begin your eight weeks of boot camp!" Lewis took delight in telling them this. Then, loving every minute of it, he watched their changing expressions.

The looks on their faces said loud and clear what their voices could not: *What do you mean start tomorrow! This last week has been the worst one of my life! It counts! I want credit!*

Another commercial airliner took off from the airport next to the recruit depot. The roar of the jet engines was so loud that Lewis had to stop speaking. The airliner rose up into the sky, leaving behind a trail of dark exhaust fumes. Many of the recruits wished they were on it. The first official day of training was July 7, 1967.

Meanwhile, in correctional custody Private Bain was meeting some rather bizarre characters. One of them later abducted a drill instructor's wife at knifepoint and fled the base. The last Bain heard of the incident was that the woman was driving the private out the main gate as he held a bayonet to her throat. Another guy attacked a captain and tore the bars off his uniform. The last Bain heard of him was that he was being dragged off and getting the crap kicked out of him. There were about eighteen guys in the Correctional Custody Platoon, with a rapid turnover. Bain spent his days sanding boards and going out on forced marches. It was very boring and the time passed slowly.

"I need you to help me get out of the Marine Corps!" one correctional custody inmate told Bain.

"I'm not looking to get out," Bain told him.

"Hear me out! Just tell them we're a couple of fags."

"It don't interest me at all," Bain told him.

"Listen! It's the way to go!" The inmate explained how homosexuals were not allowed into the Marine Corps, and therefore their fake confession would be grounds for an immediate discharge.

"No! I'm not interested!" Bain said emphatically. He planned to convince Marlene Johnson to marry him when he got home on leave. He had known her since fourth grade and they had been going steady for years. As it was, he already had enough explaining to do when he got back home.

Bain's recruiter came to see him while he was doing his five days in the correctional platoon. He had Bain sign a statement that his allegations against the drill instructors and the MPs were true.

Shortly after that Bain got a good scare. Sergeant Jenkins was standing outside the correctional custody billet waiting for him. He told Bain point-blank, "You fucking little maggot! You ever come back to my platoon and I'll kill you. I'll get you for this!" Sergeant Jenkins was really pissed; he called Bain every name in the book before stomping off.

"What was that all about?" an inmate asked Bain.

"He knows I'm not coming back. He just wants to make a point that he's pissed over what I done. He knows I dropped the dime on him."

"You scared?" asked the inmate.

"I'm scared shitless!" Bain admitted.

Back in the billeting area Sergeant Jenkins told the platoon as it stood at attention, "Listen up! Private Bain won't be coming back! He's the shit bird who went AWOL! People might be coming around to ask some questions."

Sergeant Lewis interjected, "Private Bain is saying we didn't treat him very nice. Went to his congressman, or some shit. Now the Marine Corps will have to investigate!" Sergeant Lewis puckered with disapproval.

In a fatherly kind of way, Sergeant Jenkins motioned for the recruits to gather around him. He was going to take them into his confidence. "Technically, we are not supposed to swear at you."

Sergeant Lewis pretended to look shocked and appalled, and said loudly, "Oh my! How traumatizing!"

"And we are not suppose to hit or strike you," Sergeant Jenkins continued.

An agitated Sergeant Lewis loudly injected, "It don't

matter the enemy's going to try and kill your ass!" His whole face was a frown, and he didn't look particularly optimistic that the recruits could put the whole thing into perspective.

Sergeant Jenkins continued by saying, "I am only going to tell you this once. That slimy Private Bain wrote his congressman. There might be an investigation into how we treat you. What you say could have an effect on the kind of training you get. After you hear what I have to say, you'll have to decide for yourself if you want to snitch or not.

"I think you all know we are doing this for your own good. As Marines you have to be tough. If you can't handle a little swearing and hitting, how are you ever going to hold up in combat? It's my job as your platoon commander to get you ready. Most of you are going straight to Vietnam when your training is finished. How well you're trained is going to determine if you come back from Vietnam alive."

Sergeant Lewis made it very obvious to the recruits that he thought the whole idea that they were being abused was ridiculous. "If you wanted things to be easy, you don't belong here. You should have joined the army or some shit. Or maybe you should have just stayed home with Mommy."

Sergeant Taylor was close to going berserk by the time it was his turn to speak. With raised eyebrows and a crazed look in his eyes, he dared them, "Go ahead, snitch on me. Just remember our paths will cross again before you get out. And when they do, you're dead. In 'Nam, you'd better be looking over your shoulder for me. Because when I see you, I'll kill you."

Sergeant Taylor's admonition primed Sergeant Lewis for another remark. "If you snitch I won't kill you. You'll just wish you were dead! You see, it's okay for the DIs to exercise the privates!" he reminded with grin.

Sergeant Jenkins summed things up: "If anyone should ask

you if the DIs swear at or physically touch the recruits, your answer should be 'Sir! No, sir.'"

In spite of the threat of a congressional investigation, the behavior of the drill instructors remained unchanged. If they had any concerns about how the recruits would respond to questioning, it didn't show.

A couple of weeks later, the platoon was standing in formation in front of the billet when a well-dressed civilian flanked by a Marine in uniform approached. A worried-looking Sergeant Jenkins shouted, "Platoon! Attention!" The recruits immediately snapped to attention. So did Sergeant Taylor and Sergeant Lewis! Whoever the civilian was, he was clearly someone of importance.

"Morning, Sergeant Jenkins!" the uniformed Marine said rather abruptly.

"Sir! Good morning, sir!" Sergeant Jenkins responded, looking concerned about the surprise visitors.

"We have a few questions that we would like to ask your recruits in private," the uniformed Marine told him, while the civilian stood by patiently.

"Sir! Yes, sir!" Sergeant Jenkins replied. He turned to his recruits and said, "Listen up! We have some visitors. They would like to ask you a few questions. You will not be punished for anything you say. Sergeant Lewis, Sergeant Taylor, and myself will leave the area. We will not be present to hear your answers. You are to give truthful answers. Is this clear?"

"Sir! Yes, sir!" the platoon shouted. Right away they knew this had something to do with Private Bain; they hadn't forgotten there might be a congressional investigation into their treatment.

"Thank you, Sergeant Jenkins," the Marine said, looking appreciative of the platoon commander's apparent willingness to cooperate. The silence cued the drill instructors that they were dismissed. Sergeant Jenkins did an about-face and walked out of the area with Sergeant Lewis and Sergeant Taylor in tow.

The civilian immediately began to go from one private to the next asking questions. "How do you like boot camp?"

"Sir! Fine, sir."

"Do your drill instructors exercise you much?"

"Sir! Yes, sir!"

"Are you exercised excessively as a form of punishment?"

"Sir! No, sir!"

Determined to get at the truth, the civilian continued to probe the recruits. "Do your drill instructors ever swear at you?"

"Sir! Yes, sir!" answered the private being questioned. The silent platoon became more silent. At last, the civilian found the private he was looking for.

"Does your drill instructors ever physically touch you or hit you?" the civilian probed.

"Sir! Yes, sir!"

"Tell me about it."

"Sir! Yesterday, Sergeant Taylor punched me in the mouth! Sir!"

"He did?"

"Sir! Yes, sir!" the private snitched.

The civilian closed his fist and said, "Like this?" He punched the private in the mouth so hard his head snapped back. The civilian screamed, "You slimy puke!"

A disappointed Sergeant Jenkins walked back into the area followed by an angry Sergeant Lewis and a berserk Sergeant Taylor. Sergeant Jenkins walked right up to the private with the bleeding lip and snarled, "You dumb shit!" Sergeant Jenkins turned and walked back to the front of the platoon and stated, "You're only as strong as your weakest link."

Everyone knew what that meant; their physical condition was about to get beefed up. To help them better operate as a team the drill instructors exercised them to near total exhaustion. The day the real investigator showed up no one ratted on drill instructors. In return for their solidarity they got nothing. It was business as usual at MCRD.

Unknown to them, Private Bain was released from the correctional custody platoon after doing his five days and was reassigned to a different platoon, where he successfully completed his boot camp training.

Recruits are not allowed to have pop or candy in boot camp. Someone mailed a box of candy to one recruit. The drill instructors stated that because there were not enough pieces for everyone, the private had one minute to eat it all, including the box it came in. With tears rolling down his face, the private gobbled them up.

On July 18, Mr. and Mrs. Baltes opened a letter from their son. His letter started with a puzzling request without an explanation. To emphasize its importance, he wrote in capital letters "DON'T SEND ME ANYTHING BUT LETTERS!" His letter went on to say, "One kid was UA (unauthorized absence). He's in correctional custody. A couple of other kids were sent to the pig farm. A place you go if you are weak or fat."

Bruce Sommer was born June 7, 1949, in Sisseton, South Dakota. He was the oldest of eight children and had two sisters and five brothers. At a young age his family moved to Minnesota, where Bruce became the neighborhood paperboy for a long time. On the morning of January 3, 1965, he came across a two-year-old boy who had wandered out of a house into subzero weather. Bruce quickly brought the child to a nearby subscriber and called the police. The child's hands were frostbitten and he required medical attention. Bruce was credited for saving the boy's life and received a special carrier award. In 1967 he graduated from Fridley High School and, by the end of June, was on his way to Marine Corps boot camp.

Bruce Sommer was short in height, so his position in the platoon placed him toward the rear near Cusick, Schmidt, Sauro, and Paulseth. Sommer managed to fly under the drill instructors' radar, because he was quick to learn, always did things right, and never spoke a word. He could blend into the background and remain unnoticed.

His anonymity ended the day he took a drink of water at the wash racks. It happened when all the recruits were busy washing their clothes with soap and a scrub brush. Sommer incorrectly assumed it was okay to take a drink from the water faucet. Sergeant Taylor saw the infraction, and Bruce got to experience what it was like to get punched in the gut. Bruce learned from his mistake and quickly faded back into obscurity. He was one of few recruits in the platoon who managed to do almost all the right things at almost all the right times.

David Paulseth was a shoo-in for the short end of the platoon. He was five feet four inches tall and weighed 135 pounds. Before high school he worked on a dairy farm milking forty cows by machine. In return for that he got room and board and fifty dollars a month. He was very independent and self-supporting. He liked fast cars and owned a high-powered 1965 Chevelle. After high school he held down two jobs working fifty hours a week so that he could pay his college tuition. Paulseth's course in life changed when he learned some girl's husband was looking for him. He joined the Marines at age nineteen because for him it was the best way to get out of town in a hurry.

6

ESPRIT DE CORPS

In order to graduate from boot camp the platoon had to pass three tests. One of them, the drill test, involved marching in perfect step while performing the manual of arms with precision.

Sather looked like the Marine on the recruiting poster. He had no unsightly physical characteristics to clash with the stunning blue dress uniform. The drill instructors decided to take advantage of his classic looks by putting him up front as squad leader. Unfortunately, Sather could not march in a straight line. After two days of watching him veer the platoon off course, Sergeant Jenkins shouted, "Take his ass out of there!"

Platoon 3011 passed the drill test and went on to win the series marching competition. They passed the fitness and academic tests with flying colors and came within tenths of a point of wining all three streamers for the platoon flag.

Skip Schmidt was highly motivated to make it through boot camp. At night, while others slept, the high school dropout studied under his blankets in the glow of a tiny pen light. With this extra studying, he passed all the written tests.

As the smallest member of the Minnesota Twins Platoon, he made his mark during the combat readiness testing. For the fireman's carry, the drill instructors playfully paired Schmidt up with the largest member of the platoon. Schmidt dumbfounded everyone when he took off running with the gigantic recruit draped over his shoulder. The larger recruit, who had to pretend to be wounded and unconscious, couldn't believe what was happening, and neither could anyone else. Schmidt raced across the finish line within the allotted amount of time with the big guy's knuckles and toes dragging on the ground. Despite the risk of being punished, the recruits burst into a cheer for Private Schmidt. Two of the drill instructors were shocked and speechless. The other, Sergeant Lewis, summed it up by saying, "Private Schmidt! You a *determined* little bitch, aren't you!"

Sergeant Taylor referred to the series as having two sets of platoons: one set filled with hoodlums from Chicago and the other with farm boys from Minnesota. The ongoing rivalry between the platoons added spark to an incident that occurred when Platoon 3011 was joined by the three other platoons from the series for a week of mess duty.

When the recruits enlisted, no one mentioned that a week of boot camp would be devoted to washing dishes and peeling potatoes. They just assumed somebody else would be doing that, but that was not so. The hours spent at the mess hall were long and hard. The recruits got up at 0330 and didn't hit the sack until 1900 hours. Lack of sleep, boring work, and the hot and humid working conditions caused tempers to flare.

Paulseth was washing some pots and pans when he accidentally splashed water onto a white recruit from Chicago. Without warning, the recruit grabbed a thirty-inch iron frying pan and swung it like a baseball bat into Paulseth's face. Blood went flying in every direction as Paulseth fell to the floor. He was a horrifying spectacle to see when he stood back up. His face was ripped in three places and his white utilities were mostly red. There was a steady flow of blood coming from a deep cut above his eye. His nose was split down the middle and bleeding. Next to his nose was another bleeding gash.

The sergeant in charge took immediate control of the situation. He ordered Paulseth to report to sick bay for medical attention. Paulseth set off on foot, dripping blood and wondering what it took to merit an ambulance ride. By the time he arrived to sick bay, his face was as white as a ghost. He was stitched up and given a day of bed rest.

A few days later, Paulseth and the recruit from Chicago stood tall before the captain. They had to explain about the ruckus in the mess hall. Paulseth's hope for justice went out the window when the captain stated, "Competition between platoons is good. I am going to let you both off. Keep the fighting to a minimum."

For two days Buske's right leg felt stiff. The problem started after he injured his heel running through the obstacle course at full speed. Standing at attention caused a sharp pain to radiate up his right leg from his heel. He told no one about his injury and kept the pain to himself, which worked for a while. Unfortunately, the time spent running became longer and the speed of the runs became faster as the platoon prepared for the notorious three-mile run, a graduation requirement. The entire platoon had to run three miles in formation, wearing combat gear and carrying a rifle, in less than twenty-six minutes. To pass the test, every member of the platoon had to make it.

One morning, as they practiced for the run, the pain in Buske's heel became unbearable and he started to fall behind. After the platoon passed the two-mile marker, Sergeant Jenkins noticed that Buske was dropping back. He ran up behind Buske and kicked him in the butt. Buske accelerated, causing more stress on his foot. The pain became too great for Buske to conceal his injury. Sergeant Jenkins saw Buske running with a limp and he knew it could mean trouble. There was a saying,

"No foot, no Marine."

Sergeant Jenkins ordered Buske to report to sick bay. The doctor on duty examined Buske and asked if he had injured his heel. Buske lied and said, "No."

The doctor reviewed the x-rays and announced, "You have a heel contusion. I want you in the casual company for three weeks. I want you on crutches for the first two weeks. Then return to the clinic in two weeks for a checkup."

Buske was devastated, for he knew what that meant. Going to casual company meant being set back! Whatever training day he was on when he left for casual company would be used to place him with another platoon after his recovery. When the examination was over the doctor handed Buske a folded note and ordered, "Give this to your drill instructor."

Buske did not want to be set back or assigned to another platoon with a different bunch of guys. He stopped short of the billeting area. After looking around to make sure no one was looking, he unfolded the doctor's note intended for the drill instructor and read it.

July 18, 1967
0828
Casual Co.
Crutches x 2 weeks
Whirlpool TID x 3 days
RSC II weeks

At the bottom of the paper was the doctor's signature.

Buske knew what he had to do: he walked to the nearest trash can and deposited the note. A few minutes later, he yelled, "Sir! Private Buske reporting as ordered, sir." The door to the duty hut swung open and out stepped Sergeant Jenkins, sour faced, expecting the worst. He asked for the medical chit, and then grew impatient as he watched Buske's bogus attempt to come up with the note. Finally, Buske ran out of places to search. He announced sheepishly, "Sir! The private lost it, sir."

Sergeant Jenkins berated Buske for losing the note and asked, "Well, puke, what did the doctor tell you?"

"Sir! The doctor said everything was fine, sir!"

While Buske continued his training, the pain about drove him nuts. He did not return to the clinic for his two-week checkup, even though the stiffness and pain remained. On August 19, a day short of four weeks, Buske sought some relief and returned to the clinic. A different doctor examined his leg and told him to return in two days for another assessment.

On August 21, Buske returned with renewed determination and updated the doctor, "My leg is better now and there is no tenderness."

Although the doctor saw through Buske's sham, he went along with it anyway. The doctor returned the recruit to duty without any restrictions. Handing an ace bandage to Buske the doctor said, "Use this to wrap your right calf."

Burke's injury healed gradually. He continued to hide his injury from the drill instructors and successfully continued his training without missing any days.

In the fifth week of boot camp, the platoon was moved forty-five miles in green cattle cars from the recruit depot at San Diego to Edson Range at Camp Pendleton for two weeks of rifle training. At Edson Range the recruits were issued M14 rifles. What the drill instructors had been drumming into them from the moment they were issued their rifles was now strongly reinforced. Their most important piece of equipment was their rifle, never to be let out of their sight—not for a second. They slept with it and learned how to clean it by taking it apart and putting it back together while blindfolded.

A good deal of time was spent inside the classroom learning the fundamentals of marksmanship. Known-distance firing was taught so each recruit had the ability and confidence to kill with one well-aimed round. They were taught such things as: how to sight and aim, trigger control, rapid fire, sight adjustments, effects of weather, and firing positions. Outside the classroom they practiced firing from various positions. The kneeling position, in particular, required a higher degree of muscular flexibility. Getting into the required positions was one challenge, while learning to hold that position for an extended period of time proved to be another. This painful and unforgettable experience was called "snapping in exercises."

It became obvious to the recruits that the drill instructors were under a lot of pressure to get them all to qualify on the rifle range, for it was a graduation requirement. Coaches and primary marksmanship instructors gave one-on-one instruction to make sure everyone qualified at one of three levels — marksman, sharpshooter, or expert. A lot of time was spent teaching the recruits how to sight in their rifles. There was no room for error in war; Marines had to be able to fire their rifles with deadly accuracy. Tensions mounted as the day of qualification neared.

Private David Seldon was a concern because of a hand tremor. His affliction could have kept him out of the service had he not convinced the recruiter it wasn't going to be a problem. And it wasn't a problem until Seldon got to the rifle range. Seldon's tremor was involuntary and brought on by stress. Seldon didn't notice that his hand quivered slightly each time he pulled back on the trigger, but the drill instructors were painfully aware of it.

No one would have guessed that Seldon came from a privileged background. His father was a successful businessman who had the resources to send him to St. John's Northwestern

Military Academy in Delafield, Wisconsin. Afterward, Seldon attended Breck School, a private college-preparatory high school that prided itself in being able to send just about all of its graduates to college. Seldon graduated from Breck without a desire to continue into higher education. Instead, he wanted to serve his country and fulfill his military obligation.

His parents were horrified when their son enlisted and reacted by contacting their U.S. senator, Hubert Humphrey, asking for help to get their son out of the Marine Corps and out of harm's way. Military school was one thing, but in effect Seldon was volunteering to go to war in Vietnam. The Seldons believed that their son's hand tremor should have excused him from military service. To the surprise of his parents, there was no basis for granting Seldon a medical discharge. He was reported to be doing just fine in boot camp.

The drill instructors knew something had to be done to stop Seldon's hands from shaking and quivering. Sergeant Taylor took a personal interest in helping Seldon. When normal teaching methods didn't work, Sergeant Taylor was ready to try something different: he duct-taped Seldon's head to the butt of the rifle. After wrapping the tape many times around the recruit's head, Sergeant Taylor put in a fully loaded magazine clip and set the rifle on automatic fire. The idea was to teach Seldon that the recoil was nothing to fear. Like a jackhammer going through concrete, the rifle recoiled multiple times per second. Things didn't work out exactly as planned. By the time the clip was empty, Private Seldon's right cheek was noticeably swollen. The following morning Seldon showed up at the firing range with a black eye, an enlarged face, and a hand tremor that was worse than ever.

It was a matter of pride for the drill instructors to have all their recruits qualify on the rifle range. Sergeant Taylor continued to single out Seldon for special attention. The night before qualification, Sergeant Taylor ordered Seldon into the duty hut. His newest idea was to have Seldon stand with his arms extended straight out and repeatedly scream at the top of his lungs, "Stop shaking!"

That went on for most of the night. Sergeant Taylor still didn't know stress and fatigue aggravated Seldon's condition. By morning Seldon's tremor was out of control; he was in no condition to qualify. Sergeant Taylor had almost run out of ideas. He took Seldon back into the duty hut and persuaded a corpsman to sedate Seldon with tranquilizers. When Seldon left the duty hut, he was feeling no pain. When his time came to get on line and fire at the targets from varying distances, Seldon qualified. The drill instructors had overcome a major hurdle!

As graduation day neared, so did the physical readiness test with its notorious three-mile run in full combat gear. The final test would be very official, with stopwatches and observers. The drill instructors made it very clear that the three-mile run was a test of the entire platoon. If a single Marine in the platoon didn't make it to the finish line within the twenty-six minute time limit, the entire platoon failed.

On the day of the test the temperature soared to 98 degrees Fahrenheit, which seemed to make the drill instructors nervous. All morning, the recruits could hear them whispering to each other about the heat. There was speculation among the recruits that the run might be postponed. That ended when Sergeant Jenkins ordered them to fall out and be back on the road in five minutes with their combat gear on. The humidity caused them to perspire before they even started.

Each drill instructor had some words of advice. Sergeant Jenkins told them, "Be sure to take your salt tablets. You're going to need them."

Sergeant Taylor added, "Remember it is the platoon that is being tested. This means you all must cross the finish line, every fucking one of you."

Sergeant Lewis said, "You is only as strong as your weakest link," and then waited for them to answer. He often made a statement and treated it like it was a question.

"Sir! Yes, sir," the platoon chorused.

His final words were, "I don't give a shit how you do it: upright, head first, feet first, backwards, upside down, alive, dead. It don't matter to me. Just make sure everyone of you crosses that finish line before the time runs out. Is this clear?"

"Sir! Yes, sir," the platoon responded.

The recruits started the three-mile run looking good, with everyone staying in formation. By the end of the first mile, their fatigues were wet with sweat. The spotter looked worried as the platoon passed by his stopwatch at the one-mile marker. By the end of the second mile, many of the recruits looked rough, with some struggling to keep their places within the formation. The extreme heat was starting to take its toll.

"You got to hurry it up. You're running out of time! You're running too slow!" Sergeant Lewis yelled as he ran alongside the platoon. Even the drill instructors were showing signs of fatigue due to the ungodly heat, and they weren't wearing the heavy equipment.

The recruits began to communicate with one another with their eyes. Not being allowed to speak in boot camp had taught them that skill. Through their stares they told one another, *Here's our chance to show the DIs what we're made of. And we can make them suffer in the process, without getting into any trouble!*

Their pace began to quicken. The harder the drill instructors ran to keep up, the more determined the recruits became to stay ahead of them. The drill instructors were not about to let that happen and caught up.

Sergeant Lewis was sweating profusely. He looked absolutely miserable because the sweat was ruining his perfectly creased, starched utilities. Sergeant Jenkins cut across the course to get to the finish line ahead of them. He wanted to know how much time they had left. From the way he was jumping up and down and waving his arms, they knew it wasn't much.

The hot sun turned their steel helmets into hot plates. Their faces were bright red and hot to the touch as they poured it on, trying to get to the finish line in time. The last quarter mile turned their faces dark red and left them gasping for air. Their sweat-soaked fatigues stuck to their bodies, which restricted movement. As they labored down the final stretch, Sergeant Jenkins screamed, "Go faster! Go faster! You're not going to make it! There's less than a minute left!"

Sather became a victim of heat exhaustion. He was running near the front of the platoon when his legs started to quiver uncontrollably and turned to rubber. Just as his knees buckled and he began to fall, Mulvihill and another large recruit ran up on opposite sides of Sather, and each grabbed an arm. The sight of Sather being dragged toward the goal line sparked the rest of the platoon. Inspired by what they saw, they began to accelerate their pace.

To the utter joy of the drill instructors, Platoon 3011 was no longer running as a herd of individuals but as a team. The drill instructors watched with pride as the entire platoon thundered across the finish line, with more than one Marine being dragged by another. The entire platoon made it across before time ran out . . . but just barely. Passing the physical readiness test not only showed that the members of the platoon would be physically able to carry out their future assignments, but more importantly, the manner in which they passed the test showed they had esprit de corps, which the Corps viewed as a major factor in its world famed battle record.

7

GRADUATION DAY

In the weeks leading up to graduation, the recruits got a small break on Sundays. In the morning the recruits were allowed to sleep an extra half-hour with reveille not until 0530. Church service was held in the base theater located at the far end of the parade grounds. The theater stood like a modern-day coliseum, with six large pillars at its entrance, and it could seat some fifteen platoons. Inside, the recruits could practice their faith and get a break from their drill instructors.

After the church service there was some light exercising and close order drill to improve their marching. Later in the day the recruits got some free time to wash their clothes with a scrub brush. Sunday was the day for sewing up damaged clothing, spit polishing their boots and shoes, and writing longer letters home.

The Sunday prior to graduation, however, was special; the recruits were allowed to have visitors for the first time, but only family members. Word came down as to who was to report to the visitors' area. Private Schmidt was one of them. Waiting to see him was his father Eugene, his sister Diane, and her husband John Van Bergen, who was in the navy and stationed in San Diego. He was a seaman aboard the USS *Sioux*, a fleet tug.

"It's a heck of a place isn't it, Skipper," Eugene said.

The way Skip laughed and said, "It sure is," suggested to

Eugene that boot camp hadn't changed much since he had passed through.

"I'm proud of you," said Eugene, as he embraced his son.

"We're all so proud of you," said Diane, as she stepped up and also gave Skip a hug. John was equally happy as he congratulated Skip.

It was a very special day for Skip and his appearance matched the occasion. Schmidt stood upright with perfect posture. There were no wrinkles in his starched uniform, and his black boots were shined to a high gloss. The wide smile on his face reflected his pride in his accomplishment. From the concession stand Skip and his family headed for the open picnic tables carrying paper cups filled with nonalcoholic refreshments. Skip remained the center of attention while everyone sat around him. He was eager to let his dad know that his boot camp platoon had a lot of esprit de corps and was made up of a tight group of guys.

"Our drill sergeant had three days off but didn't have enough money to go home to see his dying mother, so we all chipped in so he would have enough money to go home," Skip proudly told his father.

"Skip, they're still doing the same thing! The drill instructor's mother was dying when I went through boot camp. They told us the same story! They said if everyone chipped in the sergeant would have enough money to go home," Eugene said. He shook his head and chuckled.

For the entire two hours Skip just beamed. He felt confident about following in his father's footsteps, and more importantly, about himself.

"Visitation will end in five minutes," crackled the announcement over the loudspeaker. With handshakes and hugs, Skip bade his family farewell and stood erect as he watched them leave. When Eugene, Diane, and John reached the exit gate, they turned and looked back. Skip was standing in the same place, holding his paper cup in one hand. The smile that had been on his face all afternoon still remained. He looked so happy he almost glowed. Never before had his life been filled with so much purpose and meaning.

Private Sauro was notified by the drill instructor that his brother was in the visiting area waiting to see him. He questioned it. "Sir! There must be some mistake. My brother lives in Minnesota. He is just fourteen years old. My mother would not have sent him out here for a visit, sir!"

Sergeant Jenkins blew up and screamed in Sauro's face, "You puke! The Marine Corps does not make mistakes! Now get out of here!"

"Sir! Yes, sir!" Sauro replied and quickly proceeded to the visiting area. His visitor was Wayne Stanley; the two grew up in Woodbury, Minnesota, next door to each other, from age eight to sixteen. Wayne was one year older, and he had enlisted in the navy and was stationed at the San Diego naval base. In order to visit Sauro, he had to say he was his brother. Their discussion quickly got around to comparing boot camp experiences. It wasn't long before Stanley told Sauro that he would have told the Marine drill instructors that he would not put up with that kind of treatment.

"Oh really! Well, here's your chance," Sauro said, as he nodded his head toward the Marine coming up behind Stanley. "Here comes Sergeant Lewis. He is one of our DIs. Go ahead! I want to hear you tell him that you would not put up with that kind of bullshit."

Stanley turned his head around and saw the approaching drill instructor, whose broad shoulders rhythmically tipped back and forth, right to left, while his Smokey the Bear–type hat remained upright and perfectly level. Sergeant Lewis could have carried a glass of water on the top of his head without spilling a drop. The large drill instructor with massive arms shot the two of them an unfriendly glance as he passed by. His face was in a frown and his lips were curled downward.

Without saying a word, Stanley quickly took his eyes off Lewis and looked back at his childhood friend, who was staring back at him and grinning from ear to ear.

August 31 was Platoon 3011's last day at MCRD. Graduation Day was both a joyful and somber occasion. It started with an upbeat formal military ceremony filled with pomp and circumstance. All the recruits took great pride in having made it through boot camp. They might have been more jubilant to be a part of the world-famed fighting force, known for its battle record and esprit de corps, if times were more peaceful. A few days prior, the drill instructors had told them, "Ninety percent of you will spend Christmas in Vietnam."

The ceremony concluded and the time came for them to leave MCRD. The recruits were given a four-hour base liberty before their departure for Camp Pendleton, where they would receive advanced training. As the members of Platoon 3011 stood in their dress uniforms before their drill instructors for the last time, they wondered what parting words the drill instructors would have for them.

"Knuckle push-ups! Ready! Begin!" Sergeant Jenkins shouted out. Reluctantly, the platoon dropped down into the push-up position and followed orders. Knuckle push-ups were the worst kind, especially because the drill instructors never asked for them unless the surface beneath them was asphalt or concrete, which made the push-ups more painful and slightly bloody. The message the drill instructors were sending was open to the former recruits' individual interpretations. Many believed it was their way of saying, *Don't let this graduation go to your head. You still have a lot to prove.*

Without question, Marine Corps boot camp had forever changed them all. As one graduate wrote in a letter home, "When Tuffy [the family dog] first sees me, she won't even know who it is."

8

ADVANCED TRAINING

After graduating from boot camp, the recruits of 3011 took a fifty-mile bus trip to Camp Pendleton for basic infantry training . They were assigned to 2nd Battalion, 2nd Infantry Training Regiment, with most going to companies A, N, and Q. Each company comprised about 250 men, who were spilt up into four platoons. Troop handlers replaced drill instructors, and in the eyes of their new instructors, they were still not Marines and required a high degree of supervision. Although their treatment was much better, they were still slapped up and knocked around for the more serious foul-ups.

At Camp Pendleton they were taught the basic skills required to be an effective infantryman. They swam in deep water carrying sixty pounds of combat gear. Large-scale infantry maneuvers took place day and night. They were taught how to use a variety of weapons, from hand grenades to a string of wire. One month later they were able to claim proudly the title of U.S. Marine!

The excitement and anticipation of going home on leave was almost overwhelming. On the last day of advanced infantry training, one troop handler had a few surprise announcements. "Those of you from the Midwest may not have enough money to buy round-trip airline tickets to go home on leave. But don't worry, the Marine Corps will advance you your pay. You will be able to fly home and see your families before reporting to your next duty station."

It took a few minutes for the news to sink in. The main reason they had enlisted was not monetary; the low pay of a private was never an issue. But none of them expected to go home on leave owing the Marine Corps money. As it began to occur to everyone that serving their country would put them in debt, the laughter started and became so widespread the troop handler had to yell, "Hey! Listen up. I have one more announcement. The following Marines should not purchase airline tickets home. They will not be given leave at this time." A hush fell over the entire company; some 250 Marines did not utter a sound.

The troop handler read off thirty-three names. Nearly half were from the Minnesota Twins Platoon: Carter, Cirkl, Cusick, Ehn, Fimon, Gregor, Knutson, Marlowe, Mathewson, Mudgett, Olsen, Parisse, Paulson, Sauro, Smith, and Sundeen. Instead of going home on leave, they were given orders to report immediately to the Landing Force Training Command at Coronado, California.

The reason their leave home was cancelled was due to the critical shortage in Vietnam of trained embarkation personnel as a result of the rapid troop buildup. At the start of 1967, the supply system was having trouble keeping pace with the number of combat troops being sent over to fight the war. As the number of troops increased, so did the need for supplies. The Corps urgently needed to get more logistics people to handle the massive troop deployments and supplies going into Vietnam. Some Marines lacked such basic necessities as socks and uniforms. The condition of their equipment when they left Vietnam, after completing their tour of duty, was alarming.

Mildred Sauro went out the restaurant delivery door and across the street to her mailbox. Inside was a letter from her son, Chris:

> *Dear Mom,*
>
> *In one day, I add up over 400 million numbers. If I pass embarkation school I'll be the one who makes loading plans for troops that are going to Vietnam. I have to gather information from the different units and figure out where the things will be stored, so they can be unloaded according to their priority number in a certain amount of time. I also have to take into consideration the weight of each item, the cubic feet, and square feet to see if they will fit where I want them to. I will have to provide space for the troops, get the shore parties to do the loading, get the military police to direct the traffic in the staging area (after I have checked to make sure the staging area is big enough). I can't even begin to list all the things an embarkation officer's assistant does.*
>
> *In the class I am in, there are also some army sergeants and staff sergeants, navy chiefs, and some Marine staff sergeants, plus PFCs and privates. It used to be an eight-week school. We won't know if we pass until three days before the end of the course, because they give just one test. (I am really sweating it!) Well if anything new comes up I'll let you know.*
>
> *Your son,*
> *Chris*

Life at Coronado was plush, and the Marines in charge treated the embarkation students with some degree of dignity. They were housed and fed just like the sailors, and every meal was fit for a king. Going to embarkation school was like having a regular job, with nights and weekends off. Outside the classroom there was one thing on their minds—girls!

At age nineteen, Cusick was slightly older than most. When a civilian, he was able to attract good-looking girls, so his fellow Marines expected great things to happen to him on liberty. The first time Cusick returned from liberty, a small crowd was waiting in the barracks to interrogate him. His fellow Marines wanted a full account!

"I was approached by two girls on a street corner in San Diego," Cusick said matter of factually. "They asked me if I wanted to go to their place." His last comment initiated a lot of pushing and shoving as the Marines jockeyed around Cusick for a good listening position. "Once they got me to their place, they took out their beads and began to chant. When I saw they belonged to a sect and weren't interested in me, I bought a scroll and left," Cusick finished with a sigh. Suddenly Cusick found himself standing alone. His audience of listeners went flocking toward another Marine returning from off-base liberty, hoping he might have something more tantalizing to report.

The popular dance place Cinnamon Cinder was one of the few places Marine recruits could go to meet girls because it did not serve alcohol. California's legal drinking age was twenty-one, which left the majority of underage Marines on the outside looking in when it came to the local bar scene.

The next time Cusick returned from liberty and entered the barracks the Marines inside again rushed over to interrogate him. Cusick enjoyed the attention and proceeded to fill them in. "I met a girl at Cinnamon Cinder. I walked across the dance floor and asked this girl sitting at one of the tables to dance. She accepted!" Cusick reported to his fellow Marines, who longed to hear about the opposite sex.

"You being a Marine didn't scare her off?" one Marine asked skeptically, because many of the Marines returning from off-base liberty were reporting that the local girls didn't want much to do with them. The young women were well aware that Marine recruits had been isolated from the opposite sex for three months. Also, if they were looking for any kind of long-term meaningful relationship, a recruit didn't fit the bill because upon completion of their training, they were almost always sent to Vietnam.

For the second time Cusick had their undivided attention, as he told them about his night out. "After she accepted my offer to dance, I turned and headed for the dance floor expecting her to follow. At first I couldn't figure out why people were giving me dirty looks. When I turned around I discovered why! The girl I had asked to dance was shuffling behind me with her arms outstretched in front of her. She was blind!"

"Well that explains why she accepted," one Marine said to another.

"So what happened next?" an impatient Marine wanted to know, hoping the story might end like one of his fantasies.

"We had a good time together. We danced a number of times and talked."

"That's it?" asked one listener.

"Yes!" Cusick honestly told them.

It was not what they wanted to hear. For a second time, Cusick suddenly found himself standing alone. Cusick could hear his friends saying, "Let's find someone who went to Tijuana!"

On November 3, 1967, Twins Platoon members Carter, Cirkl, Cusick, Knutson, Marlowe, and Sauro graduated from embarkation school. They were among those to receive their diplomas with orders for Vietnam. Before going to Vietnam, they would get one chance to see their loved ones. Their leave, however, was cut back to seventeen days, including round-trip travel time between California and Minnesota.

Skip Schmidt successfully completed his basic infantry training at Camp Pendleton and remained there to start battalion infantry training specialty (BITS) school. At BITS he received special training to become an "assaultman." He was taught to fire a wider range of weapons, like the .50-caliber spotting rifle, 106mm recoilless rifle, 3.5-inch rocket launcher, and flamethrower. There were sixty-three students in Schmidt's class at BITS, including four familiar faces from boot camp: Gerald Baltes, Robert Barrette, Larry Jones, and Kenneth Goodman. BITS lasted three weeks.

On October 25, 1967, Skip and the four other Twins Platoon members graduated with honors. Out of sixty-three students, all five were in the top ten of the class! Skip's proficiency and conduct marks went from "good" to "excellent," which was another rewarding accomplishment for him. With the excitement of graduating came the apprehension of getting new orders. When the troop handler handed Skip his new orders, it stated that he, like most, was being sent to Vietnam.

In Vietnam, communist forces were preparing for a major military action. Top U.S. military leaders continued to be concerned about the substantial increase in guerrilla warfare and the growing number of enemy troops in and around the demilitarized zone (DMZ). The number of enemy troops operating in the I Corps area was estimated to be as large as three divisions. Some twenty-seven-thousand enemy troops were massing to battle with the Marines in I Corps. The massive enemy buildup combined with the shortages of supplies in I Corps left the American troops faced with a major problem, which was exacerbated by a stated policy that prohibited Marines from engaging the enemy north of the DMZ. It was a serious tactical disadvantage that allowed the enemy to deploy forces along the DMZ, while denying the Marines their most effective means of fighting offensively.

On December 1, 1967, Skip Schmidt was promoted to private first class ahead of schedule. His self-confidence increased, making him even prouder to be a Marine. The week before Christmas, Skip phoned his sister Diane, who was still living in Chula Vista, fifty miles away from Camp Pendleton.

"Diane! Some girls from Minnesota are up in Los Angeles. They want me and my buddy to go out with them! We've got a date with them for this weekend, but we have no way to get there," Skip said, sounding both excited and frustrated. This was to be his last liberty before leaving for Vietnam.

Diane offered Skip the use of her car. It was a gray 1963 Volkswagen bug on its last legs. There was no extra money to pay for any repairs, extra gasoline, or unseen expenses. In 1967 the salary of a navy sailor was as dismal as that of a Marine; it was not enough to make ends met. Combined, John and Diane's salaries barely raised their standard of living to be above the poverty line.

Skip and his buddy scraped together the bus fare to get to his sister's house. When they arrived, John told his brother-in-law, "Skip, take the Volkswagen for the whole weekend. Just be sure to have it back here Sunday night, because Diane and I both have to go to work Monday morning."

Skip and his buddy looked troubled. "We don't have any money for gas," Skip confessed. "If we could get up there, I know we could find somebody who would give us the three or four dollars to get back home." With the war escalating, Los Angeles was crawling with Marines on liberty and leave. Skip knew the two empty seats in the back of the Volkswagen were easily worth the price of gas. Plenty of Marines would jump at the chance to get a car ride from Los Angeles to Camp Pendleton for only three or four dollars, which would be cheaper than taking a cab and better than a long bus ride.

"Okay we'll gas it up," Diane said. She turned to John and asked, "Honey, you got any money?" John opened his billfold and watched the moths fly out. Diane glanced down at her purse. She had a lot of things in it, but money wasn't one of them.

"I got some money!" She returned carrying a piggy bank, which she broke open to get the coins out. It was barely enough. "This should get you there!" Diane said, filling Skip's hands with quarters, nickels, dimes, and pennies.

"The Volkswagen isn't working real good. We have to push it to get it started," John warned.

Diane and John awoke Monday morning to find Skip had not returned with the car. The two nervously got ready for work with no way to get there. Just as they were about to throw their hands up in the air in desperation, they saw the Volkswagen pull up in front of their apartment.

"Don't turn the car off," John and Diane both shouted to Skip as they hurried down the sidewalk. "Well, old man, how did your weekend go?" John asked as he slid in behind the steering wheel.

"It was great," Skip said and smiled.

"Did the big man behave himself?" John asked the other Marine.

"We didn't get any sleep," the other Marine replied with a happy face.

John laughed, put the bug in gear, and pushed the accelerator to the floor. The fully loaded Volkswagen drove off puffing black smoke.

John braked the car to a halt in front of the plant where Diane worked. Her job brought her close to the war. She worked as a machinist in a shop that made ball bearings for helicopters. Because the fighting in Vietnam had intensified, her employer was granted special permission by the government to allow women employees to work extended hours to keep up with the shipment of needed parts.

It was time for her to say good-bye to Skip. The weeks Diane and Skip had spent together in California gave them the opportunity to really get to know each other well. Before getting out of the car, Diane turned around and looked at her uniformed brother sitting in the back seat. In a choked up voice, she said, "Skipper, we'll be anxiously waiting for you to come home."

The look on Skip's face was something Diane would never forget. Skip didn't say a word. He just looked at Diane and shook his head, as if to say, "No Diane. I probably won't make it back alive."

As Diane watched the Volkswagen drive off, she worried that she might never see her brother again.

Kenneth Goodman completed his Marine training in November and received orders for Vietnam. Before shipping out, Kenny was given his first leave, so he returned to Stewart, Minnesota, proudly wearing his Marine Corps uniform. For Eileen McGraw, one of Kenny's most endearing and charming qualities was his blue eyes and great smile.

"We're invited out to the relatives' for dinner tonight," Kenny said to Eileen with a smile. Both sets of parents had grown up and gone to school together in Stewart, and over the years, they had become best friends. The McGraws were also good friends with Kenny's uncle, aunt, and grandfather. Such closely knit relationships were not uncommon in small rural towns like Stewart, where things changed little from one generation to the next. With each new generation, a good number of neighbors became relatives through the marriage of their children, drawing those in the community even closer together.

"I'll see you later tonight at dinner. I have to go to St. Paul this afternoon to see my aunt," Kenny fibbed. When Kenny was supposed to be at his aunt's, he was, instead, in a jewelry store purchasing a diamond engagement ring.

That night the Goodmans and the McGraws were at a relative's home for dinner. They were at the table eating when Eileen noticed Virgil and Bernice whisper something to her parents. Her parents smiled and looked happy. Suddenly it hit Eileen; she figured out what was going on.

Kenny stood up and in front of everyone asked Eileen, "Will you marry me when I return from Vietnam?" It was the moment she had been waiting for. Inside she felt great. She knew this day would come and was not totally surprised by Ken's proposal. Without hesitation she accepted the proposal of the man she loved. When Kenny placed the ring on her finger, everyone clapped and toasted the childhood sweethearts.

Larry Rademacher was a stocky five feet six and one-half inches tall and weighed 160 pounds. He enlisted in the Marines at age seventeen with an interesting array of skills. He had four years of auto mechanics, one year on the Shakopee High School wrestling team, played the cornet in music, and could type thirty-six words a minute. He and Buske had become good friends in part because they always received orders that keep them stationed together. It started with boot camp, continued through individual combat training, and finally endured through amtrac school. Both received twenty-three days of leave at the same time. While home on leave the two got their families together for a visit. What the two families had in common, besides seeing their sons sworn into the Marine Corps at Met Stadium on June 28, 1967, was that both Rademacher and Buske had orders for Vietnam.

PART TWO:
IN VIETNAM

9

THE CUA VIET

Rademacher and Buske arrived in Da Nang, Vietnam, on December 30, 1967, where they received new orders that kept them together. The two were directed to where they would board the small landing craft that would transport them up the Cua Viet River to the 1st Amphibious Tractor Battalion, their final assignment. The first words out of Rademacher's mouth as they started upriver were, "This is unbelievable! We should have been issued a rifle or something. Remember how it was in California? We had to eat and sleep with our rifle. We were told never to leave it out of our sight! Then they send us to 'Nam, put us on a boat, and send us up to the DMZ without so much as a slingshot. Is this crazy, or what!" Rademacher exclaimed as he continued to harass Buske.

Upon reaching the Cua Viet port facility, the two young Marines' destination, they were split up for the first time since they'd been sworn in at the Twins game, which already seemed a lifetime ago. Buske was assigned to 2nd Platoon, Company A, 1st Amphibian Tractor Battalion, and Rademacher was assigned to the battalion's headquarters and service (H&S) company.

Ocean freighters came to the Cua Viet to offload their cargo and equipment. It was a new port facility directly below the DMZ and about nine miles from North Vietnam. It was used to supply the Marines operating along the DMZ, and in the nine months it had been in operation, the landing ramp tripled the daily tonnage that could be brought in by ship. Smaller watercraft carried the cargo farther inland to supply the Marine bases that ran along the DMZ. Although the new ramp helped the situation, trying to keep the Marines well supplied remained a troublesome burden.

Buske was hoping to avenge the death of his high school friend, Tom Healy, who had been killed in Vietnam in 1966. He still wondered how someone as tough as Tom could have gotten killed.

On the morning of January 19, 1968, a short-timer told Buske, "If I had as many days left in country as you do, I'd shoot myself."

"So how many days do you have left?" Buske asked.

"Thirty," replied the short-timer. With eager anticipation Marines nearing the end of their standard thirteen-month tour of duty counted the remaining days and told others, "I'm short!" With the help of a "short-timer calendar" they tracked the last hundred days left to serve in Vietnam. Generally, the calendar was a poor drawing of a gorgeous girl scantly clothed. In their letters home they often referred to the number of days they had left in Vietnam.

"You're not out of here until your out of here," the short-timers' peers reminded them. Short-timers knew the risk of being killed in Vietnam had no relation to the number of days left to serve. For those serving in 1968, a leap year, there was one extra day to sweat it out.

Bad news came from headquarters. The enemy had opened up on a column of amphibious tractors (amtracs) with rocket-propelled grenades (RPG) and mortars. It was a surprise attack and casualties were said to be heavy. Third Platoon was totally disabled and fighting desperately to hold on until reinforcements could arrive.

Buske's platoon mobilized quickly; the Marines grabbed their rifles, cartridge belts, flak jackets, and helmets. It took just a few minutes for them to suit up and hit the road. They departed the base compound determined to cover quickly the three miles that separated them from 3rd Platoon. Buske stayed close to the short-timer.

Without warning they came under fire. The seasoned veteran dashed for cover with Buske trailing close behind. When the short-timer dove for cover behind a large mound, Buske did too. Buske could see numerous other mounds of similar size and shape, then it occurred to him that they were pinned down in a cemetery. Over the snap of bullets the short-timer yelled to Buske, "Get your damned legs around here or you'll get 'em shot off."

Buske pulled his legs in fast and assumed a fetal position behind the grave mound. The short-timer was experienced in combat. Whatever Buske could learn from him could mean the difference between life and death.

Buske saw flashes from a rifle barrel in the tree line ahead. He aimed his rifle and returned fired. Other members of 2nd Platoon maneuvered into position. Two UH-1 Huey gunships equipped with side-mounted rockets passed overhead. No one had to tell Buske to put his head down. The gunships fired their rockets, and the explosions followed within seconds. The two choppers never circled back; they continued their course toward the trapped 3rd Platoon. The tree line was still hazed over with smoke when the order to "move out" was given.

Buske got up from behind the dirt mound, but the short-timer did not. Buske went over to see why. The eyes he saw staring back at him were glazed over, lifeless. Right in the center of the short-timer's chest was a large gaping hole. Buske was stunned. The two were lying side by side, and he had not seen it happen. He knew there was nothing he could do to help the short-timer, so he hurried off to join the others.

An enemy soldier put Buske in his sights and opened fire. Buske heard the popping sounds of gunfire and saw the water in the puddle next to him start to splash.

"Shit! This is real!" Buske thought as he dashed for cover.

The Marines advanced toward the tree line, exchanging fire with the enemy. It took nearly a half-hour to reach the trees, so by the time they got there, the enemy was gone. They had been fighting a few snipers whose purpose was to delay the reinforcements for 3rd Platoon.

When 2nd Platoon reached the ambush site, they came upon what was left of 3rd Platoon. Out of some forty men, just seven were still alive, and their condition was critical. A few hours later, 2nd Platoon returned to the cemetery. Buske helped lift the body of the short-timer onto a poncho liner. Then they carried his body over to a waiting amtrac that was piled high with the bodies of 3rd Platoon Marines.

Buske had never got around to asking the short-timer his name. In the days that followed, all he could think about was the short-timer's family back in the States.

On his nineteenth day in Vietnam, Buske gained a deep insight into how someone as tough as Tom Healy could have been killed.

Rademacher was an amtrac crewman without an amtrac. Property damage losses from incoming rounds had recently become so great that the amtrac he was assigned to operate had to be dismantled. This interfered with his unit's ability to carry out their mission, but it did not stop them. His unit retrained him to fire rockets and put him to use as an infantryman.

On January 20, 1968, 1st Amphibian Tractor Battalion was conducting a two-company operation in conjunction with the South Vietnamese's 2nd Army of the Republic of Vietnam (ARVN) Regiment when a platoon of Marines came under attack by a larger enemy force. The opposing forces fought one another on the northern bank of the Cua Viet River by the hamlet of My Loc. Rademacher's unit was mobilized to assist in the fighting, which escalated as more Marines arrived on the scene. Fifty artillery rounds hammered Marine positions as cover for the enemy's withdrawal.

When Rademacher had arrived, the fighting was already over and the area had been secured. The Marine tractor battalion had suffered thirteen dead and forty-eight wounded. Rademacher's job was to help load the dead onto the amtracs. Rigor mortis had set in, making it difficult to put Marines who had died in peculiar positions into the body bags. Rademacher hoped Buske was not among the casualties. The dead Marines were loaded into the bottom of the amtracs and the wounded climbed in on top of the pile.

The amtracs crossed the river, leaving a trail of blood in the water. Rademacher watched the red wake fan out across the river. He figured it was just a matter of time before his number was up.

The month of January brought a noticeable increase in enemy activity in the Cua Viet area. Navy landing craft filled with supplies were routinely attacked en route to Dong Ha. Those attacks led to Rademacher's next assignment, to ride aboard the landing crafts to provide security. In addition to his rifle he would have a weapon that was new to him, the M72 light antitank weapon (LAW). This weapon fired a shaped-charge warhead with the lethality of a hand grenade from a disposable telescoping plastic rocket launcher. Although he didn't expect to see any Viet Cong (VC) tanks to shoot at, the LAW was great for attacking enemy bunkers. After a few quick lessons and a couple of practice shots, Rademacher was ready to ride the river.

There was nothing scenic about the Cua Viet River. Its clay bottom tinted the water a brownish red color. Marines traveling the Cua Viet knew the enemy were lurking in unseen places and watching them the whole way. On the river, they were sitting ducks, for if they were attacked while aboard a landing craft there was no place to go.

Five landing craft set out; Rademacher was aboard the last one along with a few other Marines for security and a half-dozen sailors. The landing craft carried a communications truck lashed to the deck, for delivery to Dong Ha.

Any hopes for a peaceful trip ended with a large explosion. The first vessel hit a mine, causing it to rise up out of the water and flip over backward. Rademacher frantically looked for the men aboard to surface. He expected any second to see sailors and Marines pop up out of the water. When that didn't happen, he was convinced Vietnam was some kind of hellhole. Each time an incoming round missed its target and exploded beneath the surface, water sprayed high up into the sky. "Get up on the truck. You'll see more," the sailor on the boat tower yelled to Rademacher. But before Rademacher had an opportunity to react, an RPG hit the tower, destroying it and killing the sailor.

Rademacher and the Marine next to him dove for cover in the hull of the ship. Rademacher's face was pressed to the deck when he heard another loud explosion. It was so loud he reacted by trying to push his whole body into his helmet. Windshield glass from the truck sprayed all over. The enemy round had hit right where the sailor had suggested he should go.

The Marine next to Rademacher stood up, but then another explosion blasted in the boat. When Rademacher looked up he saw the Marine standing headless, still holding his rifle. Then the body of the decapitated Marine crumpled to the deck. When the partially filled helmet went rolling by, it made for a sight that Rademacher would never forget.

The explosions continued in rapid succession. Rademacher wondered where the rounds were coming from. Amidst all the confusion he saw something that gave a hint of an answer. A sailor aboard one of the landing craft was firing a 40mm automatic cannon at a Buddhist temple set back from the river's edge. The 40mm tracer rounds served as a guiding light to the distant pagoda. Suddenly, an RPG hit the other landing craft and blew up the 40mm and the sailor behind it.

Rademacher spun into action; he raced to get his LAW. The others aboard began yelling and pointing, "Hey, it's coming from that pagoda!" Rademacher was worried that the pagoda might be out of range, so he extended the tube and graduated the sights for maximum distance. When Rademacher fired his rocket launcher, the projectile sailed upward over the river before it reached its highest point. Then it began its downward descent toward the distant pagoda. The rocket went right through the roof of the pagoda and exploded. A much louder secondary explosion blew the pagoda into a million pieces.

Rademacher was too green to realize he had just destroyed a supply of enemy ammunition. All he knew was that the fighting was over. The convoy continued and successfully reached its destination. When he got back to Dong Ha the executive officer had him ceremoniously promoted to lance corporal.

10

ATTACK ON KHE SANH

A secret enemy offensive was to get under way with a surprise attack planned for February 1, 1968, to coincide with the start of the most important Vietnamese holiday of the year, Tet. North Vietnam desperately wanted Tet of 1968 to mark the fall of the U.S. military presence in South Vietnam.

Largely undetected, the enemy moved vast amounts of supplies and some hundred thousand soldiers into the cities of South Vietnam. U.S. intelligence sources indicated that the 325C North Vietnam Army (NVA) Division was moving toward Hill 881 North, just four miles north of the Marine base at Khe Sanh. Another NVA division, the 304th, had crossed the Laotian border and was moving into position southwest of the base. The 324B Division and elements of the 308th and 341st NVA divisions were spotted along the eastern half of the DMZ.

Of the half-million American troops in South Vietnam, only about 20 percent were Marines. The Marines occupied I Corps, which comprised the four provinces located just below the DMZ. The enemy forces pouring into I Corps so heavily outnumbered the Marines that General William Westmoreland, the U.S. field commander, ordered the deployment of the U.S. Army 1st Cavalry Division to reinforce the northern I Corps area.

Kenneth Goodman arrived in Da Nang, Vietnam, on December 8, 1967. Twelve days later, he learned that he was being deployed to a base that he had never heard of in the uppermost northwestern corner of South Vietnam. When he wrote home, he misspelled his destination: "I don't know the company I'm going to, but it's a place called Kason. There's not much fighting going on there, but it should be interesting. There's tigers, elephants, and lots of monkeys there."

On December 21, 1967, 3rd Battalion, 26th Marine Regiment went out on a five-day sweep of the hills surrounding Khe Sanh in search of a large North Vietnamese force said to be in the area. Along the way the battalion found plenty of evidence to confirm a large enemy presence. They saw well-worn trails, hidden bunkers, and empty, freshly dug fighting holes.

In Washington, D.C., the fate of the Marines at Khe Sanh was a subject of major concern. The unfolding events mirrored those that led to the defeat of the French at Dien Bien Phu. In Saigon General Westmoreland told his assembled staff, "We are not—repeat—not going to be defeated at Khe Sanh. I will tolerate no talking or even thinking to the contrary." General Westmoreland had formulated a plan that called for doubling the number of Marines at Khe Sanh from three thousand to six thousand. Goodman was one of those Marines being moved into the troubled area.

On Christmas Day, Goodman attended the Catholic Church service. As for Christmas presents, he already had his. He had received them when he was home on leave in November. His family had celebrated both Thanksgiving and Christmas early just for him. It was the first time he had ever opened his gifts in November, but that's what his family wanted.

On December 27, 1967, Goodman was on a flight to Khe Sanh dressed in full combat gear. His orders read to report to

1st Platoon, Kilo Company, 3rd Battalion, 26th Marines, where he would assume the dangerous job of machine gunner.

The Goodman family was spending a lot of time thinking about Kenny. News reports said that North Vietnam was preparing for the winter-spring offensive and some thirty-five to forty-five thousand communist troops were massing just above the DMZ. The Goodmans were eager to know where their son was, because they couldn't find "Kason" on the map. Kenny's next letter clarified that point: "I am at Khe Sanh, pronounced Kason. It's really too bad there's a war on here, cause right here where I am, it's beautiful. Boy, it's a beautiful day. The jungle is full of birds and they're really singing. The monkeys are pretty, too. They make a loud scream that's pretty."

Bernice put her son's letter down. She had thought that knowing his exact whereabouts would make her feel better. It didn't.

Goodman was part of a column of Marines headed for Hill 861, which was about three miles northwest of the main base. To get there they went up high ridges and down deep ravines. In some places they came upon jungle grass that had sharp, serrated edges and was fifteen feet tall. Getting through it was nearly impossible; their boots stuck between the thick stalks before they reached the ground. The best way to forge a trail was for each man to follow directly behind the other. At the end of the day, the tired group reached the top of Hill 861.

Rolls of concertina wire encircled the top of the hill. Behind the wire were Marines peering out over the top of narrow trenches and a smattering of sand-bagged bunkers. The hilltop looked large enough for helicopters to land. Goodman got a good view of the main combat base down below. Two miles to the northwest were two steep-sided hills named for their elevation, 881 North and 881 South, which were also occupied by Marines overseeing the approaches to the main base.

The Marines at Khe Sanh were informed that fresh NVA regiments were moving into the surrounding mountains, with several more on the way, including those of the famed 304th Division, whose fighting prowess in the Battle of Dien Bien Phu in 1954 had brought about the defeat of the French.

Goodman went out on patrol a few days later. He was surprised to see Vietnamese people living so primitively. They didn't wear much for clothes, lived in grass huts, and carried spears. In the nearby lowlands, Goodman saw Vietnamese people farming the rice paddies with wooden plows pulled by water buffalo. When the little kids saw the Marines, they ran over to beg for food and cigarettes.

When Goodman was not patrolling the high mountains, steep ravines, and small valleys surrounding Khe Sanh, he wrote to his loved ones back home. Bernice Goodman read Kenny's letter dated January 12, 1968, out loud to the family. Little Jan was too young to understand, but Bob and Mary weren't. Their older brother's closing lines were, "Dear Bob, I want you to know I'm thinking of you constantly. You too, Mary and Jan."

In the same day's mail there was another letter from Kenny addressed to his twelve-year-old sister, Mary. She took her letter into her room to read it in private. Lying across her bed, she read, "I got a letter from Eileen today. She said you wrote her the nicest letter. I'm sure glad you like Eileen the way you do, because Eileen really thinks a lot of you, too. You should see the pretty flowers here in the jungle. The flowers are all colors and sizes. There are monkeys, too. I'm trying to catch and tame one for a pet."

Mary rolled over and looked up at the ceiling. That was just like Kenny. He wanted her and his future wife to be close.

Kenny loved animals and had all kinds of pets, such as rabbits and baby raccoons. She remembered the time Kenny was out at the gravel pit and came upon a dead mother fox. He looked around until he found her two pups and brought them home, and the whole family helped raise them. There were other memories, too. Like the time Kenny woke her up at two o'clock in the morning.

"Mary, Mary. Wake up. It's Kenny. Grab your blanket and follow me. I have something to show you," Ken whispered. At the time Ken was sixteen years old and Mary was eight. Without hesitating, she climbed out of bed, grabbed her blanket with one hand, and took Kenny's hand with the other. Kenny was more than just a brother; he was her best friend, which is often how it is in small towns like Stewart, where few children lived nearby. Mary followed her older brother outside.

"Wow! Is this ever neat, Kenny," Mary said looking up at the aurora of bright green lights dancing on the horizon. The colors radiated upward into the sky like flames of fire. "What is it, Kenny?"

"It's the northern lights," Kenny explained, as he wrapped the blanket around her shoulders. The two sat quietly together and watched the flickering light show.

In early January 1968, General Westmoreland ordered the development of a massive aerial bombardment program code-named Niagara to help defend the Marine base at Khe Sanh.

On January 10, Goodman looked down from his position on top of Hill 861. The sound of whirling rotor blades caused him to turn his head. A CH-46 transport helicopter passed directly overhead, where Goodman could see helmet-headed cargo staring back at him through the portside windows. The chopper continued its rapid descent toward the airstrip below. When the CH-46 landed, about twenty-five Marines hurried down the lowered tail ramp, crossed over the open runway, and disappeared into a trench on the opposite side. It was a scene Goodman would see repeated many times over in the days to come.

For the Marines manning the trenches at Khe Sanh, the steady stream of choppers flying in reinforcements fueled the speculation that the enemy was going to try to overrun the base. The rumored size of the enemy force grew daily. When the number reached twenty thousand, all Goodman and the others could do was laugh nervously and joke about it. Goodman didn't want his family to worry, so he didn't write about what was really taking place.

Two days later a Marine patrol returned to base carrying enemy gear found hidden in a tunnel near Hill 861. Everyone knew it was just a question of time before the North Vietnamese would try to overrun Khe Sanh. The upcoming battle was viewed as the fight that could decide the outcome of the war.

By mid-January twenty-thousand enemy troops had taken up their positions around the Marine base at Khe Sanh. Many believed the enemy's first targets would be the Marines occupying hills 881 North, 881 South, and 861. Taking control of these hills would deny the Marines a view of the surrounding valleys and provide the North Vietnamese with a clear shot at the main combat base. The steep sides of hills 881 North and 881 South made Hill 861 the most likely to come under attack.

On January 13, Ken Goodman responded to the letter he had received from his worried and concerned family: "Man, I'd like to know how you're all going to find time to say all those prayers. When I stand watch at night, I always say a rosary and I think that's almost every night. So I'm getting my share of praying in, too.

"If I ever get off this hill and get to a post office, I'll mail home the three pots we captured from the NVA in a tunnel."

Bernice Goodman wrote another letter to her son on the same day: "How are you? According to the news you have a lot of action there now. Sincerely hope you take every precaution to take care of yourself. Thanks for writing such cheerful letters. It's just like you not wanting to worry us. But it's also like you to enjoy the country and to lighten and cheer up your environment regardless of the circumstances or dangerous as it may be. [That's] why you always had so many friends and why we all love you so. And like dad says, that's my boy!

"Sure is nice of you to write so often; got three letters last week, keep it up. I can't tell in words how much it means to us. Dad comes home running with your letters and the kids pretty near wear them out reading them. We are all praying for you, wherever you are my love. God Bless You."

News of the enemy buildup around Khe Sanh continued to make headlines all around the world, as it became increasingly clear that the major battle was imminent. The Goodmans anxiously checked the mailbox every day for a letter from Ken, but there was nothing. All the Goodman family could do was worry.

On January 19, Goodman spread black grease paint on his face, neck, arms, and hands. Routine patrols were a thing of the past. All the patrols were now considered high risk. One group of Marines had gone out on patrol and never returned. The triple canopies of foliage, which covered the hills surrounding the base, hindered observation of the area from the air. If you wanted to hide thousands of North Vietnamese troops, the hillsides around Khe Sanh were the place to do it.

Combined U.S. intelligence sources revised the number of enemy troops surrounding the base to forty thousand with

some sources placing the count as high as fifty thousand. Ho
Chi Minh was confident his well-equipped army could overrun
six thousand Marines. His plan called for cutting off all supplies
to the Marine base. The offensive was timed to correspond with
the onset of the monsoon season, so the heavy cloud cover, rain,
and fog would limit the use of American aircraft.

There was talk at the highest of levels of pulling the
Marines out of Khe Sanh. It was argued that the base could be
abandoned more easily than it could be defended. The main
purpose for having the Marines at Khe Sanh was to keep the
Ho Chi Minh Trail under surveillance. The trail was located
twenty miles away, inside the neighboring country of Laos.
North Vietnam relied heavily on the trail to move troops and
supplies into South Vietnam. With the base under siege, there
could be no effective ongoing surveillance of the famed trail.
"So why keep them there?" many asked.

General Westmoreland saw the massive buildup of enemy
troops around Khe Sanh as an opportunity to kill communist
soldiers in large numbers. He believed the Marines could
defend their positions while a program of massive aerial
bombing was directed at the enemy. The aerial attacks would
cause communist casualties to soar to such heights that their
ability to wage war in the northern provinces would be severely
crippled. Supported by the Joint Chiefs of Staff back in the
Pentagon, General Westmoreland announced that the Marines
at Khe Sanh would stay and fight.

The two factors that weighed heavily in the outcome were
the weather and the ability of the United States to resupply the
Marines at Khe Sanh. President Lyndon Johnson worried Khe
Sanh might turn into another Dien Bien Phu. He followed the
events there closely and went so far as to have a sand-table scale
model of Khe Sanh built in the White House basement.

U.S. intelligence sources obtained an updated version of

Ho Chi Minh's Resolution 13. The plan called for the elimination of Khe Sanh and the launching of the Tet Offensive at 0100 hours on January 31, 1968.

While Marines like Goodman wondered about the days ahead, an enemy defector revealed a portion of the assault plan against Khe Sanh. Once Hill 861 had fallen, a reinforced regimental-sized force was to attack the main base. One NVA heavy mortar platoon on the northeast side of Hill 1015 would attack the Marine heavy weapons on Hill 950, while another heavy mortar platoon would fire on the parked helicopters at the airstrip. Both mortar platoons would have antiaircraft gun platoons to protect them against U.S. air attacks.

On January 20, after a night of shelling suspected enemy targets with 105mm howitzers based at Khe Sanh and long-range 175mm guns firing from nineteen miles away at Camp Carroll, Goodman's company left Hill 861 in search of blood trails and bodies. Before they ever had a chance to complete their mission, they received an urgent radio communication to return immediately.

Back on Hill 861 the Marines were put on 100 percent alert. A large enemy force was taking up position on the cloud-covered ridge directly across from them. The dense clouds that blanketed the area prevented the Marines from seeing the NVA. Goodman and the others made it back to their positions on the hill without incident. Although they couldn't see the enemy surrounding them, they could hear the NVA banging pans and blowing horns. Enemy soldiers in a steep-sided ravine opposite Hill 861 yelled over to the Marines in broken English, "Death tonight."

Back in Stewart, Minnesota, on the Sunday afternoon of January 21, 1968, Bernice Goodman sat down and wrote a long letter to her son. "I sure hope you're okay. According to the paper, you're right in the midst of it." The rest of the letter was upbeat about the things that were happening back home.

Goodman's platoon, 1st Platoon, Kilo Company, was notified that it was about to be attacked by a large enemy force. The attack began at 0330 on January 21 with a deadly barrage of rockets and mortars, and RPGs slammed into the Marines' bunkers. From a nearby hill .51-caliber machine guns opened fire on the Marine positions. A tremendous amount of firepower was directed against Hill 861. On the heels of the rocket and mortar attacks, Goodman's platoon was assaulted by two NVA infantry battalions. The fighting on Hill 861 was brutal as the NVA advanced up the hill with their AK-47s blazing. They penetrated the concertina barriers on one side of the hill and overran the Kilo Company command post. Bullets were flying everywhere. An enemy soldier out in the jungle was keying a radio headset to jam Marine radio communications.

Fifteen minutes into the fighting North Vietnamese soldiers poured through the wire. Sappers advanced quickly through the dense fog, guided by their own illumination flares.

The North Vietnamese ground offensive to seize Khe Sanh was under way. What had once been an elusive enemy force was now charging up the hill. Goodman opened up with his M60 machine gun. Other Marines of 1st Platoon did the same, using their assigned weapons. The Marines nearby on Hill 881 South shot off illumination flares to confuse and misguide the advancing NVA. They fired so many rounds trying to stop the NVA advance that their mortar tubes became red hot.

The battle on Hill 861 remained intense. Soon the hill was a mass of people fighting, some hand-to-hand. Enemy soldiers charged forward with their bayonets affixed to their rifles. Off in the direction of the main base came a gigantic explosion, as the largest ammunition dump at Khe Sanh blew up after being hit by enemy artillery. The ensuing fire illuminated the night sky, making the fighting on Hill 861 look like a scene from hell. When it was over, there were dead bodies everywhere. In spite of being heavily outnumbered, the Marines held their ground. The North Vietnamese suffered so many casualties they had to call for reinforcements.

Goodman fought on. When he heard someone yell that the corpsman had been hit, he looked around and saw Marine casualties lying everywhere in need of medical attention.

Before joining the Marines, he had graduated from the Medical Institute of Minnesota as a medical histologist (a person who studies the microscopic structure of tissues) and had worked with a doctor on a cure for cancer at the Lake Region Hospital in Fergus Falls, Minnesota. "A lifetime spent helping other people is the least a man can do," is how he explained his medical career choice to others.

Like so many of the Minnesota Twins Platoon, Goodman did not have to be there. When his draft number came up, he was carrying out his studies in medicine and doing quite well. He could have obtained a college deferment, but instead, he enlisted in the Marines.

Ken Goodman's compassion for others took over. He went from one wounded Marine to another using his medical background to do what he could.

At dawn the guns of Hill 861 fell silent. Twelve Marines of 1st Platoon were dead and nearly all the others were wounded. The NVA, who had failed in its attempt to take the hill, left behind a hundred dead. For now, Hill 861 was still controlled by the Marines.

"Goodman, I'm making you team leader because you did so well last night," squad leader Mike James told him the following day. Goodman was really proud to have been promoted so quickly. In fact, he was promoted ahead of a lance corporal and another private first class. Word spread about how well Goodman performed in combat and how he had put his medical background to work when the corpsman was wounded.

The following day, January 22, news of the fierce fighting on Hill 861 reached Stewart. Filled with worry, Bernice Goodman wrote, "I sincerely hope you get this and are still amongst the living after going through such a major battle. There's not one moment that we all aren't thinking or praying for you. All the news reports describe that you're in the fiercest fight of the war so far. Of course, we are worried and, if you are wounded and in a hospital, please have someone write immediately. I have enclosed a stamped envelope. We are all praying hard for you, somewhere our love."

Bernice stopped writing to make supper for her family. Heavy on her mind was the news of intense fighting between the Marines occupying the hills surrounding the base at Khe Sanh and the ever-growing size of the North Vietnamese force that surrounded it. Bernice picked up on how worried Virgil was, and that only added to her fear. After supper she added another page to her letter.

"Please, please try to take care of yourself. Now, son, if you do get wounded please don't ever conceal it from us. You know your dad and I aren't the type to go to pieces. We have faith in the Lord for the best. We are very thankful to the Lord for giving us you and know he'll double his blessings with your return & Eileen. God Bless you, Mother and Dad."

At the bottom of her letter appeared a few lines from the rest of the family. From Ken's twelve-year-old sister: "Thanks for the nice letter. I will write you another letter real soon. All my love, Mary." From his fourteen-year-old brother, "Dear

Kenny, I miss you very much. I will try to write you real soon too. Love, Bob." His seven-year-old sister, Janet, wrote five large words at the bottom, "Ken I Love You, Janet."

On January 23, Bernice Goodman still had not heard from her son. She heard on the news that more troops were being sent to Khe Sanh.

Around noon on January 24, during a lull in the fighting, Mike James, a corpsman known as "Doc," another Marine, and Goodman were sitting around a foxhole. Without warning an incoming mortar round exploded behind them. The loud blast sent James diving for cover. Miraculously, he wasn't even scratched. The first thing he did was yell out, "Doc! Goodman! You okay?"

The silence that followed was deafening. Fearing the worst, James looked around the foxhole. His heart sank when he saw the others; they were all hit by shrapnel. Doc and the other Marine were dead; Goodman was crumpled over and comatose from multiple wounds. James broke out a battle dressing, but realized things were too serious for that. Besides the arm injury, Goodman had sustained a life-threatening wound to the back of his head and was unconscious. James took off for help. He brought back three corpsmen. The way Goodman cared for the wounded just a few days earlier was being repaid threefold. An urgent call went out for an emergency medevac.

Normally, help was twenty miles away at the Marine airbase in Phu Bai, where five medium helicopter squadrons were operating. But because of the previous attacks, and the large number of enemy troops closing in on the Marines at Khe Sanh, help was much closer.

As Major W. H. Shauer Jr., the commanding officer of one of the helicopter squadrons, wrote in his narrative summary: "Since the attack of 21 January, when Khe Sanh was first hit by mortars, rockets and artillery, HMM-362 has maintained two aircraft there [Khe Sanh] on a twenty-four-hour-a-day basis. During this time the two aircraft of HMM-362 evacuated over a hundred medevacs, mostly from Hills 881, 861, and 950. Substantial battle damage to aircraft and crews did not lessen the ability of HMM-362."

Bernice mailed Kenny her fourth letter within the last five days. It said in part: "Today the news was that more troops were sent to Khe Sanh, so I suppose you're still there. We just thank God for every day that passes knowing you're okay. Please take care & God Bless You, Love, Mother Dad and All."

Goodman's buddies placed him aboard the medevac chopper. The chopper lifted off and made a beeline for the main combat base. After the chopper departed, one of the corpsmen said something they all feared: "There's not much of a chance." As the aircraft lifted off, many Marines were thinking about Goodman. His unique personality and friendly smile had made him many friends.

Within a half-hour of being wounded Goodman was in the medical facility at the Khe Sanh combat base. At 1300 the examining doctor pronounced Goodman dead. He determined that Kenny Goodman had died from his head wound. The official cause of death was listed as "massive hemorrhage." The Marine who had once said, "A lifetime spent helping others is the least a man can do," was placed in a body bag, but not before the last rites of the church were given to Kenny by navy chaplain Lieutenant W. L. Driscoll.

11

"DEAR MR. PRESIDENT"

Overnight, the Tet Offensive of 1968 changed how Americans viewed the military action in Vietnam. American servicemen throughout all of South Vietnam were simultaneously under attack. The fighting was front-page news and widely reported by the television networks. What people saw on their televisions was not a conflict, it was an all-out war.

In nearly every neighborhood, American families worried about their loved ones stationed in Vietnam. When the communists launched their offensive, the war in Vietnam suddenly reached out and touched the personal lives of people all across America in the worst way possible.

It was a cold Sunday morning in Stewart, Minnesota. Virgil Goodman was walking with his three children to St. Boniface Church, which was just two blocks away from his home. Vince McGraw beeped the car horn as he drove past. Virgil waved back and laughed; Vince laughed too. It was an inside joke the two had between them. Virgil had always said he lived too close to church to drive and too far away to walk. When the neighbors met as they walked up the front steps of the church, Lenora McGraw asked Virgil, "Where's Bernice?"

"She got up early and went to the eight o'clock mass." As Virgil made his way through church with his children it was "Hello" and "Good morning" to everyone he saw.

After the mass ended and as the pews began to empty, a long, slow-moving line formed. As Virgil patiently waited for the line to move ahead toward the door, he visited and joked with the people around him. Today, the line seemed to be moving slower than usual. People seemed to be congregating outside to talk about something. Eventually, Virgil passed through the front doors of the church and into the bright sunlight.

Churchgoers were clustered in small groups, busily talking to one another. The usual smiles and sounds of laughter were missing. As the people congregated on the sidewalk noticed Virgil, they stopped talking and averted their eyes. *Why're they talking about me?* he thought. Virgil suddenly realized that a number of people in the congregation were looking down the street toward his house.

He heard one person say to another, "Why else would it be there?" From another direction he heard someone else say, "A Marine car is in his driveway." Virgil hurried to the front of the crowd to see for himself. There it was, a strange car parked in his driveway. When Virgil recognized the familiar globe, anchor, and eagle on the car door as the Marine Corps emblem, he took off running for his house.

Father Henry Sterner came out of the warm church to see why so few were leaving. Some ladies were holding their hands over their mouths in shock. Others were digging for their handkerchiefs and tissues. Father Sterner heard someone say, "Something must have happened to Kenny. Why else would the Marines be there."

"And Virgil's got high blood pressure," another lady expressed in a tone of deep concern. When Father Sterner spotted Virgil running down the middle of the street toward home, he whispered, "Lord, no! Not this!" Prayer book in hand, the priest hurried down the street toward the Goodman home.

The McGraws arrived home in time to hear the telephone

ring. Vince McGraw picked up the receiver. He barely recognized Bernice Goodman's voice at the other end. "Get over here as fast as you can!" was all Bernice could say before she hung up.

Vince turned to his wife and said, "We've got to get over to the Goodmans! Something has happened to Kenny!" They grabbed their winter coats and ran out the door.

Mary Goodman left church and headed for home virtually unnoticed amidst the hubbub. As she got closer to home, she wondered, *Why are there so many cars parked in front of our house? Why is everyone going over to our house?* As she neared the driveway, she noticed the car with the Marine Corps emblem on the door. Putting these things together, she concluded Kenny was dead, and she started to cry.

Mary entered the house her eyes full of tears. The inside of her home was jammed full of people; she wondered where they all had come from. When she saw her father, she went to pieces. Virgil was lying on the couch with the family doctor at his side. It looked to her as if he was dying. "His blood pressure's gone just nuts," Mary heard one lady say.

Two uniformed Marines stood quietly in the living room. Whenever a Marine is killed in action, two uniformed Marines deliver the tragic news. The tradition was well known to Virgil and very much on his mind when he had run down the street for home. Virgil and Bernice were both in rough shape.

Father Sterner wanted desperately to be of help. He saw that all the Goodman children were at home and accounted for. He felt that he could help the children and instructed Mary, Bob, and Janet to get their rosaries, a familiar devotional tool. The priest led the children in reciting the Lord's Prayer on the larger beads and the Hail Mary on the smaller ones. After every ten beads, he coached the children to say, "Glory be to the Father."

His heart was in the right place, but his effort didn't work for Mary. Saying the rosary was the last thing she wanted to do. What she wanted to do the most was cry. She felt hurt and betrayed. How could God do this to her family? They worshipped him and followed his law. Knowing she would never again see her brother alive made her so angry. As Father Sterner led her in prayer, she began to turn away from God and religion. When she said, "Glory be to the Father," she was too overcome with grief to mean it.

The doctor stayed at Virgil's side for hours. Everyone was especially worried about him.

Kenny's fiancée, Eileen McGraw, was not in Stewart the day the two Marines drove into town bearing the tragic news. She was in San Diego attending nursing school and living with her sister, Hannah. Hannah was married to a naval officer who didn't like what he had heard on the news about the events at Khe Sanh. He was aware of how dangerous the situation was for the Marines surrounded at Khe Sanh, and he told his wife and Eileen he was concerned about Kenny.

On that Sunday morning Eileen heard the phone ring and saw Hannah answer it. Her sister acted a bit strange. "Who was that?" Eileen asked after Hannah had hung up.

"Oh! It was Mom and Dad. They called to see how everyone was doing."

There was something odd about the call, but Eileen couldn't put her finger on it, so she soon forgot about it. About five hours later there was a knock at the door. Eileen opened the door to find her solemn-faced parents. They didn't have to say a word; she knew right away why they were there. She buried her face in her hands and wept.

Eileen's dad couldn't bring himself to say it, so her mother did: "The Marine Corps came and told Virg and Bernice this morning Kenny was killed." It was all downhill after that.

Eileen became nearly hysterical and waved her loved ones to keep away. She did not want anyone to say or do anything. All her parents could do was to let their daughter vent her emotions and stood by to wait for the right moment.

For Vince and Lenora McGraw, Kenny's death was more than the loss of a future son-in-law, it was like losing a child. They had known Kenny all his life. He had even worked for Eileen's dad and brother.

After Eileen was able to regroup, she went over and hugged her grief-stricken parents, and they all broke down in tears. "How are Virg and Bernice doing?"

"We'll all leave for Minnesota tomorrow," was all her father would say as he took his daughter into his arms.

There was an incredible outpouring of support. Stewart had a population of five to six hundred people and it seemed like all of them stopped by to offer words of encouragement. Concerned friends and relatives kept the Goodman house full. One neighbor took it upon himself to show up daily and scrub the floors on his hands and knees.

As the North Vietnamese continued to tighten their grip on Khe Sanh, priority was given to getting the wounded out and supplies in. That meant a prolonged stay in the morgue for Kenny Goodman and the others who had been killed in action.

Back home, details of Kenny's death were sketchy. Information as to the time of his death was conflicting. The date of his death was first listed as January 21, 1968, and the cause was listed as a gunshot wound to the head. On February 7, 1968, the first reported date of death was corrected to January 24, 1968. The family wrongly took the news to mean that Kenny had suffered terribly for three days before dying from his gunshot wound.

The ensuing month was a long one for the Goodman family. Each day came and went without a word as to when

Kenny's body would be returned. They were finally notified that the body was en route. At last the Goodman's could make final arrangements.

Virgil and Bernice couldn't imagine what their son's body might look like, so they requested that the casket remain closed for the visitation and funeral. Mary overheard the phone conversation her parents had with the mortuary. It sounded to her like the mortuary was fairly insistent about showing the body. She was surprised to hear her parents give in to having an open casket. That was not what they wanted! After her parents had finished their conversation with the mortuary, Mary took it upon herself to phone the McGraws.

"They talked Mom and Dad into showing Kenny's body. That's not what they really want. He's been dead for over a month. He can't look the same with a bullet through his head."

"Mary, we'll be right over."

The final decision was for a closed casket. On the day of the funeral the casket was surrounded by flowers and covered with an American flag. On top of the coffin was a photo of Kenneth Goodman in a stand-up frame. People showed up in record numbers. The funeral procession was so long that the first cars reached the cemetery before the last cars were able to pull away the church. Hundreds of phone calls and letters poured in. One lady Eileen had known for years confided that she, too, had lost her fiancé during World War II.

From February through April letters trickled in from Khe Sanh from Marines who had served with Kenny. Gene Groeschel was one of Kenny's good friends. They had met in California at staging battalion and received assignments that placed them in the same company but in different platoons at Khe Sanh. Groeschel wrote a frank letter detailing their friendship and the events that ended Ken's life. His letter ended with, "I wish to extend my sympathy to you, Mrs. Goodman, the rest of the family, Eileen, and all his friends. All of us here miss Ken. He was a kind and generous person, and a friend to all."

Kenny's squad leader Mike James wrote, "I hope this letter does more good than harm. I know it will hurt, but I put myself in your place and thought I would want to know what happened."

First Lieutenant Jerry N. Salisbury, Goodman's company commander, wrote, "It is difficult for me to express the regrets and sorrow felt by all the Marines of this company and myself of the untimely death of your son."

Then there came the difficult task of adjusting to life without Kenneth Goodman. At first it was simply too painful for the Goodmans to talk about it. A large picture of Kenny was put up in the living room. Then they added a cabinet to be filled with letters, a flag, photos, and other memorabilia. The in-home shrine was one way to reward Ken Goodman for a life well lived, but the cost to the family was dear. They paid for it in sad memories every time they passed the display. Eventually, they put everything out of sight to try and forget. That helped, but only a little.

Kenny's personal effects became valuable keepsakes. When his loved ones went through his things looking for items to cherish, they came across a letter in an old billfold. It had been written twenty-one months earlier, while he was still in college. Kenny's letter was addressed to Lyndon B. Johnson, the president of the United States.

Dear Mr. President:
I have to do something to help my country, which I dearly love. I feel in this day and age people, citizens of the United States, are dead, unpatriotic. We're letting organizations like Communism influence us. We let the

press distort our minds, and because of this we see men burn draft cards, demonstrators, strikes, sit-ins, flag burning, etc. I realize Mr. President that this is just the minority, but where in hell is the majority? I want to do something about it.

Tonight I was arguing with my roommate, and in the end he kind of laughed at me and said, "Oh Ken, don't be so darn patriotic." Well Mr. President I am patriotic, because I love my country so much that I'll even die for her.

Sincerely,
Ken Goodman

12

ATTACK ON DA NANG

On January 30, 1968, a rocket attack temporarily destroyed part of the Da Nang airstrip, and some two hundred enemy troops were spotted just across the river southeast of the Da Nang airbase. Mark Mulvihill's unit, H&S Company, 3rd Amphibian Tractor Battalion, 1st Marine Division, was deployed to assist the Marines fighting along the river and on a small island on the outskirts of Da Nang. His unit was being used as a blocking force.

Mulvihill's occupational specialty was amtracs. The Landing Vehicle Track Personnel Mark 5 (LVTP5), the most common amtrac model in Vietnam, was rectangular in shape, solid green in color, and full tracked with nine pairs of road wheels on each side. It had a gun turret on top near the front mounting a .30-caliber M1919A4 machine gun. An amtrac's size varied depending on the model, with the LVTP5 being some thirty feet long, twelve feet wide, and ten feet tall. The LVTP5 could carry up to thirty-four combat-equipped Marines, although in Vietnam fifteen Marine infantrymen was a more typical load. It was operated by a three-man crew consisting of a crew chief, a driver, and a gunner. The gunner would often place an additional .30-caliber, or even .50-caliber, machine gun, outside the gun turret and surround it with sand bags for better protection.

Because the amtrac was originally designed to transport troops and supplies from ship to shore, it was designed more to float than to protect. In Vietnam, however, it was mostly used on land to transport men and supplies. Amtracs were vulnerable to armor piercing rounds that could penetrate their thin side armor. The steel ramp on the front was much thicker.

Mulvihill never felt safe inside an amtrac. Under the deck plate were twelve fifty-gallon fuel cells. Mulvihill knew that if the cells ever ignited, the amount of air rushing in through the open hatch to fuel the fire would create a suction so strong that it would pull anyone trying to get out back into the inferno. He figured he had only seconds to climb out to keep from being fried. He was very outspoken about the danger of being burned to death and told his buddies, "If the fuel cells ever ignite, it's not going to be a pretty picture. It's not going to be a pleasant way to die. If I'm going to die over here, I want it to be some other way."

For three days Marine artillery units hammered enemy positions on the island. Jets flew over to drop napalm canisters, which tumbled awkwardly and slowly through the air toward the ground. When they exploded on impact, a large area instantly became engulfed in flames. The jellied gasoline consumed so much oxygen that some enemy troops died of suffocation. Others who were splashed with the sticky substance tried frantically to wipe off the flaming gunk sticking to their bodies. Their attempts to wipe off the burning material would only spread it over a greater area, setting even more clothing and skin on fire. The heat was so intense that some enemy soldiers, who had no actual contact with napalm but were near the area of the explosion, were severely burned.

On the third day of fighting the amtracs started across the river to sweep the island. A grisly sight awaited amtrac drivers on the other side. As they splashed ashore, they were met by the unforgettable smell of burned human flesh. Mulvihill saw more dead soldiers than he could count, as the dead numbered in the hundreds. Several scorched bodies were stuck to the branches of charred trees. As Mulvihill looked at their burned remains, he remembered hearing that the enemy had been offered terms of surrender but they had refused. *Wow! Are these guys tough!* Mulvihill thought as he viewed the awesome carnage.

David Paulseth was in the same unit as Mulvihill. He was on top of another amtrac driven by a sergeant who was on his second tour of duty. They were traveling parallel to the river when they came to a large open area of sand that looked like a flood plain. Four enemy soldiers who were hiding behind some scrub brush opened fire, trying to kill as many Marines as possible in one final burst of glory.

Paulseth had been in country only a short while and didn't know what to expect when the bullets started to fly. One NVA soldier dropped his empty weapon and started to run away across the sand. The sergeant drove after the fleeing soldier, who kept looking back over his shoulder at the approaching amtrac. As the fleeing soldier became tired, the distance between the two decreased until all that separated them was inches of space. Paulseth wondered if the driver was deliberately being cruel and thought, *Don't tease the guy! If you're going to run him over, just do it!* The enemy soldier stumbled and fell, and the sergeant never hit the brake.

After the fighting was over the body count began. Paulseth helped lift the crushed NVA soldier onto a vehicle piled high with enemy dead. Seeing his mangled body next to those that were scorched and burned made his death look more humane.

The sweep of the island continued, with Paulseth walking alongside an amtrac holding his rifle at waist level. Then something right out of a Camp Pendleton training exercise happened. An NVA soldier popped up from a spider trapdoor and threw a grenade that landed right at Paulseth's feet. He looked down at the grenade and braced himself for death. Paulseth never heard the explosion; the grenade malfunctioned. Realizing he had a second chance, he leveled his rifle at the NVA soldier and fired. The soldier's head did what Paulseth's head would have done if the grenade had exploded.

Later, in a letter home, Paulseth wrote, "This is going to be short. I'm writing by flashlight. We're on 100 percent alert and lights are out. I got back this morning from an operation in the field. One of the biggest things 3rd tracs have had in over a year. We swept two islands. We killed close to two hundred VC and took fifty prisoners. We had six killed and the same wounded. I shot a guy, and believe me it doesn't feel good afterwards."

Gerald Baltes was assigned to 2nd Platoon of K Company, 3rd Battalion, 5th Marine Regiment, 1st Marine Division. His military occupational specialty (MOS) was 0351 flame-throwers and rocket launchers. On January 3, 1968, he wrote to his parents to say, "All I need is a small Bible."

A few weeks later Baltes received a package of goodies from home. Tucked inside was a small pocket Bible with a message on the inside cover from his parents: "With this book goes our love and our thoughts, which are many and varied. We hope that it will give you the comfort that it is giving us to send it to you. We hope, too, that it will give you the insights you seem to be looking for right now. We think it will."

Baltes' unit was assigned to flush out the enemy and drive them into the South Vietnamese army, which was dug in to block the enemy's retreat. On February 6, Kilo Company moved through its assigned area without incident. On the return trip, the company veered through a rice paddy and into a

rear," while I gave cover. As he bent over to help the injured Marine, I noticed Gerry got hit in the shoulder. I then ran over and gave them as much support as I could. I finally directed two more Marines to come up and give us some help. I checked Gerry over and he was all right, except being hit in the shoulder.

Well, when he got to the rear and got ready to move farther back, another weapon opened fire on him and the other Marines. At this time he took a bullet through the side and in the leg, but yet your Marine kept going and he finally made it to the rear and was sent to a hospital. When I got back I talked to a corpsman that treated him in the field. He said he was in great shape and was smiling when he got on the chopper. Well, there it is. Please, whatever you do, don't worry, for he is OK. I say this, for I know he is in good hands.

I figured I should at least let you know for he won't be able to write for a while. All I have to say Mr. and Mrs. Baltes is your son did his job well and performed as an outstanding Marine in my eyes.

A Friend of Gerry's,
Royce
P.S. Please say a prayer for us Marines. We need them all.

Larry Jones was in the same battalion as Baltes with India Company. On January 30, 1968, Jones climbed aboard one of twelve waiting helicopters. All he knew was that they were going to help some outfit in trouble. When the helicopters landed in an open field, Jones and everyone else piled out the side door in rapid succession. They came under fire almost immediately. Jones and the others ran for cover.

When Jones reached the taller grass surrounding the landing zone, he popped his head up to see what was going on. When he saw lots of small-arms and automatic gunfire being directed his way, he ducked down and waited for the signal to advance. When the command was given, they didn't get far due to the intense enemy fire. As Jones fired his 3.5-inch rockets at the tree line, his platoon tried unsuccessfully to root out the enemy in three attacks. Just before dark, around 2030, the fighting subsided and the Marines dug in for the night.

India Company was being used to help the South Vietnamese army encircle an NVA battalion and a VC force. As darkness approached the circle was complete, leaving the enemy with no avenues of escape.

India Company was placed on red alert, because an enemy attack appeared imminent. The attack came at 0230 and matters could not have been worse. The silence was shattered by gunfire and explosions as the NVA and VC forces assaulted the Marine line, determined to break through and make their escape. Both sides popped illumination flares. Marines and North Vietnamese soldiers were throwing hand grenades at each other. The fighting was hand to hand in some places.

Jones fought until he was out of ammunition. He abandoned his weapon and took an M16 rifle from a dead Marine. Illumination flares from both sides popped open to light up the area. Enemy soldiers continued to pour out of the heavy vegetation in large numbers and run through the shattered Marine lines. Lying dead next to Jones was his squad leader and assistant machine gunner. Ten feet away were two more dead Marines.

Jones saw the radioman was severely wounded and unable to fight. A Vietnamese woman and a young boy jumped over the rice paddy dike. They began pistol whipping the radioman about the head. The two had apparently run out of ammunition and were going to beat the helpless radioman to death. Jones knew what he had to do; to save the radioman, he shot and killed both the woman and the boy.

Nearby, an M60 machine gunner fired his bipod-mounted weapon at the enemy, then he screamed a chilling, primeval scream. Jones looked up and saw the gunner slouched behind his weapon. He crawled over and discovered one of the gunner's eyes was hanging outside the socket and his left hand was nearly blown off. What remained of it was attached by only a few bits of loose skin.

"Chris!" Jones yelled as he tried to get a response from the critically wounded Marine. Chris was unresponsive but alive. "Corpsman up!" Jones yelled, not knowing all four company corpsmen were dead.

The first thing Jones did was to try and stop the flow of blood from the severed limb. In a frantic effort to do something, he removed his own dog tags and tried to use the chain as a tourniquet. As he twisted the chain around Chris' wrist, a mortar exploded behind them. The blast hurled Jones forward and snapped the chain. Jones lay unconscious on the ground with blood coming out of his ears, nose, and mouth. A piece of shrapnel had entered through the armhole of his flak jacket and had punctured a lung.

Jones regained consciousness with a severe headache and wheezing for air. His right lung was deflated. Casualties were everywhere. He found his M16 rifle lying on the ground nearby. It was useless. All the plastic had been blown off and the barrel was bent. Jones dragged himself over to the dike and collapsed. As he lay against the dike, he did something that was out of the ordinary for him: he began to pray. He prayed to either get better or to die fast. He did not want to be taken prisoner, and he decided that under no circumstances would he allow that to happen.

Marine reinforcements arrived the following morning. The silent battlefield said it all. They placed the dead on ponchos and covered them over until body bags arrived. A navy corpsman noticed Jones walk by in a trance, dragging three rifles by their slings. The tall Marine's face was covered with mud and blood. The corpsman knew something wasn't right when he saw the way Jones winced in pain as he reached down to pick up a radio. The corpsman hurried over and made Jones lie down on the ground. A disoriented Jones looked up and said, "I can't breathe." The corpsman gave him a shot of morphine and marked a big "M" on his forehead with a black grease pencil.

A helicopter took Jones to the Da Nang naval hospital, where a surgeon cut a hole in Jones' side, parted his ribs with what looked like a shoehorn, and twisted a tube through the hole. For the next three days, Jones remained in the hospital drifting in and out of sleep.

Jones awoke to the voices of doctors talking about him. The first doctor to see that Jones was conscious went to his side and asked, "How are you feeling today?"

"Relaxed," Jones answered. The morphine made him feel better than he was.

"We're sending you to the hospital ship USS *Repose*. The piece of metal that punctured your lung is still in you. We're concerned about that."

Jones was transported by helicopter to the USS *Repose* on February 10. The doctors examined Jones and told him, "We are going to leave the metal in you rather than risk the surgery to get it out."

Unlike Mulvihill and Paulseth, Jones and Baltes were both still recovering from their wounds when Major General Donn Robertson gave his congratulatory message to the 1st Marine

Division on February 10, 1968:

> I view with great pride the stalwart defense of the Da Nang area by all division units and, in particular, the efforts of the 11th Marines; the 3rd Battalion, 5th Marines; the 2nd Battalion, 3rd Marines; and the 196th Light Infantry Brigade, USA, which units bore the brunt of the enemy main effort. The enemy has been unable to occupy a single objective in the Da Nang area while he has suffered in excess of 1,100 casualties.

13

THE BATTLE OF HUE CITY

arine Medium Helicopter Squadron (HMM) 362, also known as the "Ugly Angels," had the unique distinction of being the first Marine aircraft unit to operate in the Republic of South Vietnam. The squadron consisted of twenty-five UH-34D Sikorsky helicopters.

After reporting in to HMM-362, Christy Sauro Jr. headed for the sleeping quarters under a pouring rain. It was a flimsy hut with one big room crammed with double bunks, footlockers, and sea bags. The air reeked of people who didn't bathe. The upper half of the exterior walls could be pushed out for ventilation, but they were kept closed to keep things dry. Many fully clothed Marines were sleeping sprawled facedown across their bunks. The unmade empty racks exposed yellow mud-stained sheets.

"Is that bunk available?" Sauro asked as he pointed to an empty one.

"You can have it," the Marine on the next bunk told him. "By the way, you need to pick yourself a 'mama-san.' It's a great deal. You pay her five bucks a month in piaster and she'll clean up your area and do your laundry."

"Piaster?" Sauro questioned.

"Yeah, piaster. It's Vietnamese money. We call it 'funny money'; it looks like monopoly money. If you haven't got any, you'll have to get some from the paymaster. You're not allowed to use American currency over here," he warned.

The next morning the same Marine urged Sauro to get going. "Hurry up! Go pick out a 'mama-san' before all the nice-looking ones are gone." Sauro walked the road circling the airstrip until he came to an area in which a small handful of Marines were surrounded by a dozen Vietnamese women.

All the women were identically dressed in black pajamas and cone-shaped straw hats, and jabbered away in Vietnamese. None of the Marines understood what they were saying, but it was clear that each was trying to get picked for the job. Most of the women were young girls trying overly hard to look seductive and inviting long enough to get hired. Flirtatious smiles and blinking eyes were used to edge out the competition. Not surprisingly, the prettiest ones were chosen first. When Sauro joined the group, he got the usual treatment. All the women smiled and waved at him like he was a long-lost friend.

The eyes of one woman in particular caught his attention. She was much older than the rest, and the passage of time had robbed her of beauty. Etched into her face were the harsh lines of old age. The prolonged use of betel nut had changed the color of her teeth from white to black. The smile on her face was forced, as the years of war had left her eyes filled with sadness. When Sauro pointed to the old woman as his choice, her eyes brightened and she grinned. Immediately she stepped forward to take charge of the situation. She grabbed Sauro by the arm and led him away from the group while casting a defiant glance back at the younger girls.

As they walked along, Sauro listened to his mama-san chatter away in Vietnamese. He had no idea what she was saying, but her gestures indicated she wanted to be taken to his sleeping quarters to be shown his bunk bed.

"Looks like you didn't get there fast enough," the Marine joked when he saw Sauro with the aged woman.

The mama-san immediately rifled through Sauro's dirty clothing. She frowned and looked upset about something. Sauro got the idea when she pointed back and forth at his green utilities and at the ones the other Marines were wearing. She was right; his uniform was different than the others. Sauro asked the Marine sitting on the next bunk, "Say! Where do I go to get my jungle boots and jungle utilities?"

"From supply, but good luck. I waited a month to get mine."

The thought of wearing stateside utilities in Vietnam was cause for panic. Stateside utilities had tiny little pockets, with no big, deep pockets on the sides in which to put extra gear. Stateside boots were made of solid black leather; they did not have the green mesh siding needed to keep the feet cool and dry. Worst of all, wearing stateside utilities was like hanging a sign around your neck that read, "Hey, everybody, I'm the new guy."

Sauro looked at his mama-san and shrugged his shoulders. The old woman nodded that she understood and grumbled something in Vietnamese.

Sauro went to work as the squadron embarkation assistant. He learned his position had been vacant for some time and that he would be working for an embarkation officer whose primary duty was piloting a helicopter. For that reason, the embarkation officer was rarely around for help or guidance.

At the end of the first day, Sauro heard a siren go off on his way back to the barracks. He noticed that all the Vietnamese stopped working and started walking toward the main gate. He saw his mama-san in the line of Vietnamese workers being escorted off the base. She was easy to spot because her walk was more like a shuffle. When she saw him, she smiled and waved. He waved back.

"What's with the siren?" Sauro asked a nearby Marine.

"The siren tells them when it's time for them to leave. They have to get off the base before dark. It's for their safety and the security of the base."

"Where do they come from?" Sauro asked.

"Hue City, it's spelled h-u-e, but it's pronounced 'way.' The city is eight miles north of here. Our trucks pick them up in the morning and bring them back at the end of the day. You have to feel sorry for them. Their economy is in a shambles. This is a big deal for them to be able to work here. The couple bucks we pay them are, by their standards, a lot of money. For them it's a high-paying job."

"It's a good deal for everyone then, because I hate making my bed and doing laundry," Sauro commented.

"It's not all good. By working for us they take a chance of getting killed."

Sauro learned that the Viet Cong killed and tortured those Vietnamese workers they believed to be sympathetic to the Americans. He was told the previous base barber got both his hands chopped off by the VC, presumably because the VC believed it was a fitting punishment for someone who used his hands to aid the Americans.

Back at the barracks Sauro found his bunk was made. Placed in the middle of it was a pile of neatly folded, clean clothing. On top of the pile was a pair of freshly polished jungle boots. "Well, I'll be!" Sauro said as he lifted up the jungle boots, which were exactly the right size.

As he put his clean clothes into his sea bag, he came across a set of jungle utilities in his size. The owner's name, which is normally stamped in black ink over the shirt pocket, had been scrubbed off. Sauro reached into his sea bag for his name stamp and inkpad. "There," Sauro said, as he held up the utility top that now had his last name stamped clearly over the breast pocket.

That night an ill-tempered Marine came stomping through the barracks looking for his name over someone's shirt pocket. "Some son of a bitch stole a set of my jungle utilities!" he said in a voice loud enough for all to hear. He stopped in front Sauro and stated, "You're new here."

"Yeah, I just got here yesterday."

"How in the hell did you get jungle utilities so soon?" the Marine challenged suspiciously.

"Hey! I didn't steal your clothes," Sauro said as he looked the Marine in the eye.

"So how did you get jungle utilities so damn fast?"

"You just got to know the right people," Sauro replied with a smile.

"You work in supply?" the Marine asked.

"Well, kind of. I am in embarkation and that is a part of the S-4 supply department," Sauro explained.

"And they tell everyone they're out of jungle utilities. Shit," said the Marine in disgust as he walked off in the hope of finding the culprit who had stolen his clothes. Later, another Marine came storming through looking for the "asshole" who had taken his jungle boots.

Millie Sauro received a letter from her son in Vietnam. Among other things, he wrote, "I got this mama-san. She's sort of old. Nobody pays much attention to her, but I flatter her all the time, giving her all these compliments and stuff. When the wash comes back everybody's always missing all kinds of stuff except for me. I always end up with about three or four pair of extra utilities and socks. She sort of likes me I guess, 'cause she does extra things none of the other mama-sans do, like polishing my boots.

"The people over here are really nice and really appreciate us being over here. We had a couple USO shows put on by the

Vietnamese Catholics from Hue City. They came to the base and sang Christmas carols. They thanked us for being over here and for helping them resist communist aggression. I'll probably see you in about fifty-three weeks."

Sauro had his work cut out for him. None of the squadron's sections and departments had up-to-date packing slips or cargo manifests. Most of the department heads didn't know what they were and could care less. They weren't interested in pushing papers and told him so. No matter what department or shop Sauro went to, everyone was working hard at something. Everyone he talked to told him the same thing: "Our number one priority is keeping those birds flying." Sauro got the message: Get lost.

There was no mistaking the dedication and commitment they had for their jobs. It was impressive to see how hard every man worked. Everyone was performing with minimal supervision. The problem for those in charge seemed to be getting their men to stop working. "Ortega! You've got to get some rest," Sauro overheard a gunnery sergeant say to a short corporal in the hydraulics shop. In the maintenance shop, he overheard another sergeant tell one of the mechanics, "Go on! Get out here! Go get some shut-eye!"

"I will later. We got another bird down. One of the ARVNs accidentally discharged his weapon and put a couple rounds in the clutch fan compartment," the mechanic responded. By listening to what they were saying, Sauro learned that what mattered the most was keeping the birds flying. Meeting the needs of the grunts in the field was what the squadron was all about. For the wounded Marine, a helicopter ride often meant the difference between life and death.

It was inspiring to see everyone working so hard to keep the choppers operational. In the month of January alone the twenty-five helicopters of the Ugly Angels took to the air 2,344 times. Of those sorties, 205 were for medevacs. The only way to keep up with the damage caused by the heavy fighting was for the squadron personnel to work until they dropped. That's why the barracks were in such disarray and why so many air wingers were collapsed across their bunks, facedown and fully clothed.

Sauro routinely popped into the different departments and shops to talk about what needed to be done to help the squadron redeploy quickly. To pull up stakes and move to a new location was no small undertaking; it was an event that took both time and a great deal of effort. Upon reaching the new destination, more time and effort was needed to unpack and set up before the squadron could be fully operational again. Heavy fighting could suddenly break out at any time during the deployment. If the squadron couldn't respond because the helicopters were tied up moving personnel and equipment, the results could be disastrous. Critically wounded Marines didn't have the luxury of time.

The best way to make sure the choppers would be available for missions was to make a "rapid" deployment. To do that required a high degree of organization, which could not come about without pushing papers, marking boxes, and a lot of other seemingly not-mission-critical activities. When Sauro stopped talking about "maintaining a high level of embarkation readiness" and starting talking about "keeping the birds flying," his fellow Marines stopped throwing his materials in the trash after he left. He never became their favorite person to see, but things did start to change. The squadron personnel began to do the mundane things necessary to make a rapid redeployment possible.

On January 13, 1968, six helicopters of HMM-362 completed an emergency extraction of forty-two troops from a hot zone. Small arms and automatic weapons poured in on the choppers as they whisked their comrades to safety. There

THE BATTLE OF HUE CITY

were no celebrations when the choppers returned to Phu Bai. Everyone on the flight line was unusually quiet. The crew chief went off to be alone. During the extraction his port-side gunner was killed by a round from an enemy small-arms weapon. On January 17, two more choppers took heavy fire while making another emergency extract. One returned to Phu Bai filled with bullet holes.

Major W. H. Shauer, the commanding officer of HMM-362, reported in his command chronology for the month of January: "In the Phu Bai area, the squadron has encountered increasing enemy fire. This has been attributed to the increased build up of both the Viet Cong and the North Vietnamese Army in the area. One aircraft was seriously damaged with shrapnel from a land mine, which may have been command detonated while on a medevac pickup. Two aircraft, while hoisting a U.S. recon team out, came under heavy grenade and small arms fire. Toward the end of January, the number of fire incidents in the Phu Bai TAOR [tactical area of responsibility] has steadily increased."

As the Tet holiday neared, Marines at Phu Bai were put on full alert and prepared for a full-scale attack. Many, like Sauro, were assigned to their unit's reactionary platoon. By day they performed their regular duties, and by night they manned their assigned section of the base perimeter.

Millie Sauro received another letter from her son dated January 31, 1968. It said in part:

Dear Mom,
We got hit again with rockets and mortars last night,
about 4:00. I woke right up and was in the bunker in a
flash. I am supposed to get my combat gear and go to my
position, but I didn't because they were hitting so close
that the bunker was shaking and I decided to wait. After

*about twenty minutes they stopped pounding the base, so
I went and grabbed my gear and me and Mike Mauthe
went to our position.*

*We have been getting attacked quite a bit lately, but
it will be a lot before they will ever be able to take this
base. I have enclosed a clipping from the Stars and Stripes
that tells about the time they attacked before (the one I
wrote you about).*

Well if anything new comes up I'll tell you.

Right after Sauro mailed his letter, the enemy launched their Tet
Offensive of 1968. At 0340 on January 31, 1968, at the same
time Sauro and Mauthe reported seeing an intruder in front of
their position, the North Vietnamese Army began pounding
the nearby city of Hue with artillery. Under the cover of a
low-hanging fog, detachments from eight North Vietnamese
and Viet Cong battalions entered the city from the south, and
elements of the 6th NVA Regiment attacked the Military
Assistance Command, Vietnam (MACV) Headquarters in Hue.
The 1st ARVN Division headquarters in Hue also came under
attack. News that Hue City had fallen into enemy hands was
quick to reach the Marine base at Phu Bai, which was just ten
miles to the south.

Widespread fighting erupted overnight throughout all of
South Vietnam. It was more than most Americans could have
imagined. The population of Hue City was in excess of two
hundred thousand. To put things into perspective, had Hue
been located in Minnesota, it would have been the third largest
city in the state; only the cities of Minneapolis and St. Paul
would have been bigger. The entire country of South Vietnam
was 20 percent smaller in size than the state of Minnesota,
which covers 84,068 square miles. South Vietnam covers 66,897
square miles.

Imagine waking up one morning to discover that 90 percent of Minnesota's main population centers and 80 percent of the major cities are under attack by an invading army. Imagine hearing that overnight Minnesota's third largest city, Duluth, had been taken over by an invading army. Imagine every major military base and installation within the state simultaneously under siege by enemy troops, with some completely surrounded and heavily outnumbered. Imagine fighting so widespread and severe that the U.S. National Guard and all the military reserve units had been called out to become involved in the fighting. This is what it was like for the American troops and the people of South Vietnam on the morning of February 1, 1968.

Four understrength U.S. Marines infantry companies were sent to Hue by piecemeal to counterattack. Company A, 1st Battalion, 1st Marines, left Phu Bai by truck with orders to reinforce the MACV compound on the morning of January 31. Following close behind on February 1 and 2, companies F, G, and H, 2nd Battalion, 5th Marines, were also dispatched from Phu Bai to Hue. Their mission was to help the ARVN forces recapture South Vietnam's most beautiful city.

Help would not arrive in time for more than three thousand citizens of Hue. Before the Marines could get there, many citizens were shot, clubbed to death, buried alive, and even decapitated. To hide their atrocities, the communists buried the bodies in the nearby river beds, coastal salt flats, and forest clearings. When their bodies were later exhumed, many were found tied together. Their remains told the world that these victims' last moments on earth were filled with terror.

The hard-fought battle to liberate the city of Hue would prove to be one of the bloodiest battles of the Vietnam War. Operation Hue Citadel officially ended on March 2, 1968. After twenty-six days of heavy fighting, the number of NVA and VC killed totaled 5,113, with another 89 captured. There was no way to account for the number of wounded enemy troops, or those who died later from their injuries. The ARVN lost 384 killed and 1,800 wounded. The U.S. Marine Corps reported 147 men killed in action and 857 seriously wounded. Close to half of the Marine infantrymen committed to the battle were killed or wounded.

The once-beautiful city was forever changed. Eighty percent of the buildings were damaged, more than one hundred thousand people, two-thirds of the city's population, were homeless, and nearly six thousand civilians were killed or missing.

Personal accounts of the fighting in Hue made their way back to Phu Bai. There were reports that the civilian casualties ran high and many had died at the hands of the communists. Sauro was worried about the old Vietnamese woman. Was his mama-san still alive? Was she being tortured for working on the base? Was she one of those civilians who got caught in the line of fire? Was she all right?

Even though the Battle of Hue City was over, the enemy never stopped fighting. On March 21, enemy gunners fired twenty mortar rounds and rockets into Phu Bai. Two Marines were wounded and several buildings suffered structural damage. On the morning of March 26, between 0300 and 0330, the compound was hit with 108 rockets and nearly eighty mortar rounds. Two Marines and two ARVNs were killed in the attack and forty-six were wounded, most of whom were Marines.

Finally, the civilian workers began to return to their jobs at the base. Each morning on his way to the S-4 office, Sauro passed the growing line of Vietnamese workers returning to work. The old woman was not to be seen. He tried to question some of the workers, but it was no use. All Sauro knew how to say in Vietnamese was, "I do not understand" and "Quick! Get out of here." Neither phrase could help him find out what he wanted to know. The Vietnamese workers patiently listened to his questions and watched his charades, but they could only shake their heads in the negative. Either they didn't know what it was he was trying to ask or they didn't know what had happened to her.

Sauro didn't hire a replacement worker. He let his dirty clothes pile up, washing only what he had to and hoping one day the old woman would show up to reclaim her job. Then one morning he saw her in the line of workers coming onto the base. Sauro was glad to see her and asked, "What happened to you?"

"VC number ten! Americans number one!" she kept repeating over and over, her face filled with anger. It was the only English he had ever heard her speak.

"I'll bet in Hue you said, 'Americans number ten and the VC number one,'" Sauro joked.

"No! No! VC number ten! Americans number one!" the old woman insisted soberly.

"So what happened to you?" Sauro asked with concern. The old woman seemed to understand. She reached down, pulled up her pajama leg, and revealed a deep gash in her leg that started below the knee and ran almost to her ankle.

"How did that happen?"

Again the old woman seemed to understand. She used her arm to simulate something falling over onto her leg.

"Did a wall fall on your leg? Were you in your house? Were you fleeing the city?"

The old woman didn't understand his words and repeated her earlier gesture for him. Sauro could only wonder what might have happened. He wondered if her home had been destroyed in the fighting.

"Come with me," Sauro said with a smile. He walked her over to the barracks. When she saw his laundry bag heaping with dirty clothes, she smiled at him. Then she put her hands on her hips and looked at him with a frown, as if to say, "Didn't you do a thing while I was gone?"

The end of the week was payday for both Sauro and his mama-san. This time Sauro paid the woman with a roll of bills. She looked down at the wad of piaster being given to her with an amused smile; Americans never could get it right. Shaking her head no, the old woman counted out the correct amount and handed most of the money back to him. The private shook his head no and handed the wad of bills back to her. She shook her head emphatically and handed the extra bills back to him. She had counted right and wasn't about to cheat the mistaken American. This time, Private Sauro placed the wad of bills into the palm of her hand and folded her fingers over it.

Suddenly, she realized what was happening. She looked down at the money, then back up at him. Sauro said to her, "I don't even know if you have a home anymore. Even if you do, you're going to need this money more than I do."

The old woman managed a weak smile; there was sadness in her eyes. It was as if she sensed the two would never see each other again. The old woman looked back down at the money and then slipped it into her pocket. Hue was a shambles. Two-thirds of its people were homeless and out of food. Emergency food supplies had been transported into the city to keep the people from starving. Sauro was confident the money would be well spent.

Sauro knew something he couldn't tell her. This was her last payday. The word had been passed down, "No more mama-sans." The Vietnamese workers would soon be told they had lost their jobs. Those in command either knew, or suspected, that the civilian work force had willingly, or unwillingly, provided information to the enemy that jeopardized the security of the base. For the safety of the troops the combat base was about to be off-limits to all civilian personnel.

14

DEFENSE OF KHE SANH

During Tet 1968 no place was of greater concern than Khe Sanh, where six thousand Marines remained surrounded by some forty to fifty thousand heavily-equipped enemy troops. Minnesota Twins Platoon members Brad Borreson, Robert Barrette, Charles Rice, and Dave Seldon (to name a few) were there.

Robert Cusick had no reason to believe he would be doing much more than some distant cheering for the unfortunate Marines, who belonged to the 26th and the 9th Marine Regiments at Khe Sanh. He was with the 3rd Marine Division.

Shortly after the NVA began its attack on Khe Sanh, Cusick was flown thirty-seven miles north, from Phu Bai to Dong Ha, where 3rd Marine Division had set up a forward command post. Dong Ha was thirty-two miles northeast of Khe Sanh; it was the supply center for all the III Marine Amphibious Force units operating in Quang Tri province. In no time at all, Cusick was standing, with clipboard in hand, on the airstrip at Dong Ha, monitoring the flow of men and supplies going to and from Khe Sanh.

Without adequate water, food, and supplies, the Marines at Khe Sanh had no chance of surviving the siege. Important to the resupply effort were the two logistics men operating from inside Khe Sanh. They radioed Dong Ha to tell their counterparts what supplies made it in and what went out. At the other end were logistics personnel, like Cusick, who used the information to keep track of what got lost or didn't make it back.

Mostly what went out of Khe Sanh was the wounded. As the walking wounded passed by Cusick's clipboard, he always gave them a friendly smile. The more seriously injured went by on stretchers, while the worst off were in body bags. When Cusick counted the number of Marines in need of medical attention, it never seemed to end. The disturbing remarks made by the returning helicopter crewmen made Cusick count his blessing. He heard that Khe Sanh was under constant bombardment, it had been leveled by incoming, and there was nothing left standing, not a damned thing. Pilots complained that the runway was pitted with holes and that the enemy started shooting at their aircraft before they touched down and didn't stop until they were gone.

On February 7, 1968, Cusick was called into division headquarters for the worst news of his life. He entered the S-4 billet expecting another routine assignment but was stunned to hear, "You're being assigned to temporary duty with the 26th Marines," the lieutenant told Cusick. He just stood there, not believing what he just heard. "It's your turn to go to Khe Sanh," the officer told him.

To hear he was going to Khe Sanh was like being told he had cancer. It was a near-certain death sentence. For the rest of the day, Cusick went about the difficult task of preparing himself for a life suddenly cut short. In order to have any chance of fulfilling his life ambitions, he would first have to survive Khe Sanh. The chances of that sounded slim.

The following morning Cusick was in the cargo hold of a KC-130, along with another logistics man. Both were dressed for combat. The twenty-five-mile flight to Khe Sanh went quickly. The crew chief yelled over the roar of the four propeller engines, "We're not going to come to a complete stop.

Once we land and start turning the aircraft around, you guys jump out. Run like hell! Got it?"

The camouflaged Hercules descended rapidly through the cloud cover. Cusick hung on for dear life as the cargo plane nosed into its steep dive. Suddenly the clouds were gone and Khe Sanh popped into full view. The runway was straight ahead and coming right at them. From the sky, it looked like the hard-fought battle was over and all the troops were gone. The KC-130 nosed up sharply and leveled off just in time to keep from crashing into the runway. The three-point landing was made in bounces as the pilot hurried to reach the end of the runway, where he could turn around and take off. After putting on the brakes to keep from going off the end of the runway, the pilot turned around for an immediate takeoff. As the plane pivoted, the crew sent the palletized cargo rolling down the lowered tail ramp.

"Hurry up! Get the hell off!" the crew chief screamed. Cusick and the other Marine ran down the ramp. The two men they were replacing raced by, going up the ramp. Before the palletized cargo had rolled to a stop, the KC-130 was traveling down the runway in a burst of speed. In a short distance the mighty giant was airborne. Four trails of black smoke spewed from its engines as it made its nearly vertical climb into the clouds.

In less time than it took the enemy to aim and fire their weapons of destruction, the plane had landed, unloaded its cargo, and departed. The procedure worked for now, but the North Vietnamese remained determined to cut off all supplies to the base.

Cusick ran like hell and jumped into the first trench he saw. Explosions began erupting along the runway in places where the KC-130 had been just seconds earlier. Cusick caught a whiff of something that wrinkled his nose. The other Marines in the

The special pre-game swearing-in ceremony at Metropolitan Stadium for the Minnesota Twins Platoon on June 28, 1967. Before the baseball game ended, the new recruits would be on their way to San Diego. *Millie Sauro*

Christy Sauro at Phu Bai in 1968. *Author's Collection*

Robert Gates
displays a skull that
the VC had placed
on a stake to intimidate
the Americans.
Clearly, Gates
was unintimidated.
Robert Gates

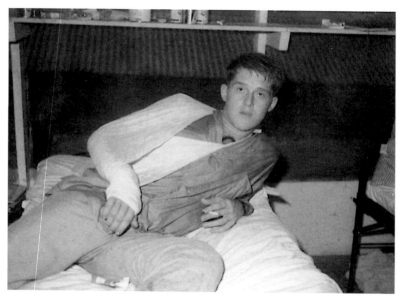

Gates recovering from his wounds in the 1st Medical Battalion hospital in Da Nang. *Robert Gates*

The men of the
1st Amphibian Tractor
Battalion earned
themselves the
nickname "amgrunts."
Larry Buske

Larry Buske shows the
damage caused by
a small land mine. The
secondary explosion
from a ruptured
fuel tank destroyed his
amtrac. *Larry Buske*

Mark Mulvihill receives the Bronze Star in 1970, awarded for his heroic actions on June 13, 1969. The ceremony took place in the hangar at Wold-Chamberlain Airport, in the same area Mulvihill had passed through as a recruit headed for San Diego in June 1967. *Mark Mulvihill*

Wallace R. "Skip" Schmidt's sisters and mother (left to right): Diane, Shannon, Monica, Colleen, and Jackie. *Diane Finneman*

Shannon Schmidt placing flowers on her brother Skip's grave in the Fort Snelling National Cemetery prior to a 1997 remembrance ceremony. *Cliff Buchan*

Skip's proud parents, Monica and Eugene, holding his Silver Star citation and medal, awarded posthumously in 1998 at a ceremony in the Minnesota state capital building. *Cliff Buchan*

The Twins Platoon's drill instructors (left to right): Sergeant B. Lewis, Staff Sergeant R. K. Jenkins, and Sergeant T. L. Taylor. *U.S. Marine Corps*

David Seldon, with a bandaged and swollen right eye from a previous unorthodox training session, gets some additional pointers from a primary marksman instructor. *U.S. Marine Corps*

The Minnesota Twins Platoon 3011. *U.S. Marine Corps*

Skip Schmidt standing
squared away between
his brother-in-law
John van Bergen
and his father Eugene.
Diane Finneman

An incoming round hits an above-ground fuel bladder at Cua Viet. *Larry Buske*

Larry Rademacher being promoted to corporal onboard the USS *Yorktown*. *Larry Rademacher*

Larry Buske standing by a C-4 outpost bunker in range of enemy artillery positioned north of DMZ. *Larry Buske*

With some helpful tugging from his girlfriend Eileen, Kenny Goodman just barely fits into his father's World War II Marine uniform.
Mary Goodman

Catholics from Hue City sing for the Marines, thankful for the Marines helping them fight for their freedom. When the communist soldiers invaded Hue City, the Vietnamese Catholics who put on the December 3, 1967, USO show for the Marines at Phu Bai were in danger. The Viet Cong soldiers routinely sought out American sympathizers for torture and execution.
Rudolph Holzinger Jr.

The amtrac that David Paulseth walked behind on patrol. This amtrac was mounted with a rocket launcher and a bulldozer blade. It led the way while the troops followed a safe distance behind. The ten-inch teeth at the bottom of the steel blade cleared the way by unearthing enemy mines. *David Paulseth*

The explosive power of the amtrac that Paulseth walked behind. *David Paulseth*

The well-populated city of Da Nang. *David Paulseth*

A C-123 hit on March 6, 1968, as it approached Khe Sanh, killing all aboard, including forty-three Marines. *Robert Cusick*

Three VC sappers killed in the May 5, 1968, raid on the Marine compound where Mark Mulvihill and David Paulseth resided. There were 5,267 North Vietnamese soldiers, 326 South Vietnamese soldiers, and 154 Americans killed during the May 5–13, 1968, Communist Offensive (Mini Tet). *David Paulseth*

Robert Cusick steering the USS *New Jersey*. *Robert Cusick*

Cusick by the No. 3 gun turret. *Robert Cusick*

Timothy Sather on Hill 10, Golf Battery, Gun No. 3, wearing his first Purple Heart. *Timothy Sather*

Sather (right) on Hill 10, Golf Battery, taking a break from cleanup and restocking. *Timothy Sather*

The HMM362 "Ugly Angels" Helicopter Squadron in 1968 . While on temporary assignment to the 9th Marine Amphibious Brigade, the squadron was deployed aboard the USS *Iwo Jima*, USS *Princeton*, and USS *Okinawa*. *Christy W. Sauro Jr.*

Larry Jones. *Larry Jones*

David Paulseth
by a machine gun.
David Paulseth

Mark Mulvihill (in sunglasses) driving an amtrac.
Mark Mulvihill

Hill 861—home for seventy-seven days.
Brad Borreson

HMM362 Reactionary Platoon returns to their squadron area to find the devastation from the latest round of rocket attacks.
Christy W. Sauro Jr.

Robert Cusick (right) receives the Navy Achievement Medal with combat "V" for valor for his actions at Khe Sanh during the Tet Offensive of 1968.
Robert Cusick

trench burst out laughing and told him, "Get used to it. Everyone stinks here. We live below ground and we got no place to wash or clean up."

Two days after Cusick arrived, on February 10, he witnessed a grim sight that would become a historical event. A Marine KC-130 carrying six bladders of highly flammable helicopter fuel approached the runway for landing. The North Vietnamese opened fire with antiaircraft weapons and machine guns. The incoming aircraft caught on fire. Shortly after it crash-landed on the runway, the fuel bladders exploded. All those aboard were incinerated as they tried to run clear of the burning aircraft. Two days later the Khe Sanh runway was closed to all C-130s.

Incoming rockets and mortars were an everyday occurrence. If the explosions weren't too close, everybody kept working. The nights were unnerving; everyone knew the North Vietnamese were most likely to launch a ground attack under the cover of darkness. To counter the threat the Marines filled the night skies with outgoing artillery. The boom-boom sound of outgoing artillery was constant.

Cusick's job required that he be out on the airstrip. The runway remained closed to C-130s, but helicopters and some fixed-winged aircraft still dared to land. After what happened to the KC-130 on February 10, it took nerves of steel and a lot of courage for pilots to land at Khe Sanh. Normally, not much happened until late morning, when the fog lifted and the runway became visible to approaching aircraft.

Cusick heard the distinctive sound of an approaching helicopter. Fresh in his memory was a Marine who had been killed when a piece of shrapnel passed through his open flak jacket. Cautiously, he raised his head and peered over the sandbag wall that encircled the assembly area. Like he had done countless times before, he helped evacuate the wounded.

As part of his embarkation duties, Cusick counted the Marines around him. Not one was standing. They were all on stretchers and wrapped in green blankets. He made his way over to one who lay face-up on a stretcher and whose blanket was in disarray. Like a caring mother, he drew the young man's legs together, tucked the blanket in, and secured the bottle of plasma for the rough flight ahead.

A loud explosion shook the ground as the helicopter approached. Incoming rounds began raining down on the staging area. Cusick leaned over the stretcher and shielded the wounded Marine with his own body. For the shrapnel to reach the vital organs of the Marine on the stretcher, they would first have to pass through Cusick. His actions were preserved in a click of a camera. Unknown to Cusick, Robert Ellison, a freelance photographer, had taken his picture. It would appear in the March 18, 1968, edition of *Newsweek* magazine. The headline on the front cover was "The Agony of Khe Sanh." The caption below Cusick's picture within its pages read, "Marine shields a wounded comrade from enemy mortar barrage."

On February 22, 270 incoming artillery rounds rained down on the Marines at Khe Sanh, killing seven and wounding twenty-four. As a countermeasure U.S. air strikes and bombardments were stepped up around the base.

On the weekend of March 3, American watch teams in Saigon and Honolulu manned the war rooms, waiting to hear if the big ground assault on Khe Sanh had begun. They had reason to expect the big attack would occur by early Monday morning. When it didn't happen, they anticipated the big attack might be launched March 13 to coincide with the anniversary of General Giap's infamous attack on the French at Dien Bien Phu. As a precaution, the aerial bombardment of the areas surrounding the base was significantly increased. The stepped-up bombings seemed to work, for the celebrated anniversary came and went without a large-scale ground attack.

On March 6, an air force C-123 cargo plane was on approach to land. Aboard were forty-three Marines, four air force soldiers, one navy soldier, and one civilian—the returning freelance photographer, twenty-three-year-old Robert Ellison. The aircraft aborted its landing to avoid a midair collision with a single-engine Air America plane. The NVA anticipated that the C-123 would circle around and make a second approach. When it did, the enemy was ready and shot it down. The plane crashed in flames beyond the Marine lines. Except for one corpsman, everyone aboard was killed in the crash.

The number of aircraft being hit or shot down while trying to fly in and out of Khe Sanh was alarming. After the crash of the air force C-123 the runway was closed to all aircraft. Still, the resupply of the Marines had to continue without interruption.

KC-130s began flying high overhead to drop supplies by parachute. Other American planes flew in only twenty feet over the runway to dump their cargo out the rear tailgate without ever landing. As the planes passed over the runway, the crews popped parachutes attached to the pallets inside. When the chutes opened, the pallets went flying out the back of the plane onto the runway.

David Seldon was with 3rd Battalion, 26th Marines. He watched the enemy soldiers trenching closer to his section of the perimeter. To try and stop them, F-4 fighter planes were called in to drop napalm and do some strafing. Under conditions of extreme danger, the Marine pilots flew in low to the ground and passed over enemy positions to rake them with machine-gun fire and drop canisters of napalm. In one afternoon Seldon saw four F-4 fighter planes shot down in front of his position.

Fatigue became a problem; Seldon manned his position with just two hours of sleep per night. He completed his watch and retired into the bunker. He was in a deep sleep when sappers tried to breach the wire in front of his position. A firefight followed in which the Marines and NVA tossed hand grenades at one another. Seldon slept right through it.

Another time he was on watch, using a handheld radio to check in at designated intervals, and was overcome by fatigue and fell asleep with his radio clicked on. His snoring could be heard over the entire radio network. The lieutenant on duty ran from position to position until he found the sleeper.

Seldon was assigned to a detail that was to go out beyond the wire to pick up the bodies of some thirty replacements aboard a plane that had been shot down. Previous attempts to recover the bodies had failed because of enemy ambushes. The rescue detail Seldon was on made it to the crash site. He helped place ten of the deceased into body bags. They were all unrecognizable and the stench was unforgettable.

The enemy closed in and tightened their hold on the besieged Marine base each day. They dug more trenches and underground tunnels to bring them closer to the main perimeter. To keep Khe Sanh from being overrun, tactical aircraft flew an average of once every five minutes over the base. They unleashed thirty-five thousand tons of bombs and rockets on the enemy each day. That slowed the NVA down, but it did not stop them.

For the Marines hunkered down at Khe Sanh the possibility of being killed could come at any second. Some of the life-threatening incidents that occurred were random and brief. One time an incoming enemy round landed so close to Seldon that it caused his trench to cave in on him. He dug his way out and continued to man his position.

One afternoon, three high-altitude B-52 bombers passed overhead unseen and unheard by those on the ground. Each one carried eighty-four internal 500-pound bombs and twenty-four external 750-pound bombs. The B-52 bombers began dropping their payload. What fell from the 450,000-pound giants left mass destruction with uncountable results. Without any warning, a kilometer-long strip of earth erupted not more than one thousand feet outside the base perimeter.

Seldon watched dirt and debris sail five hundred feet into the air. The gigantic bombs continued to explode in rapid succession. The awesome and frightening spectacle lasted for many minutes and put a quick end to the enemy soldiers trenching their way toward the perimeter. The seventy-five thousand tons of bombs dropped on the enemy by just three B-52s left immense craters carved deep into the ground just smidgens beyond the perimeter. The bombings created a virtual Armageddon for the communist soldiers surrounding Khe Sanh and prevented the enemy from massing for a major ground attack.

In the final days of the siege the gun emplacement next to Seldon's took a direct hit. The next day they began putting together a replacement gun crew. Seldon stepped forward. He knew the Marines who had been killed and wanted the chance to even the score.

In the early morning hours of March 30, an NVA battalion entrenched one mile south of Khe Sanh came under attack. By afternoon the gun crew Seldon was a part of began firing on the coordinates they were given. His weapon, a 106mm recoilless rifle, had an open breech in back and a huge back-blast area. Each time a round was fired the concussion knocked Seldon's flak jacket hard against his chest. The weapon was extremely loud and required the wearing of earplugs and headphones to protect his hearing, but there were none. Every round fired increased the ringing in his unprotected ears.

On March 31, 1968, Operation Pegasus was launched using Marines, U.S. Army, and ARVN forces. Their objective was to open Route 9 from Ca Lu to Khe Sanh, destroy the enemy forces within the area of operations, and relieve the Marines at Khe Sanh. Two weeks into the operation, U.S. casualties totaled 92 killed and 667 wounded. ARVN losses came to 48 killed and 206 wounded. Enemy losses were eight times greater, with an estimated 1,044 dead. On April 8, Route 9 was clear. The last significant threat to Khe Sanh was eliminated.

On April 11, 1968, General Westmoreland informed President Lyndon B. Johnson that the Battle for Khe Sanh was over. The seventy-seven-day battle had claimed the lives of 205 American servicemen. The American death toll would have been substantially higher had it not been for the many pilots and crewmen who had braved enemy fire to rescue and evacuate 1,622 of their comrades. The death toll for the North Vietnamese was estimated to be a staggering ten to fifteen thousand. An exact body count was impossible because of the heavy ordnance used to bring about their defeat. The combined forces of the U.S. Army, Navy, Air Force, and Marine Corp fired ten times more artillery rounds than the enemy. During the height of battle, there were three B-52 bombers flying overhead every ninety minutes.

After being under siege for ten weeks, the entire 3rd Battalion, 26th Marines, was ready to go on the offensive. Their target was a heavily armed NVA battalion positioned a mile and a quarter from Hill 881 North. A full-scale assault was launched to relieve the Marines on hills 861 and 881 South. Seldon took part.

Company B, 1st Battalion, 26th Marines, attacked with a vengeance that left 115 North Vietnamese soldiers killed. The final battle, part of Operation Pegasus, came on April 14, with

U.S. Marines attacking and defeating the NVA forces at Hill 881 North.

The gun crew Seldon was a part of accounted for fifty kills. Their gun emplacement fired more than a hundred rounds. That was a lot for 106mm, in fact, more than the gun could handle. The rifling inside the barrel had melted down and the gun had to be retired from service. The parapet surrounding the gun had been shaken down to nothing. Afterward, Seldon was sent to the hospital ship USS *Repose* to be checked out. His chest was completely black and blue from the repeated striking of his flak jacket during each firing. Three weeks would pass before Seldon would be able to hear again.

Over the course of the siege, the howitzers within the base and the U.S. Army's 175mm guns at nearby at Camp Carroll fired nearly one hundred thousand rounds into enemy positions. In the final hours, gun crews like Seldon's cleared the way for the Marines advancing on Hill 881 North. The commanding officer of the 26th Marines, Colonel Bruce Meyers, used words like *superb* to describe the regiment's use of special weapons. The Marine air wing provided the needed air support using fixed-wing aircraft and helicopters. On the ground Marine infantry troops did their part by fearlessly storming one enemy position after another, with individual acts of heroism in abundance.

For the NVA, there was no repeat performance of what it had done to the French at Dien Bien Phu fourteen years earlier. Why the well-equipped NVA force was unable to defeat the Marines was clearly visible. The joint air assault, code-named Operation Niagara and conducted by the U.S. Air Force, U.S. Navy, and Marine Corp, dropped uncountable tons of bombs over the five square miles surrounding Khe Sanh. The landscape surrounding the Marine base looked like the surface of the moon.

After delivering this crushing defeat to the enemy, Seldon's unit left Khe Sanh for Quang Tri. When they arrived the first thing they did was strip. During the ordeal, Seldon had lost thirty pounds and his ribs showed. They were told to throw all their clothes in a pile. Most had not changed their utilities for three months. The smell was so bad that their clothes were burned.

Before being marched to the showers, they were given the packages that had been mailed to them by their loved ones and held for them during the siege. Seldon's girlfriend and soon-to-be fiancée, Patricia Vetsch, could not have given Seldon a better gift. It was a bottle of Prell shampoo. Feeling pretty smug, Seldon showed his buddies that he had shampoo. Once in the shower Seldon ran into a problem. No matter how hard he scrubbed he couldn't get the green shampoo to lather up. What his girlfriend had really sent him was lime vodka. Seldon smelled so rank that he didn't smell the alcohol until after he had poured out the entire bottle.

After they finished showering, they were given clean clothes and were in for a few more surprises. The first one came by helicopter; the crew came out carrying a hollowed out napalm bomb casing full of ice and beer. The defenders of Khe Sanh were in for a well-deserved celebration. They certainly deserved a break from the fighting and were told they could spend the rest of the day in tents, opening their mail and getting happy. They didn't have to worry about keeping the base perimeter secure; the Marines stationed at Quang Tri would take care of that.

After several hours of drunken revelry Seldon retired to a clean bunk and passed out. The next surprise was not a pleasant one. Seldon was shaken awake in the middle of the night. There was enemy movement just outside the wire and everyone was to saddle up. Seldon was still in an alcohol-induced stupor when he tried to tie his pack together. Seeing a piece of rope hanging from his pack, he reached over and grabbed his buddy's K-bar knife. But instead of cutting down and away from himself, Seldon put the blade under the rope and cut upward. The recently sharpened knife sliced through the rope and didn't stop until it was halfway through Seldon's nose.

With his hands cupped over his nose, Seldon went into the officer's tent and said, "Sir, I don't think I am going to make this one tonight." To make his point, Seldon opened his hands and let the blood splash onto his boots. The officer grumbled obscenities and sent him to see the corpsman. The only member of the unit who was drunker that night than Seldon was the corpsman who sewed him up. The incident left Seldon with a prominent scar on his nose that extends up into his eyebrow. Seldon's hearing in his right ear, damaged by the sound of the 106mm recoilless rifle firing, was never fully restored.

On May 23, 1968, at the White House, President Johnson cited all U.S. personnel who gallantly defended Khe Sanh. With emotion cracking in his voice, the president said:

> I believe our initiative toward peace talks with North Vietnam was greatly strengthened by what these men did at Khe Sanh. For they vividly demonstrated to the enemy the utter futility of his attempts to win a military victory in the South. Brave men such as the 26th Marines will carry the fight for freedom in Vietnam and soon, God willing, they will come home. We would like nothing more than to see that day. But until they do, we shall express at moments such as these on behalf of all American people our great gratitude for the protection they have given us and our great appreciation for their selfless bravery.

15

LAM XUAN EAST

The steady flow of casualties drained the ranks of 2nd Battalion, 4th Marine Regiment, 3rd Marine Division, to the point at which division headquarters gave the battalion priority on replacements. Wallace "Skip" Schmidt was one of them.

The battalion was always in the enemy's face, operating just south of the DMZ in northern I Corps. Under such intense conditions good friendships were forged quickly. Skip made many new friends and their relationships to one another were not superficial.

Right after Christmas Skip's sister, Diane—the one the family jokingly called "the mom sister"—moved back to Minnesota to live with her husband's mother in Minneapolis. She was pregnant and lonely. She missed her husband and brother. But it was not her loneliness that was on her mind as she drove to the nearby U.S. Naval Air Station in Minneapolis; it was her brother Skip. She was very worried something bad might happen to him. All she could think of was to turn to God for help.

The MP at the gate recognized the gray Volkswagen Beetle with the enlisted sticker on the bumper and waved it through. Once inside the base, Diane drove straight to the multiple-use building, which also served as the base church. It was after hours, so the building was quiet and empty. Diane tried the door and was relieved to find it unlocked.

Inside she found what she was looking for, a rack of candles. Being pregnant made it a chore to kneel down in front of the vigil candles. Diane lit three candles, one for her husband, one for her brother, and one for her husband's cousin—all three were in Vietnam. In the dimly lit church her faith shined bright. She prayed with all her heart, "Oh merciful God in heaven, give special blessing to my brother. Please watch over him. Please protect him."

As the candles flickered Diane continued to pray. Believing her prayers would protect her brother, she returned to the church on a regular basis to light the candles and pray. She also wrote to Skip and told him about the candles and what she was doing.

When North Vietnam launched its Tet Offensive on January 31, 1968, 2nd Battalion, 4th Marines (2/4), was deployed north of Camp Carroll to assist in Operation Lancaster II, which had started on January 25. Almost immediately, the unit started running into NVA platoons and became engaged in heavy combat. By the end of the month the battalion had lost ten men and eighty-nine were wounded. Enemy losses were more than three times greater. Skip was a bit shaken, but otherwise he was fine.

On March 5, 2/4 relieved 3rd Battalion, 1st Marines, and set up its command post in the deserted bombed-out village of Mai Xa Chanh, which had been captured several days earlier through extremely heavy fighting. The village smelled of death and was littered with enemy bodies and equipment. Skip and his fellow Marines entered the village, filling it with the jingle of combat gear and equipment. All that remained of the once peaceful setting were the two waterways built around the village.

Skip was in Foxtrot Company, which ended up on the east side of the Jones Creek. His unit set up its command post inside a Catholic Church, using its steeple as an observation post. The enemy attacked that night, first with rockets and mortars, then with a ground assault. Two Marines were seriously wounded; enemy losses were thirteen fatalities. The following morning Foxtrot Company was sent to check out a number of evacuated hamlets along both sides of Jones Creek. But first there was a mail call.

Schmidt got a letter from his brother-in-law, John Van Bergen: "Well, old man, I'll be joining you in another three days or by the time you get this letter I'll already be there. Yep, we are leaving for the southern tip of Vietnam today. I guess things aren't going very well at home for your mom and dad, but I suppose it had to happen some time. It sure does make it rough on Diane. I guess the baby is coming along just fine. Well, see you soon and remember I'll be over there with you, big man, when you get this letter. Love, John."

Foxtrot had to perform a series of assaults to reclear the hamlets. The number of enemy soldiers killed was impressive. For the first week, everything went well for Foxtrot Company. That changed on March 12, at Lam Xuan East, a short two miles farther north along Jones Creek.

Before Foxtrot's move to encounter the enemy, there was another mail call. Skip received a letter from Diane: "You know, Skip, John and I are both so very proud of you. You have proven to everyone what John and I knew all along. You have a good head on your shoulders and you know how to use it. Oh Skip I sure am lonesome for you. All the men in my life who mean anything to me are gone now. You and John are both over there and dad is out of town. I just keep thinking next Christmas we will all be together again and my baby will be six months old. That will be the best Christmas of my life, and man are we going to celebrate. Take good care and I will try to write again soon. From a very proud sister. Love, Diane."

As Foxtrot Company advanced toward Lam Xuan East, a few NVA soldiers were spotted fleeing the area. Immediately, the point squad took off after the NVA. It was a trap; enemy soldiers were hidden in well-fortified positions, waiting to spring their attack. The NVA held their fire as the point squad passed by their hidden positions in hot pursuit of the fleeing decoys. Following behind the point squad was the forward platoon. When the NVA opened fire, eighteen Marines were killed and the entire company was caught up in a battle it had no chance of winning.

Skip remained at the forefront. As the Marines continued to fall, Skip held his ground. At times all that separated him from the enemy was a couple yards of ground. His battalion commander, Lieutenant Colonel Weise, made the decision to break contact and regroup. Skip organized the few able-bodied Marines around him and dragged some of the wounded to safety. He was one of the few in his platoon to survive the ambush. The company gunnery sergeant, P. E. Brandon, wished he had a hundred Marines like Skip Schmidt. For his heroic action at Lam Xuan, Brandon put Skip in for a medal.

The same night, Skip noticed one Marine, the new guy, Martinez, was having a real rough time. It was his first day in Vietnam and the intense fighting was a little more than he could handle. Skip realized Martinez needed more psychiatric assistance than he could provide, so he brought the new guy to their commanding officer, who was able to get him evacuated to get the help he needed. A short time later Martinez was back with his unit, and he and Skip became good friends.

Then there was Private First Class Summers, the incorrigible soldier from 3rd Platoon. Summers was a hard-luck kid who had been knocked around all his life. What Summers needed and found in 2/4 were people who cared about him. Skip was always watching out for him and, after a while, the two of them became good friends.

During the month of March 1968, Skip's unit fought in many more battles and the casualties within the unit ran high at 59 dead and 360 wounded. Due to the heavy use of supporting arms, the number of NVA killed by the unit was estimated to be 474.

The surviving Marines were sorely in need of letters from home, just a few precious lines that showed someone cared and appreciated their sacrifices. The day the letters arrived from Shannon Schmidt's fourth grade class, Skip was all smiles. He watched the letters being passed out. He had written to his little sister and asked her to see if her classmates would write letters to the men in his outfit. Shannon came through with flying colors. Everyone in his unit was reading and passing around the grade-school letters.

In April, Monica received a letter from her son, and with it were some photos Skip had taken. Under each photo, he wrote what the picture was of. One picture stood out from all the rest; it was the photo of a young Asian male, in his late teens, lying faceup on the ground with his eyes closed. His arms were pulled up over his head. The dead soldier had been dragged out for the body count. Under the photo, Skip had written, "My first NVA."

The photo was Skip's way of showing his family that he was not one of the lucky ones to be assigned to some secure area. The picture showed he had the toughest job of all. When it came down to winning the war, the grunts were the bottom line. All the military planning and strategies, from the White House down, wouldn't be worth hoot if Marines like him couldn't be victorious in combat. For Skip it was a case of one picture being worth a thousand words. What made his job tolerable was the belief that he was killing for a just and noble cause.

16

THE SAPPER ATTACK OF
APRIL 1968

I n April 1968 the enemy confined its operations to guerrilla activities, while the NVA regulars began infiltrating their old positions in preparation of their next offensive. By late April the 31st, 141st, and 36th NVA regiments had been sighted in and around the Da Nang area. In response to the increased enemy sightings, Marine units stepped up their patrols.

"How's it going, 'Baby-san'?" Mulvihill asked a young corporal from Ohio.

"I got a new crew member. He just got in-country a couple days ago. That's him coming now," Baby-san told Mulvihill as he worked on his own amtrac.

Mulvihill greeted the newcomer with a handshake and a friendly smile. "You listen to Baby-san. He knows his shit. He's going to be a career Marine, a lifer. You watch," Mulvihill told the new guy.

"Why do you call him Baby-san?" the new guy asked.

"Didn't he tell you? He's just a baby. He just turned eighteen in February."

Paulseth was out of the compound on patrol. Routine patrols of the area surrounding the base helped defend Da Nang against rocket, mortar, and sapper attacks. Fighting a war with no front lines was nerve-wracking.

After three weeks out in the bush, Paulseth was happy to return to the safety of the compound. He had some free time and went to the little club on the base, which was no more than a hut with a few tables and chairs. It was a place where a few off-duty Marines could go to have a few beers and try to relax. Paulseth spent the evening of May 4 sitting alone and drinking.

While Paulseth was becoming intoxicated, Mulvihill, Baby-san, and the new guy were asleep. At the same time three mud-covered NVA sappers, clad only in shorts, were making their way toward the base perimeter.

Sappers often paved the way for a larger assault. They reduced the casualties to their own main body by infiltrating the enemy's base defenses. Their sudden appearance inside a fortified position caused terror, confusion, and disorganization to those under attack. Their objective was to destroy the base defense barriers, logistics facilities, and munitions dumps.

Sappers trained for almost a year, which was six times longer than the regular NVA soldier trained. Sapper recruits were carefully selected, with preference given to volunteers and honor graduates from basic military courses who showed a natural aggressiveness and keen senses, especially of sight and sound. They were taught reconnaissance, how to penetrate defenses, assault tactics, stealth, and demolitions. They trained for two and a half months on methods of withdrawal and how to walk over terrain without making any noise.

Paulseth gingerly made his way back to his sleeping quarters, unaware that the three sappers were slithering toward the base perimeter armed with wire cutters, a few pins to disarm mines, and bamboo sticks to prop up wires. Reaching his quarters Paulseth stripped down to his skivvies and crashed onto his cot.

The sappers went about the meticulous task of disarming a

maze of trip flares and anti-intrusion devices without detection. Using their hands and feet to probe for any ground wires that might reveal mines or bobby traps, the advancing sappers spent hours covering the last hundred meters to the fence.

A Marine manning the perimeter called for an illumination flare. As the flare whistled skyward, the mud-covered sappers lay flat against the ground in absolute stillness. When the flare popped open, turning night into day, there was nothing for the Marines guarding the perimeter to see.

The sappers reached the fence and painstakingly cut through an eight-foot section. Then they retreated, leaving the scene looking undisturbed. As they withdrew, they retraced their steps and marked the assault avenue with bamboo arrows. The sappers went to a prearranged location to make their report to the commander of the NVA sapper assault unit. Hearing that the sapper cell had prepared the way, the commander gave the order for the deadly mission to begin.

The sapper assault team went into action. A dozen sappers armed with explosives, some Bangalore torpedoes, and rifles slithered toward the Marine perimeter with the same stealth as the first unit. The larger and more heavily armed unit crawled safely over the marked avenue of assault. They slipped through the disabled section of fence carrying their satchel charges and automatic weapons.

At about 0100 Paulseth awoke to the sound of a nearby explosion. He reached for his rifle, but it wasn't there. He cursed himself for not having his rifle at his side, as he had been trained to, and he couldn't find his helmet either. As the explosions intensified, Paulseth stumbled around his billet trying to find his things.

Sappers ran through the compound, blowing up key targets, while others gunned down the Marines who rushed out of their billets to get to their assigned positions on the perimeter. As the base siren sounded the alert, another enemy unit attacked the main perimeter to create a diversion for the raiding party.

Mulvihill ran out of his billet and hurried toward the first amtrac parked in line. He was a member of the reactionary platoon and the base siren was signaling a full alert. When this happened he was to go to his amtrac, start it up, turn the radio on, and listen for the orders that would direct him where to go. Before he got to his vehicle the nearby maintenance shed exploded into flames. Following right behind Mulvihill was Baby-san and the new guy. All three mistakenly thought the maintenance shed had taken a hit from an incoming mortar round. Unaware that there were sappers within the compound, Mulvihill climbed into the first amtrac and Baby-san climbed into the third amtrac. The amtrac between them took a direct hit.

Oh my God are these guys accurate with their mortars, thought Mulvihill. Fearing enemy artillery might bracket the area, Mulvihill drove his amtrac a short distance away, parked it, and waited for his orders to come over the radio. When he saw one structure after another take direct hits, he realized something was wrong. He knew enemy artillery couldn't be *that* accurate. "Bullshit! That's not artillery. Someone is blowing these things up," Mulvihill cussed.

The amtrac occupied by Baby-san exploded into flames. Mulvihill turned off his amtrac and jumped out. As he ran to help Baby-san and the crew trapped inside, the thing he had always feared most happened. The first explosion damaged the fuel cells under the deck plate and gas inside ignited, causing a secondary explosion that sent the steel ramp on the front of the amtrac sailing through the air. The opening left by the blown ramp provided a quick escape route. Two of the three occupants came running out of the blazing inferno. Both were covered with gasoline and on fire.

Mulvihill and another Marine rushed to help the two Marines, who had fallen to the ground covered in flames. Mulvihill reached one of them and worked to smother out the fire. He discovered that it was Baby-san. The young corporal was in terrible shape. Mulvihill looked around for help and saw the new guy just watching.

"Come on! Help us!" Mulvihill yelled to the new guy, who remained shocked and useless. With help from another Marine, Mulvihill picked up Baby-san and carried him to a bunker a hundred feet away.

Paulseth gave up trying to find his rifle. Dressed in his skivvies, he staggered toward the nearest bunker to wait out what he thought was a rocket-and-mortar attack. Inside the bunker were other Marines who thought the same thing. The explosions within the compound and the distant sounds of fighting along the perimeter were enough to make Paulseth vow to never again lose track of his rife and equipment.

When things quieted down, Paulseth emerged from the bunker. He was shocked by what he saw. The illumination flares and flaming buildings made the dead and wounded Marines scattered about visible. The fighting had stopped, but grunts were running around the compound searching for something. The wounded were being taken care of and everything seemed to be under control.

The aftermath of the attack was more visible in the morning. Mulvihill learned that four of his fellow Marines had been killed and fifty-four had been wounded. He used his amtrac to help medevac the wounded. All the while he kept thinking about

Baby-san. The way he was suffering when the medics carried him off was enough to make Mulvihill cry. He kept thinking, *If only I had reacted quicker. If only I had picked up on what was really happening sooner.* He learned that the other Marine on fire was the mechanic, who had died during the night.

In the days that followed, there were updates on Baby-san's condition. They were told that more than 97 percent of his body was burned. Images of Baby-san suffering in terrible agony were unavoidable. Not a day passed by when Mulvihill wasn't preoccupied with thoughts about the young corporal from Ohio.

"It's remarkable he's alive," Mulvihill told the others, as he thought back on how Baby-san looked after the flames had been extinguished. A full week passed and Baby-san was still alive.

At two weeks the men were called into formation and told, "Baby-san is still alive, but he's in bad shape." Baby-san's condition weighed heavily on everyone's mind. The mood of the entire unit remained subdued. Conversations were minimal. At three weeks the men were called into formation and informed that Baby-san was still alive, but that his condition remained critical. Mulvihill reflected on how quickly Baby-san had been promoted through the ranks. His determination and strong will to live was incredible.

On May 26, the platoon was called to an early morning formation. It had been nearly four weeks since Baby-san was severely burned. The men were informed that Baby-san had died during the night. The young corporal was just eighteen years old. With deepening regret Mulvihill thought to himself, *If only I could have done more!*

17

CAMP EVANS

Rudolph Holzinger Jr. trained for four weeks at Camp Pendleton to become a field radio operator. It was depressing to hear that radiomen didn't last long in a firefight.

On the flight over to Vietnam he thought, *I am as good as dead.* During the layover in Okinawa, Japan, he met a career Marine who suggested they go to the enlisted men's club and "have a few." When Holzinger mentioned he was a radioman, the career Marine told him, "Once you get to Vietnam, you're as good as dead! Let me give you some advice. Da Nang is the most secure base in I Corps. If you want to be stationed in Da Nang, hand the guy your orders with the tip of a twenty-dollar bill sticking out of them."

Holzinger arrived in Da Nang on December 20, 1967. The Marine processing Holzinger's orders lowered the papers from view, pulled out the twenty, and assigned him to 3rd Force Logistics Command, which was located at Da Nang. After checking in, he was assigned to 5th Communications Battalion.

Soon the army asked the Marine Corps for a mobile unit they could use to set up a teletype. The Marine Corps obliged by lending the army a communications van along with a three-man crew that included Holzinger. His temporary duty assignment to the army's 1st Cavalry Division (Airmobile) got him deployed some seventy-five miles north into the northern Thua Thien province and southern Quang Tri province. The army troops were being used to fill the gaps between 1st Marine Division in central I Corps and 3rd Marine Division, which was operating along the DMZ.

Camp Evans was one of the bases to come under attack during the enemy's Mini-Tet offensive in the spring of 1968. Enemy rockets poured in, and there was fighting along the main perimeter. Holzinger thought the base was being overrun. When the attack started he was tucked in a fighting hole behind the army's main perimeter with his two crewmates. One of the incoming rounds landed right in the foxhole directly in front of them. The quiet after the explosion was creepy.

"There were three guys in that hole. They might need our help," Holzinger said in a shaky voice. Without any further discussion the three Marines piled out of their fighting hole and ran through the darkness toward the silent foxhole. Incoming enemy rounds continued to fall as the three rescuers raced to help some soldiers they only vaguely knew. They reached the foxhole without injury. The two other crewmen each pulled up a body, hoisted it over their shoulders, and took off at a run for the command post.

Holzinger heard a moan from the corner of the foxhole. He reached into the foxhole and groped around in the dark until he felt the arm of the wounded soldier. Figuring he would do the same as the others, he took the soldier by the hand and began to pull him up. The soldier let out one hell of a scream. The weight resistance of the soldier's body was suddenly gone and Holzinger fell over backward holding just the arm. The chill of goose bumps spread head to toe as Holzinger realized, *I just tore his arm off!* Holzinger dropped the arm and scrambled out of the foxhole. *I'm giving him up for dead,* Holzinger thought as he ran for the command post.

He was almost there when an incoming rocket exploded behind him. As a conditioned reflex, he dove for cover. When he got up and dashed into the bunker, he was unaware that he had been hit by a piece of shrapnel in the calf of his leg.

"Where's your man?" Bob looked up and asked.

"He's out there. He's dead. I tore his arm right off when I tried to pick him up."

"Go get a corpsman," Bob said to Holzinger, as he and the other Marine continued to administer first aid to the two wounded soldiers. One soldier had a stomach wound, and Bob was applying a compression bandage to stop the bleeding. The other soldier had leg and back injuries.

Holzinger took off running for sick bay a half-mile away. He ran into the medical structure out of breath and said, "We got some guys hit on the north end!" Within minutes an ambulance was speeding toward the bunker with Holzinger inside pointing the way. With everyone's help, the two wounded soldiers were loaded into the back of the ambulance. A medic went and checked the soldier in the foxhole. He returned and confirmed, "The one in the foxhole is dead."

Holzinger rode in the back of the ambulance and helped care for the wounded soldiers on the return trip to the sick bay. At the sick bay Holzinger watched the two wounded soldiers being taken away on gurneys. It was then he felt the wetness in his boot.

Looking down, he saw that his one trouser leg was wet below the knee. He pulled up his trouser leg and saw a hole the size of a quarter, where a piece of shrapnel had passed through his calf and created a flesh wound that needed stitching. He thought it must have missed the bone, but he was wrong. The treating physician informed him that a chunk of bone was missing. Holzinger kept thinking, *I hope this never happens again.* The very next night more incoming rounds hit Camp Evans.

Holzinger was given another temporary duty assignment. This time he worked as a forward air controller for a naval gunfire liaison officer. One night they went out as a four-man team looking to pinpoint the NVA troops traveling the Ho Chi Minh Trail. Their mission was to locate the enemy and call for an air strike. The navy officer did the math, and Holzinger passed the correct coordinates over the radio.

The mission took an unexpected turn. An NVA patrol happened to be walking up the trail they were walking down. Holzinger's team moved off the trail and hid in the bushes. His heart was pounding so loud he feared the patrol might hear it. He counted fourteen soldiers as they walked by. They were so close he could have reached out and touched them. The enemy patrol passed right by without detecting their presence. It was such a frightening experience the squad did not come out of the bushes until after sunup.

Holzinger's health took a turn for the worse. A bad case of dysentery left him dehydrated. Over a thirty-day period, his weight dropped from 205 pounds down to 185. After reporting his condition to his superior, he was sent to sick bay, where they pumped his stomach and put him on medication. After that Holzinger finally got back to Da Nang.

18

THE BATTLE OF DAI DO

On April 15, 1968, a long line of helicopters taxied from the flight line to the airstrip at Phu Bai. Except for the call numbers, all the choppers looked alike. One by one, Seahorses of HMM-362 turned onto the runway. It was obvious something was up; to have an entire squadron take off at the same time was not the norm. The first wave of choppers took to the sky with a roar. Fully loaded with squadron personnel and cargo, the choppers flew eastward toward the open sea where the USS *Iwo Jima* awaited their arrival.

The USS *Iwo Jima* was the first ship to be designed and built from the keel up as an amphibious assault ship (LPH). It looked like a conventional aircraft carrier but was specially constructed to carry a Marine battalion landing team with its guns, vehicles, and equipment, plus a reinforced squadron of transport helicopters and various support personnel. It was the navy's newest concept for amphibious operations.

The ship had three levels and was designed to carry 528 seamen and 2,090 Marines. The first level was flat for the launch and recovery of helicopters. Four twin-mounted guns, two forward of the island structure and two at the stern, were notched into the flight deck. The second level of the ship included a hangar deck and large berthing and messing spaces. Above the vehicle storage area was an extensive medical facility, equipped with an operating room, x-ray room, hospital ward, isolation ward, laboratory, pharmacy, dental operating room, and some medical storerooms. Two small elevators carried cargo from the hold to the flight deck. In addition, the LPH housed a complex communications center to coordinate large assaults with other ships, aircraft, and supporting fire.

For HMM-362 the pressure was on to complete its deployment as quickly as possible. A few days earlier, from April 10 to 13, the squadron had flown sixteen medevac missions and evacuated forty-six combat casualties. The entire northern I Corps area remained a hotbed of enemy activity. The urgent need for helicopters could come at any time, making HMM-362's rapid deployment essential.

The squadron's deployment aboard the USS *Iwo Jima* was a textbook example of things done right. Christy Sauro Jr. had flawlessly carried out his embarkation duties. All his planning and hard work paid off. As soon as the first wave of helicopters landed on the 592-foot-long USS *Iwo Jima,* sailors driving forklifts raced across the 105-foot-wide flight deck to scoop up the palletized cargo. The ship's two elevators ran nonstop to bring the incoming Marines and equipment below deck. Those assigned to the squadron embarkation team helped to identify and direct the high-priority items. From the tactical markings on the boxes they knew the contents and where aboard ship they were to go. With sweat and determination the squadron unpacked and was fully operational with a minimum of delay. No birds were grounded because mechanics couldn't find their tools. The very next day the Ugly Angels were back in operation.

The Marines were looking forward to sleeping at night without the fear of incoming rockets and mortars. They were ready to enjoy the comforts of their new home and wasted no time settling in. What the sailors got in return for their hospitality was a barrage of antagonistic remarks. Something about being in the company of sailors created an uncontrollable urge for Marines to say things like, "Marines are the best. Marines have it the toughest. Compared to Marines, you sailors have it easy."

Sailors were quick to learn it was pointless to try and argue the point. So, rather than get bogged down in a bottomless pit of discussion, they tended to be good hearted and laugh off the needling with comebacks like, "I don't want to hear it! You Marines are all the same! What is it they do to you in boot camp?"

The navy men upset their new guests the very first day by informing them that it would be a few days before they would be getting clean sheets. In their previous surroundings, it had been more important for the Marines to win the battles of Tet than it was to wash sheets. But in the sanitary conditions aboard a navy ship—where everything was freshly painted and spotless, food was served on trays with silverware, and the cups were made of glass—some Marines could not bear the thought of sleeping one more night on yellow-stained sheets covered with sand.

Some of the guests decided there was a way to get the navy men to understand the urgency of the situation. They slipped into the navy men's sleeping quarters and did an exchange of sheets. The returning sailors were quick to notice. There was no missing the soiled sheets that had been left on top of their bare mattresses for their sleeping enjoyment. The culprit leathernecks reasoned that the navy men might better be able to resolve the problem if they fully understood it. The sailors yelling, "No way!" certainly did.

The Marines aboard the *Iwo Jima* were from 2/4. The battalion's fighting prowess in World War II had earned it the nickname the "Magnificent Bastards." The last seven months had been especially hard on it, as the Marines inevitably found themselves in the thick of things. Every combat situation conceivable came their way, right down to fighting the enemy in hand-to-hand combat. No matter where the unit went, the crap hit the fan. Not surprisingly, casualties within the unit ran high. Some Marines assigned to 2/4 were killed within twenty-four hours of joining, while others were killed just as their thirteen-month tours of duty were nearing completion. The risk of being killed at any time was high for every Marine in Vietnam, but for the Marines of 2/4, that possibility loomed considerably higher.

Operation Napoleon/Saline had started on November 5, 1967, with the objective of providing security for the Cua Viet River system. The newly christened Battalion Landing Team (BLT) 2/4 officially began its participation in the operation on March 5, 1968, as part of Special Landing Force (SLF) Alpha, 9th Marine Amphibious Brigade (MAB).

The security of the area north of the Cua Viet River was being threatened by the increasing presence of the 320th NVA Division, which commanded some twenty battalions of seasoned troops freshly equipped for battle. The communist leaders of North Vietnam planned to use the 320th NVA Division to show the world that in spite of the heavy losses sustained by North Vietnamese during Tet 1968, they still had the ability and determination to win the war. Ten advance companies of the 48th and 52nd NVA regiments had infiltrated through the ARVN area of responsibility. Their infiltration placed them about fifteen miles inside South Vietnam.

As the USS *Iwo Jima* cruised offshore, there were signs that the communist forces were getting ready to launch a major offensive against the Marine base at Dong Ha. There were many reasons for the communists to target Dong Ha. It was the supply center for the III Marine Amphibious Force, and the base was crucial to the defense of the Cua Viet River system.

Making Dong Ha even more enticing was its location a mere nine miles south of the DMZ. The North Vietnamese did not have to travel far to attack, and if things didn't go well, they could retreat back across the DMZ to the safe sanctuary of North Vietnam. As the ominous events continued to unfold, the USS *Iwo Jima* cruised off the coast where the Cua Viet River empties into the South China Sea. A short seven miles inland was the Marine base Dong Ha.

Schmidt came aboard the USS *Iwo Jima* in April as part of a shore party. On a rotating basis the grunts in the field came aboard for routine medical and dental checkups. Once the Marines of the unit had been put ashore, they seldom got back to the ship. When Schmidt came aboard, the ship's two elevators were busy getting HMM-362 settled into its new living quarters. Somehow in the midst of all the confusion, Schmidt and Sauro spied one another. Because both were short in height, they had stood next to each other all through boot camp.

"Schmidt! What are you doing here?" Sauro asked, both surprised and happy to see someone from the Minnesota Twins Platoon.

"I'm with 2/4," Schmidt returned proudly. He said it like that was even a bigger deal than being part of the Minnesota Twins Platoon. "You with the air wing?" Schmidt asked suspiciously.

"Yeah, I'm with HMM-362—the helicopter squadron."

Schmidt gave Sauro a distasteful look, then said point-blank, "You skated! You got off easy! You're lucky you're not a grunt!"

"I know," Sauro agreed. It was true: compared to being a grunt he did have it easy. But he knew right away that's not what Schmidt was trying to say. "Has it been rough?" Sauro asked.

Schmidt looked around nervously. After a short silence and a little nervous fidgeting, he answered too low for the others to hear, "Yeah, it's been rough." Schmidt's eyes dropped to the floor. A few seconds passed, he looked back up, his eyes darted from right to left, and he repeated, "You're lucky you're not a grunt." Schmidt was most sincere.

"I know," Sauro acknowledged.

"What's your MOS?" Schmidt quizzed.

"Owe-four-three-one—embarkation," Sauro answered.

"I suppose you sit behind a desk?"

"Sometimes. Most of the time," Sauro admitted with a friendly smile. Schmidt shook his head as if to suggest that was no way to win the war. The difference between the air wing and the infantry was like night and day. Neither Schmidt nor Sauro knew quite what to say, and each figured the other might not be able to relate. "Well, guess what," Sauro said, after both fumbled around for something to talk about.

"What?" Schmidt asked.

"I'm leaving tomorrow to go on R&R in Bangkok." Sauro laughed when he saw the shocked look on Schmidt's face. R&R was short for *rest and recuperation.* Every Marine serving in Vietnam is supposed to get one R&R during a thirteen-month tour of duty.

Schmidt jabbed, "Give me a break! Like you guys really need R&R! You've only been in-country four months! How come you're getting R&R so soon?"

"We just finished our deployment. This is really the best time for me to go," Sauro pointed out.

"You guys are always skating," Schmidt grumbled, before referring to the air wing as pencil pushers.

Sauro thought that if he talked about a negative happening, perhaps Schmidt might not feel like he was getting the short end of the stick. He said, "They assigned me to the laundry detail for two weeks."

"Really!" Schmidt brightened up.

"Yeah," Sauro told him.

"Did you start yet?" Schmidt was eager to know.

"Yep, I started a week ago." Schmidt took the news well. Sauro continued, "I'll finish my second week when I get back from R&R. Say, one of the guys working in the laundry is a sergeant from your outfit. A short-timer with only a few days left in-country. And there's this sailor in charge. Boy, do we give him a hard time. He said if he hears one more time how tough Marines have it, he'll throw up."

Schmidt finally laughed. The topic of conversation seemed to relax Skip. The two began to reminisce about being part of the Minnesota Twins Platoon and their days in boot camp. Running out of time and conversation, Sauro said, "When I get back from R&R, I'll fill you in on all the exciting details."

"I can hardly wait." Schmidt scoffed.

Sauro returned from R&R on April 30, 1968. The first stop on the way back to his unit was Da Nang. He immediately went to the landing pad at which HMM-362 picked up the squadron mail at least once a day, sometimes more. Sauro eagerly checked out the incoming aircraft all afternoon without sighting one single Ugly Angel. That was very odd. As the sun slipped below the horizon, Sauro worried that something bad had happened. In the fading twilight, he picked up his sea bag and returned through the darkness to the main terminal. Finding an out-of-the-way spot, he curled up on the ground and went to sleep.

It was the same the following day; not one Ugly Angel to be seen anywhere. In the four and a half months Sauro had been with the squadron, he had never known them not to pick up their mail. With growing apprehension, he picked up his sea bag and returned to the terminal for a restless night of sleep on the ground.

Late the following afternoon, on May 2, Sauro spied a UH-34 Seahorse as it approached the helicopter landing pad. When the chopper turned sideways to land, he saw the familiar Ugly Angel insignia. Finally! He grabbed his sea bag and hustled over to where the helicopter was setting down.

"Is this the mail bird?" Sauro shouted to the crew chief. The crew chief signaled a thumbs-up. "Can I get a lift back to the *Iwo Jima*?" Sauro yelled over the usual noises. Again it was thumbs-up. Sauro tossed in his sea bag and climbed aboard. "Nobody came yesterday. What's going on?" he yelled to the port gunner.

"All hell broke loose. Some really bad shit. Not much left of 2/4. I heard they took 90 percent casualties," the gunner shouted over the loud sound of whirling rotor blades that came in through the open side hatch.

The *Iwo Jima* was clearly visible from the sky. As the chopper descended toward the LPH, the warship continued its steady course. Its steel hull cut a deep notch through the choppy waves as it steamed ahead, leaving a wide V in its wake.

The pilot eased back on the throttle to keep from overtaking the ship. The UH-34 descended like a rearing horse toward the wide white lines painted on the deck. A sailor wearing a headset stood on the carrier deck and, using hand signals, guided the chopper in for a landing. Once the bird set down, seamen ran over and chocked the wheels to keep the chopper from rolling off the carrier deck and into the sea fifty-two feet below. Once the pilot cut the engines, Sauro exited the chopper and made a beeline for the ladders that would take him below deck to S-4.

It was the first time he had experienced a rough sea. Every time the ship rolled from one side to the other, it sent him off in the opposite direction in which he was trying to go. Because he had not yet developed his sea legs, he crossed the flight deck like someone well into a case of beer. Under other circumstances it would have been a comical sight. As soon as he reached the side of the ship, he grabbed the railing and hurried down the ladder to the hangar deck below.

Crossing the hangar deck was another zigzag journey. Then he hurried down the narrow causeways toward S-4. The ship's public address system clicked on to make a telltale announcement, "Eight medevacs inbound." Just as Sauro reached S-4 and stepped through the steel hatch the public address system clicked on again. The same voice droned, "Ten medevacs inbound."

From behind a desk Lieutenant McCarthy looked up at Sauro and then over to the speaker on the wall. "This has been going on for days. Hurry up and get down to the ship's laundry. They can use the help."

"Yes, sir!" Sauro turned, retreated back through the steel hatch, and took off for the laundry.

The laundry was no place for the squeamish. The room was jammed full of pushcarts filled with bloody sheets and the place smelled like a slaughterhouse. The sailor in charge was four shades whiter than the last time Sauro had seen him. His eyes were bloodshot from lack of sleep, and the sockets around them were puffy from rubbing out the burn of sweat. He recognized Sauro as one who had worked there before and motioned for him to go over and help the short-timer from 2/4 fold sheets destined for the ship's infirmary. The public address system clicked on again: "Seven medevacs inbound."

More blood-soaked carts were coming in. The sailor in charge grabbed the first one and started to empty it. Then with a start, he screamed and jumped back. Someone asked, "What's the matter?"

"A body part!" the sailor in charge said as he tried to compose himself. Using a sheet corner, he picked up the chunk of flesh and disposed of it in the trash container.

Sauro turned to the short-timer and asked, "What's going on?"

"Two-four got ambushed. They took a lot of casualties," the sergeant answered calmly. The expression on his face was one of concern and worry.

"Is it over?" asked Sauro.

"No."

The ship's public address system clicked on: "Twelve medevacs inbound." The sergeant from 2/4 gave the speaker on the wall a cold stare, but it didn't help. The grim announcements of more and more inbound medevacs continued with wrenching regularity.

Shortly after midnight, on May 3, the sailor in charge did something out of the ordinary. He joined a couple of the Marines taking their ten-minute break. It was the first time he did not go sit with his fellow sailors during a break. "Do you think he'll have to go back out in field?" the sailor in charge asked just loud enough for the Marines around him to hear. He was looking at the sheet-folding sergeant from 2/4 when he said it.

"I don't know. Why?" quizzed one Marine.

"He's only got a few days left in-country," the sailor whispered, trying not to let his voice rise. Everyone looked at the sergeant, but he was so wrapped up in his thoughts that he never noticed he was the subject of conversation. The young sergeant was viewed as a nice guy. He never hassled anyone, not even the sailors.

About an hour later, an older career Marine wearing combat gear stepped through the laundry room door and yelled across the room, "Sarge! Saddle up. We need you out in the field."

As quickly as the older Marine popped in, he was gone. His words brought a halt to everything; everyone in the room stopped working. Not a human voice could be heard, with the only sound being the laundry machinery churning away. All eyes were on the young sergeant. The look on everyone's face spoke to how unfair this was. The young sergeant saw none of it. Without hesitation, he took off after the older grunt and was out the hatch. Everyone in the ship's laundry stood quietly, listening to the metallic echo of two sets of boots running down the steel passageway toward the hangar deck. In less than a minute the sound was gone.

The sailor in charge looked around the room at the quiet mix of sailors and Marines staring back at him. Instead of ordering everyone to get back to work, he surprised them by saying, "If I ever hear anyone say Marines don't have it the toughest, or they aren't the best, I'll set them straight!" With that said the sailor in charge walked over to a washing machine and began vigorously stuffing bloody sheets into it.

The announcements of more inbound medevacs never seemed to end. Shortly after each announcement a helicopter landed on the flight deck. The wounded were taken directly from the chopper to the deck-edge elevator, on which they were lowered to the hangar deck. From there they were rushed to another waiting elevator, which lifted them up one deck to a large door leading to the hospital. The hospital, in an emergency situation, could accommodate more than three hundred casualties by utilizing the troop berthing space near the stern. But even that was not enough; there were just too many casualties.

During the period April 28 through May 5, HMM-362 flew 462 medevacs in direct support of BLT 2/4 as well as 1st Battalion, 3rd Marines, the unit that was sent to relieve 2/4. After three days of heavy fighting the USS *Iwo Jima* had run out of places to put the wounded. The squadron had to fly the wounded to other ships and places that had medical facilities.

For those aboard the *Iwo Jima*, details of the fighting remained sketchy. The only thing anyone could say for sure was that 2/4 had been cut to shreds and there were few survivors. The ship's laundry became a place of hard work and few words. Finally, the loads of bloody sheets slowed to a near stop.

Tired and hungry Sauro left the laundry and went to the mess hall for morning chow. No longer did the Marines outnumber the sailors four to one; it was mostly sailors lining up for food trays. The usual chatter of conversation that filled the room was gone. It was strange to see most of the tables and chairs were empty. The behavior of the sailors was noticeably different. For one thing, they weren't talking, not even to each other. They were clearly mourning the loss of so many Marines. More than before the Marine green uniform stood out from navy blue.

The sailors shocked Sauro by motioning for him to cut to the front of the mess line. A couple more Marines entered the mess hall and the sailors immediately did the same. For the Marines there would be no waiting in line. It was a touching tribute.

The concern the sailors had for the Marines went beyond letting them go to the front of the mess line. The ship's commanding officer, Captain John Shepherd, told the battalion commander of 2/4, Lieutenant Colonel William Weise, something he would never forget: "Three-hundred sailors from my crew volunteered to go ashore and help the Marines fight."

Such news brought some comfort to Lieutenant Colonel Weise, who was recovering from the wounds he had received in the battle. A bullet from an AK-47 had penetrated his flak jacket and was lodged between the third and fourth vertebrae of his spine. The pain of his injury was minuscule compared to the pain of having lost so many men. He took it upon himself to go and visit every wounded Marine in the infirmary. It was a monumental task, even for somebody with two good, working legs.

Sauro went looking for Schmidt at the first opportunity. He went back to the place where he had last seen him. Like the time before, the hangar deck was full of Marines from 2/4, only this time they were in body bags. Every nook and cranny of the hangar deck was stacked high with body bags—one piled on top of the other. They were piled high against the steel cage of the squadron armory on all sides; the sturdy bars of the enclosure kept the stacks from falling over. The sergeant assigned to check the M60 machine guns in and out was gone. The armory was locked up and a makeshift sign was tied to the door; it read *Closed.* The armory sergeant had stared at the body bags that surrounded him for too long. It finally got to him and he had to leave. A temporary replacement hurried across the hangar deck toward the armory with key in hand.

Sauro stood on the hangar deck staring at all the body bags. There were so many. Everything was so still and quiet. It was a sharp contrast to all the activity that had characterized the hangar deck only a week earlier. Sailors and Marines alike were cutting a wide path around the body bags.

A Marine Sauro didn't recognize was cutting across the hangar deck. He looked straight ahead in an effort to avoid seeing all that was around him.

"Are you with 2/4?" Sauro asked as he stepped in front of the Marine to block his path. Taken by surprise, the disheveled and unshaven Marine stopped.

"Are you with 2/4?" Sauro repeated. The Marine nodded affirmatively, looking puzzled.

"You know Schmidt?" Sauro asked.

"Yeah," the weary-looking Marine answered. He said nothing more. He was either lost in thought or trying to recall what might have happened to Schmidt.

"Did he make it?" Sauro asked, raising his voice.

The verbal shake seemed to help. "I think. He might be in the infirmary. Check there." The grunt sounded unsure, but there was a chance.

"Thanks." Sauro hurried off, figuring if he went through enough doors he would stumble upon the infirmary. Not so. The ship was a steel maze of doors, hatches, and stairs. After twice ending up in the engine room, Sauro asked a sailor in blue, "Where's the infirmary?"

The sailor stopped what he was doing, took one look at the Marine in green, and said, "Follow me. I'll take you there."

Upon reaching the infirmary, Sauro asked the first person he saw, "Is Wallace Schmidt here?"

"Yes. I believe so. Would you like to see him?" asked the corpsman. Sauro nodded. The corpsman looked at his chart, but he couldn't find what he was looking for. "If I remember, he's in that row of beds, second one from the end, on the left side. If he's not there, let me know and I'll help you find him."

"You mean he might be out walking around somewhere?" Sauro asked optimistically.

"No," the corpsman replied soberly. Sauro understood what that answer meant. Schmidt had better be in one of those beds!

Some of the bedridden Marines were alert and made eye contact as Sauro walked slowly through the ward. Others were sleeping or too drugged to notice anything. Concentrating his attention on the second bed from the end, on the left, Sauro could see it was occupied. The person in it was lying on his back connected to an IV. The patient's eyes were closed. It was hard to tell if it was Schmidt until he opened his eyes.

"How you doing?" Sauro asked.

"I'm shot up," Schmidt replied. The fear was still in his eyes.

"Where did you get hit?"

Schmidt began pointing. "Got hit here; this is from shrapnel." Then in a shaky voice he said, "They shot the rifle right out of my hand! Look what they did to me!" Schmidt lifted up a bandaged hand for Sauro to see. His hand was mangled and he was missing a finger.

"Sounds like you're lucky to be alive. What happened out there?"

Schmidt leaned forward. His shrill voice reflected the horror of his experience, "We got ambushed. When they started shooting I looked for cover. There wasn't any. They caught us in the open. I hit the ground. I could see this gook shooting at me. I returned fire. He had cover and I didn't. He kept shooting at me.

"I rolled over and looked for something to hide behind. A mound, anything! There was nothing. The same gook kept shooting at me. I could see him. We were looking at each other. He wouldn't stop shooting at me. I knew I had to get him before he got me. I started shooting back. That's when the rifle got shot right out of my hand. It went flying through the air. That's when I lost my finger."

Schmidt held up his damaged hand again to show Sauro all the bandages wrapped around it. Schmidt continued, "I tried to crawl to my rifle. The same guy kept shooting at me. There was nothing to hide behind. I was never so scared in my life. I thought I was going to die! I think that's when I got hit with shrapnel. I'm not sure." In a lower voice, he concluded, "I remember hearing some kind of explosion. Not real sure what happened after that. Things got kind of fuzzy." Exhausted from telling Sauro what had happened, Schmidt let his head drop back into the pillow.

"So how did you get here? Do you remember?" Sauro questioned.

"I was dragged out of there. Some guy, or guys, dragged me out. That's what they tell me. I don't remember. I remember waiting to get medevaced. I remember lying there with the wounded. I could hear the helicopter coming. I was in a rear area." Schmidt recalled something else about the fighting — something so painful it caused him to suddenly stop talking. He turned his head away from Sauro and became quiet.

After a long interval of silence, Sauro said, "Schmidt! You okay?" No response. Sauro repeated, "Schmidt! You okay?"

Schmidt turned his head back toward Sauro and said in a grief stricken voice, "Everyone I know is dead." Schmidt was fighting back tears. His eyes pleaded for answers.

What to tell Schmidt? What to say? Sauro was lost for words. He didn't know what to say. He couldn't think of a thing. Schmidt turned his head away from Sauro. "Schmidt, hang in there. You'll be okay. I'll try to stop by and see you again." Schmidt didn't turn his head back around. If the tears were there, he didn't want Sauro to see. Marines are supposed to be tough.

On the way back to S-4 Sauro thought about how depressed Schmidt was. But who in the same situation wouldn't be? No wonder he had heard so many of his fellow Marines say, "Don't get too close, or too tight, with the people around you."

Sauro was confident that Schmidt would bounce back. He was that kind of guy. The next time Sauro went to visit Schmidt he was gone. All he could find out was that Schmidt had been transferred out of the ward.

The three days of heavy fighting centered around the little village of Dai Do, a mile and a half northwest of Dong Ha. It was by all accounts one of the fiercest fights of the Vietnam

War. What the attacking Marines first encountered at Dai Do was a well-entrenched NVA force of undetermined size. It took three days of heavy fighting for the Marines of 2/4 to secure the area. When it was over, 81 Marines were dead, 297 had been seriously wounded, and 100 Marines with less serious wounds had been treated in the field. The Marines ultimately won the battle of Dai Do. Some of the NVA soldiers captured were found to have come from two of the four regiments comprising the 320th NVA Division. One prisoner indicated that 2/4 had fought the entire 320th NVA Division. If true, that would mean that an understrength Marine infantry battalion of four rifle companies, consisting of fewer than seven hundred men, had stopped and driven back more than seven thousand enemy soldiers.

After the NVA fled the area, Marines found the bodies of 1,568 enemy soldiers, along with a substantial amount of weaponry and equipment. At the end of the battle there were more than nineteen dead NVA soldiers for every one dead Marine.

Years later, in May 1997, during a fact-finding trip to Vietnam, the plans officer of the 320th NVA Division would tell retired Brigadier General William Weise that his battalion, 2/4, had indeed fought and bested three full regiments in 1968 at the Battle of Dai Do.

19

OPERATION MAMELUKE THRUST

Robert Gates was assigned to Company B, 1st Tank Battalion, 1st Marine Division, as a tank crewman. Gates had excellent mechanical skills, and there was a lot to suggest he would be promoted rapidly through the ranks. But the twinkle in his eye and his carefree oh-what-the-hell attitude hinted that the road to advancement might not be a smooth one.

Operation Mameluke Thrust began on May 18, 1968, and was Gate's first major operation. The infantrymen assembling around his tank carried huge backpacks, indicating the operation was going to be a long one. Four tanks were assigned to escort the column of Marines as they headed north, out of An Hoa and toward a mountainous area southwest of Da Nang. They were a part of a large offensive to eliminate of the enemy forces that threatened the security of Da Nang.

The first crisis Gates encountered was a bad case of diarrhea. More than once he clung weakly to the side of the tank having liquid bowel movements. It wasn't long before Gates became dehydrated. He forced himself to keep drinking liquids. Bouts with dysentery were a common problem for the American troops serving in Vietnam. The few extra pounds the drill instructors had once eyed suspiciously were long gone.

"Gates, button up," his crew chief warned. Gates pulled the lever that dropped his seat down and activated a steel plate that closed over his head. But Gates didn't like the confinement, looking at the world through narrow window slits. It may have been safer to "button up," but Gates decided he had had enough.

"I'll never drop my hatch," Gates told his crew chief. Within earshot of the conversation was the new driver Gates was helping to train. The new driver listened more to Gates than his section leader. If the six-foot-one-inch rogue Marine wasn't going to button up, then neither was he.

A tank is very effective in combat when used for its intended purposes, but close-in fighting is not one of them. The tank's .50-caliber machine gun is good for forward suppressive fire, but is of limited value if attacked from the side or close up.

Gates was riding on top of the tank when an enemy soldier stood up alongside the road and fired an RPG-2 at the tank from close range. Gates heard the boom and saw the round coming his way. The infantrymen responded by jumping off Gates' tank and hit the ground firing their rifles at the attacker. He was shot dead, but there was nothing anyone could do to stop the RPG round sailing through the air. Gates sat spellbound on top of the tank as he watched the low-velocity rocket heading his way! The RPG hit the side of the tank and burned a hole in it as the missile exploded. Pieces of shrapnel hit Gates in the face. What happened next was even more frightening.

A well-concealed enemy force came out of hiding to press the attack. Both sides were firing at each other at point-blank range and were taking casualties. Enemy soldiers were so close that Gates could have shot them with a pistol.

In the next tank over, Gates saw the new driver sitting half in and half out of the open hatch. Just as Gates advocated, the trainee was not buttoned up. He went into action, pushing his foot down on the accelerator, and the tank moved forward with a sudden burst of speed. An enemy soldier popped up alongside the road and fired an RPG at the new driver as he passed by. The new driver took a direct hit from the rocket grenade. The top half of his body, which was sticking out of the open hatch, was suddenly gone. The tank lurched around wildly, endangering the Marines in its path.

The commander of Gates' tank tried to radio the driver of the out-of-control tank. When there was no response, he jumped down from his tank and ran after the one careening about unpredictably. Even though he was exposed to enemy fire, he chased after the runaway tank. Catching up to it, he climbed aboard the bouncing monster, looked down the hatch, and saw the problem. The lower half of the new driver was still in the seat with his the foot pressed down on the accelerator. The commander knew this was not the time to be squeamish. He grabbed the exposed spine and removed the half torso from the driver's seat. After changing places with the deceased, he took over the controls and shut the tank down.

The firefight did not last long. When it was over, the surrounding area was covered with dead bodies from both sides. The tank commander walked over to Gates, who was receiving medical attention for his face wound, and said angrily, "If he had been buttoned up, he might still be alive."

When the medevac helicopter lifted off with Gates aboard, he wasn't thinking about the unsightly scar the shrapnel wound would leave above his mouth, or about the mustache he would have to grow to hide it. Instead he was trying to come to grips with the horrible circumstances surrounding the death of the new driver.

Gates was stitched up and returned to his unit. The injury left him with a two-inch vertical indentation on the right side of his mouth.

Operation Mameluke Thrust continued as the Marines swept westward toward Laos in search of the enemy. The foot travel was at times exhausting; many suffered from dysentery and lost weight. The temperature outside the tank was hot, but inside it was like an oven. When Gates saw the thermometer inside the tank reach 120 degrees Fahrenheit, he climbed out. His leaving gave more room for the rest of the crew, which consisted of a commander, a loader, and a gunner, in addition to a driver who was in a separate compartment.

Gates wasn't out long before the gunner popped up through the hatch. Half in and half out with sweating rolling down his face, he said to Gates, "It's hot as blue blazes down there."

"No shit," Gates responded.

The grunts walked like weary pack animals with the scorching sun directly overhead. From his tank Gates could see the waves of heat rising up from the ground. There was not a shadow to be seen anywhere. The cloth cover on their steel helmets was not enough to keep the steel from heating up.

The Marines kept to the flat of the land until they approached two suspicious-looking hills. The topography of Vietnam provided the enemy with numerous ambush sites. This looked like one of them. Not seeing any telltale signs of an enemy presence, they continued the course. It was the hottest part of the day, so Marines stopped to take cover from the scorching sun. That's when the shooting started.

Heavy enemy gunfire rained down from the two hills they were passing through. The flat land in between provided little in the way of cover. The Marine infantry returned the fire. The blazing sun and intense heat started to take a heavy toll. Some Marines suffering from heatstroke lapsed into unconsciousness. Others tried to revive them by loosening their clothing and pouring canteens of water over their faces.

Gates was shocked to see two Marines walking around without rifles or helmets. He noticed others were dropping their rifles and standing up. Then without a clue as to where they were or where they were going, they begin to wander about aimlessly. The sound of enemy bullets zinging by their heads only added to their bewilderment. Looking confused and disoriented, they stepped over the dead on their way to nowhere. It was a bizarre sight. *Those guys' brains are cooked,* Gates thought as he watched the eerie spectacle. What the heatstroke casualties needed was to be immersed in cold water. Instead enemy bullets were peppering their bodies.

"They're dropping them like flies. They just keep dinging them. We got to do something," his tank crew shouted. Then, referring to the tank, one crewman yelled, "We got steel."

Seconds later Gates' tank was speeding full bore toward the front of the carnage. Cooking inside was Gates and his crew. The Marines wandering around in the open were about to get some desperately needed help. Gates positioned his tank between the enemy and the heatstroke victims. Using his tank as a protective shield, Gates provided cover while other Marines chased down the mentally confused. One by one the deranged troops were pulled down and dragged back to what little cover there was available.

As the tank continued to run interference, the grunts administered first aid by pouring canteen water over the heatstroke victims to slow their pulse and cool their bodies. Some, whose bodies were drained of fluids, could not sweat. Their faces had turned red in color, indicating their body's heat-regulating mechanisms were on overload. Some moaned in pain and doubled over with their hands over their bellies as the cramps set in.

Gates and his crew could hear the pinging sound of enemy bullets ricocheting off the side of their tank as they maneuvered about the battlefield. When no more Marines were out strolling around, they concentrated on picking up the wounded. Using their tank they ferried the wounded to the landing zone that had been set up behind them. At least temporarily the wounded were out of the line of fire.

At the landing zone were two shallow rice paddies, side by side. One was for the wounded; the other was for the dead. It was a sobering sight to see Marines being carried from the side of the living over to the side of the dead, whose open eyes never blinked. The sounds of war continued in the distance. Amidst all the chaos and uncertainty, the leathernecks functioned as if they would ultimately prevail. Gates returned to the front for another load of wounded. Other tank drivers followed Gates' lead and did the same.

"Over here!" yelled a grunt. On the ground sat a sergeant with both legs shredded top to bottom, bleeding profusely. They placed the sergeant on top of the tank.

"All we can do is tourniquets," Gates said to him apologetically and fearful that it wouldn't be enough to save him. After they tied off the sergeant's legs, Gates drove his tank toward the rear area. There were so many wounded soldiers on top of Gates' tank that he couldn't turn the gun turret for fear of crushing someone. *Damn heat!* Gates thought as he again wiped his brow. *Why does this sweat feel sticky?* Gates wondered. When he saw his hand covered with blood, he remembered the sergeant was right above him, on top of the tank. Gates and his crew continued to transport the wounded to a safer place. At the same time, enemy troops came down the slope and maneuvered to place themselves within several hundred meters of the rice paddies.

The approaching medevac chopper came under fire. The engine took a serious hit and the bird went down, puffing smoke; when it crashed, it broke in half. A small platoon of

Marines was dispatched to the crash site to see if anyone was still alive. Gates accompanied them in his tank. The first thing Gates saw when he pulled up was the pilot and the copilot. Both were still strapped in their seats with bones sticking out; both were dead. Some of the infantrymen fanned out to secure the area, while others went to the wreckage. Protruding out from under a large piece of twisted metal was the gunner. He was still strapped in his seat, with his eyes closed, and he appeared to be napping peacefully. There was no blood on his face. One Marine lifted up the piece of metal that was covering most of the gunner.

"Oh, Jesus Christ!" he gasped. The Marine turned his head away and let the piece of metal fall back down. The lower half of the gunner's body wasn't there.

Returning to their small, secure area, Gates saw six Marines with a captured NVA soldier. Those Marines were filled with hate and adrenaline. At that particular moment the code of conduct carried about as much weight as the thin sheet of paper it was printed on.

"He looks like hell," Gates said to his crew as they drove past the prisoner. When he looked back the prisoner was being struck down with rifle butts.

"What do you think will happen to him?" the crewman asked Gates.

"I couldn't tell you. They might do him in right there," Gates responded.

For the rest of the day, night, and following morning, the Marines continued to battle the NVA. Then the exchange of fire ended almost as abruptly as it had started. Gates never heard what the official outcome of the fighting was. All he knew was that they were still there and the NVA weren't. He returned with his unit to the Marine base at An Hoa, where he stenciled the words *Vengeance Is Mine* onto his gun turret.

While participating in Operation Mameluke Thrust, Gates happened upon a grisly sight on the outskirts of a small village. Sticking out of the ground was a large stake sharpened to a point at the top. Impaled upon the stake were the partial remains of a human body scavenged to bones by the jungle insects and tropical heat. It looked like the person had been put on the stake rectum first. The victim's downward descent on the stake ended at his head, which was resting on top of the stake. The victim's sun-bleached bones stood as a grim reminder of what could happen to anyone who dared oppose the Viet Cong or North Vietnamese.

Village officials and peasants were frequently tortured to extract information or as retaliation for sympathizing with the wrong side.

Gates spoke up and said, "I sure hope that poor bastard was dead when he went down that stake!"

"You know why he's still hanging there don't you," remarked a grunt.

"Yeah! They are too dammed scared to take him down," another answered.

"There's got to be VC in that village. Probably watching us right now," grumbled another.

Gates was a bad ass. He was not intimidated by the grisly spectacle and wanted everyone to know it—including the enemy. If they were watching, he'd give them something to think about. "Why not? What the hell!" Gates said, as he got down from his tank and walked up to the skeleton. He grabbed hold of the skull and twisted it off the stake. "It's mine now," he said as he tucked the skull under his arm and returned to his tank.

The Marines continued to sweep the assigned area. The platoon commander told Gates what he wanted him to do.

He said, "See those three huts over there? I want you to drive through them."

"Yes, sir!" Gates acknowledged and yelled down to his tank crew, "He wants us to drive through the damn things."

Gates drove his tank through the first hut and flattened it. The second hut collapsed beneath the steel tracks with a crunch. On the way to the third hut they drove past some dead NVA soldiers lying on the ground. "I'll be damned. They got starched new uniforms. They even have creases in them! Can you believe that?" Gates exclaimed.

The following combat required air support. Two jets took off from Da Nang. There was also a radio call for tank support. Gates immediately drove his tank to the front, where the fighting was the heaviest. The enemy troops were advancing rapidly and could not have been more than five hundred yards away. Gates drove past the point men and braked to a stop. The remaining distance between him and the NVA was closing rapidly. Before Gates had a chance to open fire, the two jets from Da Nang passed overhead. The NVA were hurrying toward the Marines. The pilots decided to thread the needle anyway, meaning there was absolutely no room for any error.

"Holy shit!" Gates yelled when he saw the first jet streak by and drop a napalm canister directly in front of him. Gates and his crew immediately buttoned up. They stayed inside the tank until the outside air cooled off. After a few minutes passed, Gates opened the hatch and peeked out. Small bits of the flaming gel were still burning on the fenders of his tank. Directly in front of his tank the landscape was charred to a cinder. There were no signs of life; the ground was black and the air was filled with the smell of death. The fight was definitely over.

Gates was promoted to tank commander. When his crew rolled out of An Hoa, it was with an element of the 1st Marine Division. They were to conduct a sweep of the main thoroughfare between An Hoa and Da Nang known as Liberty Road. Ahead of his tank went the minesweepers. Mines and booby traps were favored weapons of the enemy. It was a safe way to maim and kill from a distance or long after the soldiers who laid them were gone. Fifty percent of American casualties were caused by mines and booby traps.

The minesweepers did their best to find any hidden explosives up to three hundred feet from the road, but they missed a 125-pound bomb buried in the road. When Gates drove his tank over it, the explosion was huge. The blast totally disabled the tank by taking out all the wheels. Gates was riding half out of the open hatch and was blown twenty-five feet into the air before his body flipped over and started to descend back toward the ground. Instinctively, he put his arm out to break his fall. Consequently, the fall broke his arm and twisted his knee.

Cradling his broken arm and limping, Gates hobbled over to the medevac chopper, determined to climb aboard under his own power. He discovered it was too difficult to do with only one good leg and one good arm. The bemused gunner jumped down from the chopper and helped Gates climb aboard.

When the chopper touched down at Da Nang, Gates was put on a gurney and whisked inside the medical facility. His arm and knee throbbed with pain and the swelling added to his agony. The hospital was buzzing with activity as wounded Marines were arriving from all over I Corps. All kinds of causalities were being pushed around on rollaway beds. A doctor leaned over the top of Gates wearing a face mask. Finding Gates conscious the doctor asked, "Where do you hurt?"

"My right arm and my left knee," Gates answered in a distracted state. Another gurney was being brought in. The patient on it was unconscious; it was not a pretty sight. Gates heard the corpsmen say with urgency, "Gunshot wound!"

"I ain't so miserable," Gates said as he nodded his head toward the other Marine. The doctor looked at the other Marine and immediately went over to the gurney. As Gates was being rolled away, he could see the doctor working on the gunshot wound patient with a team of people gathered around.

Gates was moved to another area, where his clothes were cut off. Shortly after that he was resting comfortably in bed with a cast on his arm. Looking around he could see about thirty other Marines in his ward recovering from various injuries.

"Until we know more about the full extent of the injury, your knee has to be immobilized," the medical assistant told Gates. Gates looked puzzled. The corpsmen elaborated: "We don't want you to move your knee. If you move your knee you could cause further damage to the nerves and blood vessels. Plus, it'll hurt like hell. It's swollen and tender.

"We put a molded pillow around your knee and have secured it. The pillow will make it hard for you to bend your knee. You can't get out of bed for at least three days. Whatever you do, don't get out of bed. Everything you need is here. If you have to piss or crap, slide the bedpan under yourself. We'll dump it for you. Holler if you need any help," the corpsman instructed, and then he left.

Everything went fine until Gates had to take a crap. When he couldn't hold it any longer he slid the bedpan beneath the sheets. The last time he had crapped in bed he was too young to remember. This was still a first because he had to make sure he hit the bedpan. After he completed the feat, he realized it takes two hands to get toilet paper off a roll. Gates was confident he could manipulate the roll and do the wipe. With one hand in a cast and lying in a prone position, Gates discovered it was a hard thing to do without making a spectacle of himself.

Some time later Gates prided himself in having done it without drawing any attention. He looked around for the aide to empty his bedpan, but the aide was nowhere to be seen. The bad smell began to work its way out from under the sheets, which made Gates nervous. The guy in the bed next to Gates gave him a dirty look and cussed, making Gates embarrassed. The aroma continued to drift through the ward. More unsmiling heads turned in his direction. *Where was the damn medical aide?* Gates keep thinking.

"They're supposed to come and get it," Gates said apologetically. The other patients didn't say a word; they just kept staring at him, willing him to do something about the problem. Gates turned to the patient in the next bed over and said loud enough for the others to hear, "I'm not supposed to get out of bed for three days."

The other patient made a facial expression that indicated, *You created the problem. You solve it.* Gates felt humiliated. He looked around his bed and mumbled, "Where's my walker?"

After that Gates got himself a cane and kept it by his bedside. The next time Gates had to go, he used his cane to walk outside to an outhouse raised on pallets. With only one good arm and one good leg, he managed to get inside, drop his pajamas, and sit down. Getting back up was another problem, as Gates discovered he could not bend down far enough to pick up the cane or his pajama bottoms. So he sat on the toilet and had to wait for another cripple to come along. Finally, another patient came and opened the outhouse door.

Gates forced a smile and said, "I need you to help me pull up my pajamas."

Hospital life did not agree with Gates. He did not like

being an invalid or sitting around doing nothing. He liked helping better than he liked being helped. Not surprisingly, his disposition soured.

One day an officer came through the ward with a first sergeant; they were looking for Gates. They stopped at the bed of the recovering tank commander to make some friendly conversation and tell him about his Purple Heart medal. The first sergeant happened to notice the cigarette lighter Gates had on the table next to the bed. He reached over and picked it up. After reading the inscription the career Marine barked, "You don't believe this do you?"

The inscription read, "Lifers are like flies. They eat shit and bother people."

"Well, if the shoe fits wear it," was all Gates had to say.

Gates was discharged from the hospital. He returned to his unit and found all his possessions were as he had left them, including the human skull, which he had painted red. The first morning back, Gates shaved and washed his face. Next he trimmed the mustache he had grown to hide the shrapnel scar above his lip. Then he brushed teeth—first his own and then the skull's. The whole thing with the skull was being done as a joke.

Everyone watched what Gates did. They noticed that even before his cast was off, Gates was back driving tanks. Nothing seemed to stop him from getting the job done. He gave the Marine Corps all he had, and then some.

After one particularly fierce engagement, Gates returned to his base camp and put three captured weapons on display—two AK-47s and one RPG.

"Any casualties?" asked one Marine.

"Out of the ten men who shot at us, nine are dead," Gates replied as he looked at the enemy weapons

"How bad was it?" asked another.

"It was like they were on a suicide mission. At times they were no more than seventy-five feet away."

The longer Gates served in Vietnam, the higher his proficiency marks went. Fitness reports by his superiors described him as "cheerful and pleasant, above average intelligence, displays good imagination, accepts responsibility, and pays excellent attention to detail." His conduct marks were another matter. They went up and down like a yo-yo. During periods of combat he excelled. It was the idle time that spelled trouble for Gates and was the undoing of his conduct marks.

One day a bunch of South Vietnamese kids stood near the barbed wire fence at the base perimeter. A boy waved a bottle of Manila Rum in the air for Gates to see. Gates went to the fence. Before buying the bottle he wanted to check it out. The smiling boy handed him the bottle. Gates held it up to the light and shook it; he could see all kinds of crap floating around inside. By Vietnamese standards it was good stuff, and it sure beat the hell out of drinking "green lizard," better known as Mennen aftershave, which had the reputation for making everyone who drinks it shit like a goose.

Gates bought the Manila Rum from the kid and proceeded to get stiff. Later that day Gates came out of his tent wearing just his trousers. He walked with a slight stagger and had a pistol shoved down the front of his pants. "Come on. You're driving. We're going back to the main base." Gates said to the new driver he was breaking in.

The tank left Hill 10 with the new driver at the controls. It went slowly down the road like a gigantic snail. Impatiently, Gates waited for the new driver to speed it up. Finally, an inebriated Gates thought, *This guy can't drive worth a shit!*

"Stop the tank. I'll show you how to drive this son of a bitch! You, get up on top!" Gates hollered. The new driver nervously climbed out of the hatch and took his position on top of the tank, and then Gates floored it. The tank went down the middle of the road at full bore, with the new guy hanging on for dear life. With Gates behind the wheel the tank reached its maximum speed of about thirty-eight miles per hour. Trailing right behind the tank was a huge dust cloud, while ahead of it were Vietnamese merchants with pushcarts. The pushcarts got overturned as the merchants dove for a ditch.

Up ahead was the main gate to the base, which was posted with guards. The entrance gate was closed. Gates never slowed down. At some thirty miles an hour, the tank went through the main gate shearing off the two-by-ten boards that blocked the way.

Clinging to the top, the new driver looked back at the main gate. It was in chaos, but not for long. Armed guards were running around yelling into handheld radios and jumping into vehicles to join in the chase. The new driver turned his eyes back to the front. What he saw opened his eyes even wider. Straight ahead was a troop tent.

The new driver was about to have a heart attack when Gates slammed on the brakes with both feet. The tank slid to a stop just inches short of the tent. The first thing to catch up to Gates was the cloud of dust following behind. As the dust was clearing, a jeep sped toward the parked tank. It was carrying an angry colonel and Gates' first sergeant. The colonel stepped from the jeep hollering, "Who's in charge of this son of a bitch?"

Gates climbed out of the hatch and jumped to the ground. "Right here, sir," Gates said. The colonel looked at Gates, who was clad only in trousers, with a pistol shoved in his waist band.

"You got to be shitting me!" yelled the colonel.

Oh boy! the first sergeant thought when he saw that the driver was Gates.

"What rank are you?" the colonel demanded to know.
"A corporal, sir!" Gates responded.

"You're not a corporal anymore!" the colonel said as he stomped back to his jeep. "Demote that man back to lance corporal!" the colonel yelled to the top sergeant.

Operation Mameluke Thrust ended on October 23, 1968. Marine losses stood at 1,730 wounded and 267 killed; enemy losses were 2,728 killed.

The commanding general of the 1st Marine Division wrote about Gates:

> Since joining Company B, 1st Tank Battalion, on 28 January 1968 Lance Corporal Gates has consistently demonstrated a vast knowledge of tank tactics and maintenance of tanks seldom found in men of his grade and time in service. Lance Corporal Gates has been rotated through each position of the tank crew. Naturally aggressive and extremely conscientious, he enthusiastically performed all duties assigned to him in a most proficient manner. His untiring efforts, potential, and increased proficiency were recognized by his superiors and he was assigned as a tank commander on 15 November 1968. Lance Corporal Gates participated in Operations Allen Brook and Mameluke Thrust and repeatedly distinguished himself by his courage and composure under fire. His leadership skills have served to inspire the men under him and are admired by all those who observe him.

On November 5, 1968, the six-month extension Gates requested was approved. He received a meritorious combat promotion to corporal on January 8, 1969.

In August 1969 after nineteen months in Vietnam, Gates extended for a second time. During this time the Asian soldiers were being equipped to carry the burden of the land war, because a new U.S. policy referred to as "Vietnamization" called for Asians, not Americans, to do the bulk of the fighting.

In March 1970 Gates packed his belongings for the last time. His performance significantly contributed to the new wood plaque his unit so proudly displayed by its headquarters. The plaque read, "Presented to 1st Platoon, Bravo Tank, from Delta, 1stBn, 7th Marines. Given in appreciation of outstanding Tank Support from 13 to 20 February 1969."

As Gates was packing to leave, the first sergeant entered the tent and said firmly, "You're not taking that back with you." Without a word, Gates reached into his sea bag, came up with the human skull, and handed it over to the top sergeant. After twenty-five months in Vietnam, Gates was ready to go home.

20

HAPPY VALLEY

Timothy Sather was assigned to Golf Battery, 3rd Battalion, 11th Marines, 1st Marine Division. His artillery unit was on top of Hill 10, which was seventeen miles south of Da Nang in a place called Happy Valley. Their job was to protect 2nd Battalion, 7th Marines. Fifteen miles farther south on Hill 65 was another artillery battery.

The terrain in between restricted the use of helicopters and greatly decreased the chances that a wounded Marine would make it out of Happy Valley alive. The valley consisted of steep-sided valleys, jagged ravines, gorges, heavy vegetation, dense underbrush, tall elephant grass, and a jungle canopy three layers thick.

Each unit on Hill 10 had a section of the perimeter to guard. Once a week Sather went down the hill for a night of guard duty. He and three other Marines quietly scanned the darkness for three hours. They did not see, or hear, the seven sappers inching their way through the darkness toward their position.

The sappers reached the concertina wire and slowly began to make their way through without making a sound. Undetected, the sappers slowly slithered their way through the maze of coiled barbed wire. By chance they were on a collision course with a mongoose. When the rat-like critter encountered one of the sappers, it went running through the concertina wire and set off a trip flare. Sather and the other two Marines quickly opened fire; within seconds it was over.

Afterward, Sather was scared. He kept thinking, *What if that mongoose hadn't been there?* Throughout the night illumination flares popped open overhead and Sather could see the dead sappers in the wire. Their contorted positions never changed and seemed to cry out, *You killed me!*

When Operation Mameluke Thrust started on May 18, 1968, the Marines moved their artillery pieces within closer range of the enemy to allow for direct fire support that could be observed. To prepare the way, navy Seabees—with earth-moving equipment—leveled the top of a small hill near the beach. Sather's unit arrived to set up a more strategic fire support base, but as they began, incoming enemy rockets poured into their encampment.

Sather ran for cover. He spied on the nearby beach a tank that looked abandoned and seemed to offer the best shelter. After diving under the steel giant, he looked up and saw two Marines having a beer. Gates was one of them! As teenagers the two of them had often gone to Excelsior Amusement Park, outside of Minneapolis, looking for girls and a good time. They had gone to the same high school and joined the Marines under the buddy system. Both were members of the Twins Platoon. It was a joyous reunion.

"My tank is temporarily out of commission," Gates explained. "We figured this was the best time to drink the couple beers we had stashed away." After Gates handed Sather a warm beer, the incoming rounds started again. Gates didn't looking overly worried. "Just harassment," he speculated as the barrage intensified.

"You seen anybody from boot camp?" Sather inquired in between explosions.

"No. Want another beer?"

"No thanks. Warm beer doesn't taste that good," Sather replied, and then asked, "You going to get lit?"

"No. Not when I'm on an operation," Gates said seriously. He crushed the empty beer can with his hand and tossed it out. Under normal conditions he would have put the empty can into the gun breech, which he knew held exactly thirty-eight cans.

When enough quiet time had passed to suggest the enemy was hightailing along some planned escape route, Sather and Gates crawled out from under the tank and said their good-byes. They parted company with each having served five months of their tour of duty.

Almost immediately, Sather's unit began taking casualties. It started right after the Seabees cleared an area for the landing strip. Many were wounded by the sporadic incoming rounds that spewed up from Happy Valley. The well-liked second lieutenant from Georgia, who had just become the proud father of a baby girl, was killed by an incoming round.

The success of Operation Mameluke Thrust depended in part on small reconnaissance units inserted into the objective area. From well-hidden observation posts, these small teams of Marines silently and patiently watched and waited for enemy troops to enter killing zones. Then the forward observer called in the fire mission and the artillery rained down on the enemy.

"Sather, get your gear. You're going in the field. First Platoon lost their radioman and forward observer. We need you out there to call in the fire missions. Report to the 7th Marine Regiment. Tell them you're the new forward observer."

"Yes, sir," Sather responded.

On May 30, 1968, five CH-46 helicopters flew toward the drop-off point filled with the Marines of Charlie Company,

1st Battalion, 7th Marines. Sather sat quietly aboard one of the choppers with his rifle between his legs. The eight other Marines in his team, including the corpsman, did the same.

With few places for the helicopters to land, the enemy could easily anticipate where the American troops might be inserted. Unfortunately for Sather, the enemy ambush site was well chosen. The NVA attack plan was not the normal hit-and-run tactic; the enemy force in hiding was part of an anti–air mobile operation. It was a heavily armed force that planned to claim victory by annihilating every Marine.

Its attack plan called for its soldiers to hold their fire until all the Americans were out of the choppers and temporarily clumped together; then they would open fire. After the massive initial kill, the NVA planned to move in so close that the surviving Marines could not call for air or artillery support for fear of it landing on their own men. The surviving Marines would be pinned down without cover and be so heavily outnumbered that their deaths would seem inevitable.

No one aboard the choppers spoke as they neared the landing zone marked for death. The only sound was the roar of whirling rotor blades and chopper engines. They did not know they were landing right smack in the middle of an ambush, but it was a known risk that made their hearts beat as the helicopters began their descent.

The seating arrangement aboard the chopper was not haphazard. They loaded in reverse order of how they wanted to get off. First off would be the point man, followed by the automatic weapons man, then the M79 grenadier, and so on down the line. Sather's responsibility as the radioman and forward observer was to stay with the squad leader, which put him among the first off.

The pilots intentionally spread out as they made their approach in order to widen the landing zone. When the choppers touched down the Marines ran double-time down the lowered tail ramps. They weren't on the ground two minutes before the enemy opened up with everything it had. Three of the helicopters had landed outside the enemy's killing zone, but the chopper Sather was on set down right in the middle of the ambush site.

A heavy curtain of automatic fire came at Sather from two sides, immediately killing four of the nine men in his squad. Sather took off running low to the ground, flanked by the remaining five men in the squad. They were hoping to quickly set up a defensive perimeter. Incoming mortars quickly killed two of the remaining five. Sather was still running for cover when another incoming mortar round exploded ten feet away from him. He hit the ground and wrenched with pain. A small navy corpsman jumped on top of him, pinning Sather flat to the ground to stop him from writhing. It was just in time as the air just inches above their heads filled with enemy fire.

Sather looked down and saw his trousers were a bloody mess. When he couldn't see or feel his right leg, he experienced an overwhelming panic. With terror-filled eyes, he saw his leg was a mangled, bloody mess. Sather tried to move the leg, but nothing happened. The body parts needed to make it bend were either missing or destroyed. The corpsman remained focused as he applied a tourniquet to Sather's right leg to stop the bleeding, while just a short distance away the enemy troops kept firing at them.

The NVA attack plan was not aborted because three of the choppers landed outside the kill zone. Most of the Marines in the original killing zone were dead, and the few who were still alive were wounded or dying. With some quick maneuvering the enemy redirected its fire at the Marines scattering from the other three helicopters. Their intense fire inflicted heavy casualties on those Marines as well.

The NVA quickly encircled the surviving Marines, which prevented them from moving beyond the initial landing zone.

The pain in Sather's leg was so great he couldn't bear to move it. The corpsman checked the tourniquet and sprinkled a bunch of powder over the area where Sather had once had a kneecap. The corpsmen took out a syringe and gave Sather a shot, which changed the pain from excruciating to tolerable.

Sather looked up at the sun. It had yet to reach the midway point in the sky. Good! It was still early in the day, still plenty of daylight. Wounded and in pain, Sather tried to radio for help. He discovered his radio didn't work, because it had been hit by flying bullets. Sather grabbed his rifle, rolled over, and joined the few others who were able to return fire. A short time later the enemy gunfire stopped. He hoped the enemy was retreating before reinforcements arrived.

In the distance Sather could hear choppers drawing nearer. The insertion helicopters were returning with a couple of Huey gunships. The pilots could see that most of the Marines were dead, but there were still a few looking up at them. They could see the Marines on the ground had set up a weak defensive perimeter and definitely needed to be extracted.

One CH-46 went in to attempt a rescue. Just as the chopper was about to touch down, it came under intense enemy fire. Automatic fire and shrapnel ripped through the chopper's thin outer skin. The gunships responded by spraying enemy positions with machine-gun fire, but the pilots were reluctant to use their rockets for fear of injuring the Marines—that's how close the enemy had moved in. Amazingly, the helicopter that came under fire was able to get out of the hot landing zone.

There would be no fighter jets streaking downward to deliver their deadly payloads. Just as the NVA had cleverly planned, the pinned Marines would have to go it alone without air or artillery support. Three more times that afternoon the

Marine choppers went in for the rescue. Three more times the NVA turned them back.

"Do you think we are ever going to get out of here?" Sather asked the corpsman.

"We got enough medical supplies and C-rats [C-rations] for three or four days. We got plenty of water and salt tablets," replied the corpsman from Alabama. Something about the corpsman wasn't quite right. Sather watched the medic make his way over to the only other Marine in their squad who had survived. Sather could see the corpsman had been hit, too. The corpsman tended to the wounds of the other Marine and then crawled back to Sather.

"You been hit!" Sather confronted the corpsman.

"Don't worry about me. It's minor," he said, as he worked on Sather's leg.

Sather could tell the corpsman was concerned about his leg wound but tried not to show it. Sather flinched in pain as the corpsman picked out the metal fragments and cleaned the wound of dirt and debris. The white powder he kept putting on the gash over the knee area had slowed the bleeding. The way he kept looking up at the sun reflected his concern. Sather's life was on some kind of timetable that the corpsman was keeping all to himself.

The CH-46s and gunships continued to circle overhead. Occasionally, a Phantom jet streaked across the sky, tipping its wings to let the Marines, who were pinned on the ground, know that they would not be abandoned. The sound of Marine artillery was noticeably absent. Sather figured his artillery battery was standing by waiting for when it would be safe to fire upon the enemy without the risk of injuring their fellow Marines.

Soon the sun would set, and the night favored the enemy. Sather knew the few surviving Marines were in no shape to ward off a ground attack or be any match for a sapper raiding party at night. The only thing keeping the NVA at bay was the helicopters flying overhead, ready and waiting to open up with their machine guns should the enemy move into the open and try to overrun the scantily held Marine positions.

Sather looked down at his leg and wondered, *Am I going to lose it?* He looked up at the dimming daylight and wondered, *Are they going to be able to get us out of here before nightfall?* As the sun began to set Sather looked at the corpsman and said, "It looks like we get to spend the night in Happy Valley."

They both knew that the chances of them living to see the light of day were dismal. In about ten minutes the protective daylight would be gone. Then there would be nothing to stop the enemy from advancing through the dark to finish them off.

Sather held tight to his rifle. When the end came, he would go down fighting. In boot camp, when Sather suffered heat exhaustion during the three-mile run, his fellow Marines had carried him across the finish line. Now, more than ever, he needed the help of his fellow Marines, yet it seemed there was little they could do to help him.

As the final rays of sun were slipping below the western horizon, Sather heard the sound of a twin-engine plane approaching from the east. Far in the distance he could see a slow-flying cargo plane painted the conventional two-tone green with tan. The underside of the approaching AC-47 was painted completely black. It was not Marine Corps. The spooky-looking propeller aircraft belonged to the 4th Air Commando Squadron of the U.S. Air Force.

The AC-47 lowered its port wing and began circling overhead. Three six-barreled 7.62mm miniguns protruded from the left side of the fixed-winged plane. Each gun was capable of firing up to six thousand rounds per minute. When it fired, its fearsome array of Gatling-style miniguns with red tracers gave it the appearance, in the night sky, of a fire-breathing dragon. After flying just a few night missions, the aircraft had been nicknamed Puff the Magic Dragon. No other aircraft could have intimidated the enemy more. Captured enemy documents warned not to attack the "dragon" because weapons were useless against it and would only infuriate the monster.

As the sun slipped beneath the horizon and daylight faded into darkness, the AC-47 launched huge magnesium flares. At the same time, the Marine helicopters circling overhead turned on their running lights. Sather suddenly found himself under a protective shield of light. All night long the aircraft circled overhead, launching flares and shining their lights down to keep the battlefield illuminated. The same esprit de corps that had carried Sather across the finish line in boot camp now provided a constant beacon of light for the trapped and surrounded Marines on the ground.

By morning Sather's condition was worse. The corpsman knew the clock was ticking against Sather. "Can you wiggle your toes?" the doc asked.

"Yes," Sather answered drowsily through the medication and lack of sleep. No major arteries had been severed, but the bleeding was bad. The tourniquet was one of the things still keeping him alive.

The doc placed a clean pad over the open wound, trying to keep it clean. "We don't want this to get infected," the corpsman told Sather. The corpsman treating Sather always looked like he was carrying three hundred pounds of gear, because he weighed only about a hundred pounds and stood about five feet three inches tall. The last twenty-four hours had changed Sather's perception of the small sailor, for in Sather's eyes, the little corpsman stood ten feet tall.

The terrain of the landing zone was flat and open, leaving the Marines with no cover options, other than to keep hugging the ground. On one side the enemy fired from a tree line; on another side it was came from a dried-up rice paddy. Either place would provide better cover than what they had. The problem was the NVA was using it.

The squad leader's wounds were less severe than Sather's, and the corpsman's wound remained minor. The three of them stayed close together, keeping a watchful eye on the enemy. Because Sather was immobilized, he loaded the magazine clips for the corpsman and squad leader. Whenever the enemy tried to advance, the two of them fired their rifles to keep the enemy back. Not far in front of where they were pinned down, they could see their own automatic weapons man. He had been killed in the opening round of enemy fire. His weapon had never been fired. As much as they could have used it, going for it would have been too risky.

The surviving Marines outside the initial killing zone also could not be evacuated due to heavy enemy fire. For them it was the same; whenever a chopper tried to land, the enemy let loose with an awesome display of firepower. As the battle entered its second day, seven CH-46s helicopters, filled with reinforcements, hurried toward the embattled landing zone. A heavily armed Huey gunship flew far out in front of the formation.

"Look!" Sather said, as he pointed to the helicopters landing way off in the distance. The NVA also took note of the landing in progress. Its mission to annihilate the Marine insertion had nearly been accomplished. To stay and battle the reinforcements would have been foolish, as the cost to do so would have been too high in terms of casualties to its own soldiers. As part of a well-prepared battle plan, the NVA moved quickly and quietly down its avenues of retreat and were gone.

When the medevac helicopters landed, the small corpsman

from Alabama checked on Sather for the last time. Sather's eyes were closed and he was generally unresponsive. The corpsman helped load Sather on a stretcher and into the chopper. "He's heavily drugged," the pint-sized corpsman told the doc aboard the helicopter.

For Sather, waking life became like a bad dream. He opened his eyes to see a team of medical people wearing surgical masks. One was cutting away the leg of his trousers and another held a soft cloth. When the soft cloth was used to clean his knee wound, the pain was excruciating. It felt like someone was scrubbing the open wound with a steel brush. Sather's face contorted in agony as he tried to keep from screaming, and he may have screamed before he passed out from the pain.

The next time Sather opened his eyes he was lying in a hospital bed with IVs connected to both arms. There was a big sling over his bed and his injured leg was raised up over his head. Lying flat on his back he couldn't see into the sling.

"Is my leg still there?" Sather asked the first person he saw.

"Yes. The air needs to get in there to help it heel. You had some infection," the corpsman told Sather as he lowered the sling so Sather could see that his leg was still there. The wound, exposed and wide open, looked really nasty.

"We have to keep washing and cleaning it. Your leg was peppered up and down. It's a sloppy wound. You could have bled to death. The corpsman saved your life."

"I know he saved my life. He's from Alabama. You know him?" Sather asked. The doc indicated he did not. "Am I going to be able to walk?" Sather asked.

"They had to rebuild everything. You've got a fiberglass plate. You got fibers interwoven with muscles. You got muscles interwoven with bones. They took a lot of measurements to make you a kneecap."

"Am I going to be able to walk?" Sather repeated his question.

"Depends. Depends on how well you do. Depends on how you do in therapy," the doc told him.

"I'll work my butt off," Sather said.

"Not for a while. There's a pin in there right now. You couldn't bend your leg if you wanted to. In about two to three weeks, if everything goes right, you can start physical therapy."

Sather's open wounds healed and he worked his butt off in physical therapy. Enduring the pain, he regained the use of his leg through exercise. When he reached the goal of holding up twenty-seven pounds, he was discharged from the hospital. Sather was reassigned to something less hazardous, because this was the second time he had been wounded—the first time was by shrapnel during a mortar attack. Sather was sent to Hill 55 to work in the headquarters mailroom, where he sorted the mail and bagged it for delivery to units in the field.

Sather took the mail to the helicopter pad, but instead of just loading it as he was supposed to, he climbed aboard and flew to his old unit to look someone up.

"Where's the corpsman?" Sather asked.

"Which one?" a Marine from his former unit wanted to know.

"The short one from Alabama. I want to thank him for saving my life," Sather answered.

"I hate to be the one to tell you this. He was killed in action about a month ago," the Marine responded.

21

NIGHT PATROL

In June 1968, Paulseth was part of a nine-man squad on a night patrol. They walked through the dark looking for the enemy for hours. At about 0200 they arrived at the ARVN camp near Marble Mountain and received clearance to enter the camp. Shortly thereafter the camp came under attack.

Paulseth spotted a muzzle flash outside the perimeter and returned fire. The flash reappeared from the same spot. For a second time Paulseth shot back. The size of the enemy force was undetermined. To get a better angle Paulseth stood up and fired his M16 over the top of the concertina wire.

He received a shock to his arm and thought, *The damn barbed wire has been electrified.* He had worked on a dairy farm as a teenager and was familiar with the sting of an electric fence. When he looked down at his arm, he knew he was wrong and the sting was not due to electricity. The lower half of his arm looked half shot off. It was a bloody mess and hurt like hell.

"You okay?" the Marine closest to him asked. Paulseth didn't answer while standing there in shock and holding his arm. At the urging of the other Marine, Paulseth got down into a less-exposed position. He held his injured arm tight to his body. Bleeding profusely and with no end to the fighting in sight, Paulseth feared he might die.

"We got a chopper coming for ya," the squad member told

him as he wrapped Paulseth's bloody arm to slow the bleeding. Paulseth was still worried about the outcome of the skirmish.

A painful fifteen minutes later, he heard the chopper in the distance. He felt a rush of excitement as his lifeline approached. A flare was set off to guide the pilots to where they should land. As the helicopter neared the camp, Paulseth was helped over to the landing zone. Enemy gunfire hit one of the Marines trying to help Paulseth.

"You okay?" Paulseth asked.

"Don't worry. I'm all right. It's just superficial," the wounded Marine assured him, as he winced in pain.

The chopper departed the hot landing zone with Paulseth aboard. The medic tightened the wrap around the upper part of Paulseth's arm to stop the bleeding, but gave him no medication for pain. Paulseth was taken to a field hospital. Due to the serious nature of his wound, he was airlifted to the air force hospital at Cam Ranh Bay, which was about two hundred miles north of Saigon, in II Corps.

Paulseth still had not received any medication for the pain, which had become excruciating. He arrived at Cam Ranh Bay just before daybreak. An ambulance was waiting to take him to the hospital. The first thing the medical staff did was to raise his injured arm and give him a shot in the armpit to deaden the pain. Once his whole arm was pain-free, they shot sterile fluid through his wound to clean it out. A physician checked his elbow; it was intact. None of the bones was broken, but there was a hole in his arm below the elbow. Everything was sewed back together in surgery.

After a week of physical therapy Paulseth commented, "I don't have much feeling in the upper part of my hand. I can only feel the first two fingers and thumb; the rest feels numb."

The physician told him, "That's because you have nerve damage. The damage may be permanent. Right now you aren't able to feel hot and cold. You're going to have to be extra careful not to burn yourself. In time things may get better, or maybe not. But in any event, you're lucky you didn't lose your elbow. And the good news is that in a couple of days you can return to your unit."

Back at his unit Paulseth told Mulvihill, "The bastard shot me. I got this." Paulseth held up his arm to show Mulvihill all the stitches.

"Jesus, Davie!" exclaimed Mulvihill. "Another few inches over and we wouldn't be standing here talking!" Mulvihill said pointing his finger at the middle of Paulseth's chest, to his heart.

22

THE MULE OF
THUA THIEN PROVINCE

altes continued his tour of duty north of Da Nang, in Thua Thien province. He spent most of his time out in the bush, where the elephant grass cut his skin and the rice paddies filled his boots with water. The sweat dripped from his chin as he patrolled the steep inclines of the surrounding mountains.

Baltes joked in a letter to his mother that what he needed was a mule, because of all the gear he had to carry on his back when he went out in the field for extended periods of time. Shortly thereafter, he received a small package from his mother, and inside was a toy mule. Everyone passed it around and had a good laugh. Whenever spirits needed lifting, Baltes took out the toy mule.

Operation Houston IV kicked off on July 24, 1968. For whatever reasons, his unit was not being resupplied. Baltes assumed heavy fighting elsewhere preempted the delivery of supplies to his field unit. Getting the medical attention for the wounded was always a top priority.

The pain of hunger stabbed hard at their bellies, and Baltes knew it was time to be resourceful. "Wanna eat? Follow me." Baltes motioned for the others to follow him to the beach, where a strip of white sand separated the tropical vegetation from the blue waters of the South China Sea. He showed everyone how to dig up dinky little two-inch crabs. Everyone filled up on the tasty little morsels.

On August 9, 1968, Baltes was assigned to guard a bridge near the base. There was nothing to suggest the day would be anything other than boring, until incoming rounds started exploding. Baltes ran for cover trying to make every second count. A protective barrier of sandbags was just a short distance away, but he never made it. An incoming round exploded in his path. Shrapnel pierced his arm, leg, and neck. He was lying on the ground when he regained consciousness. When he looked down at his body he cried out, "Jesus! There's holes everywhere!"

His jungle fatigues were blood-soaked. He had fragmentation wounds to the right thigh, neck, and left forearm. Draining the color from his face was the wound located where his right leg connected to his torso, where the blood was pumping out fast. Already his trouser leg was so saturated with his blood that it could not absorb any more. The pool of blood on the ground around him was rapidly growing. Shrapnel had severed the femoral artery and the femoral vein of his right leg. Everyone, including Baltes, could see he was bleeding to death.

One Marine from his unit hurried over and tried to help. "You been hit and it looks kind of bad," he told Baltes. He knelt down and ripped open the trouser leg to more clearly expose the wound. The gash was wide and deep, and it had partially severed Baltes' leg from his body. The Marine took off his belt and tried to use it as a tourniquet, but that didn't work because there was no place to secure the belt above the wound.

A second wave of incoming rockets started exploding around the bridge. The Marine stayed at Baltes' side, stubbornly trying to make the tourniquet work. He kept trying to position his web belt above the wound to slow the flow of blood. As he worked Baltes' complexion grew pale. The web belt kept slipping down, making it ineffective. The

Marine was no corpsman, but he knew that he had to get the tourniquet to tighten above the severed arteries. It was the only chance Baltes had.

A corpsman arrived on the scene, and the first thing he did was to give Baltes a shot of morphine. As the morphine began to take effect, the pain disappeared from Baltes' face. A retaliatory barrage of outgoing artillery from the nearby fire base slammed into the surrounding hillside. Baltes' fellow Marines formed a circle of comfort around him and whispered words of encouragement. In a weak raspy voice, Baltes said to no one in particular, "Get me my mule." Quickly, a Marine placed the plastic toy into Baltes' hand. In his short life he had been given the last rites twice. Spiritually he was in good shape and it showed.

The 1st Marine Air Wing received an urgent call from Kilo Company for an emergency medevac. Within minutes a helicopter was on its way from Marble Mountain.

"Hey! Look, Baltes! You get the Big One!" one grunt said.

"It's the Jolly Green Giant," said another encouragingly.

Almost before the large chopper could set down, the Marines had Baltes loaded onto it. The web belt wrapped around the uttermost top of his leg continued to hold tight, just a smidgen above the mortal wound. Somehow the determined grunt had done the near impossible; he had managed to get his belt fastened in place as a tourniquet just above the wound. And somehow it managed to stay there!

The large CH-53 Sea Stallion lifted straight up in the air. When it tipped its nose slightly down, the sluggish-looking helicopter took off at record speed. For the second time the Marines of Kilo Company watched Baltes being medevaced out.

When the chopper lifted off, Baltes was still alert and holding his toy mule. On the way to the Phu Bai medical facility he slipped into unconsciousness. At Phu Bai he was rushed into emergency surgery. Then, Baltes was medevaced to the hospital at Camp Drake, Japan.

On August 14, 1968, Mr. and Mrs. Leander Baltes were notified by Western Union telegram that their son had been seriously wounded in action on August 9, 1968. Close to a month later, on September 2, his parents received a Western Union telegram advising them of his arrival at the Great Lakes Naval Hospital, which put him about 350 miles from home.

Almost immediately he was given medical leave. It was a joyous reunion when his father and brother drove from Minnesota to Illinois to pick him up. Baltes was excited to go home. The war in Vietnam had damaged his body for the last time, or so he thought. Unbeknown to him, the mosquito-infested jungles of I Corps had infected him with one of the deadliest parasitic diseases known to mankind.

Baltes wanted to see Candi Dupre. She had been with him at Metropolitan Center when he was sworn into the Marines and was among the fans who had cheered him off the ball field. The last time Gerry saw Candi, the two were waving good-bye to each other as he departed the ball field for boot camp. For Baltes, absence had made the heart grow fonder. He really looked forward to seeing and talking to her again.

Candi could have had her pick of the guys. She was beautiful, petite, and had a nice body, but she was more than just a pretty face. She was opinionated, never pulled any punches, and always spoke her mind. When Baltes phoned Candi and told her he was home and wanted to get together with her, she accepted his invitation. Because of their friendship over the years, Candi was eager to see Baltes. A lot had happened since they had last seen each other, though. She had things to tell him that would not make him happy.

Baltes picked Candi up and drove her to Mondas, a popular Italian restaurant on the east side of St. Paul. For Baltes it brought back fond memories of high school, when the two of them often ended up there on the weekend with a group of friends for late-night pizza. The chitchat and gossip always lasted longer than the food. Baltes looked forward to hearing about all that had happened while he was gone.

"Thank you," Candi said tartly, as she handed the menus back to the waitress who had taken their order. When the waitress was out of earshot, Candi said, "Gerry, I think there is something you should know." She paused to emphasize the importance of her next statement. When she spoke, her words cut like a knife. "I am opposed to the war. I don't believe we have any business being over there," she told him, her voice edged with anger and emotion.

Baltes sat quietly and said nothing. These were not the words he wanted to hear, and it showed in his eyes. An uncomfortable silence followed with neither of them saying anything. Sensing his pain, Candi reached across the table and placed her hand over his. She said, "I know your intentions were most honorable. You were only doing what you thought was right." The touch of Candi's hand felt far better than her words. "I have many friends who feel the same way as I do. In case someone hasn't told you, the war in Vietnam is wrong! I've been protesting against it for some time."

Baltes remained quiet. Her words sounded cruel and insensitive, yet Gerry knew she was just being honest. He tried to maintain a good poker face and conceal his pain. Candi saw past that. Straight from the heart she blurted out, "I just couldn't take it anymore! The last time your mother called to tell me you'd been wounded it was one o'clock in the morning! I passed out on the pool table in the basement!"

Baltes knew she had his best interests at heart. Following a brief silence, he looked at Candi and summed things up: "I am a hawk, and you're a dove. I think we are doing the right thing in Vietnam. That's my viewpoint."

There was a period of silence as both reflected back to happier times. Then Candi smiled and said, "I am just glad you're back."

It seemed like it was taking forever for the food to come. Baltes started to feel sick and began to look ill. "Are you okay?" Candi inquired.

"I don't feel so good," Baltes admitted. "Excuse me. I'll be right back." Baltes got up and staggered toward the restroom. While he was gone, the waitress brought their food. Candi started to eat, expecting that Gerry would return from the men's room any minute.

Inside the men's room Baltes tried to get his wits. One minute he was burning up, the next minute he was so cold that his teeth chattered. He stayed in the men's room for a long time. He became disoriented and confused. He dropped his wallet on the floor and left it there. Inside was three hundred dollars in back pay, which was one-fifth his annual income.

Realizing things were not getting any better, Baltes staggered out of the restroom. As he staggered back toward his table, people stopped eating to watch. They frowned and whispered as he stumbled by them, wrongly believing he was intoxicated when, in fact, he had not had a drop of alcohol. Back in the kitchen one of the workers phoned the police to have Baltes arrested for public drunkenness.

Candi was a nervous wreck by the time Baltes made it to the table. "What's wrong? You were gone for such a long time." Baltes did not respond. "Gerry, tell me what's wrong," Candi said with desperation. Baltes just kept staring down at his plate of spaghetti in a trancelike stupor. "What's wrong?" Candi kept repeating, getting more distressed each time Baltes did not answer. "I'll be right back," Candi said as she hurried over to the pay phone and called a friend to come and help.

When she returned to the table and sat back down, Baltes said his first words in more than fifteen minutes. "We can't stay. I got to go." With that Baltes got up and staggered out of the restaurant. Mentally he was not with the program. Candi hurried after him.

Baltes was more than six feet two inches tall and could cover a lot of ground fast. Before Candi could catch up to him, Baltes was out the front door. He was oblivious to the oncoming cars as he stepped into the dark street. The oncoming traffic couldn't see him. Baltes was right in the path of an approaching car when short, petite Candi Dupre put her head down and made a mad dash toward him. When she hit Baltes, it was more like a tackle, and her momentum carried them forward as the car passed, barely missing them both. The two ended up falling against a parked car on the other side of the street.

Candi got Gerry back to his car, pushed him into the passenger seat, and hurried over to the driver's side. She was about to start the car, when there was a loud knock at the passenger window that made her jump. A uniformed St. Paul policeman was knocking on the window with his nightstick.

"Mondas called. Said you been drinking," the policeman said in an accusatory manner as he looked over at Baltes.

Candi stopped the conversation short. "This guy just got out of Vietnam and he is deathly ill. I am taking him to Mounds Park Hospital."

The policeman flashed his light inside the car and saw Baltes was shivering. "We'll take a look at him."

"You won't need to, because I have already called a friend!" There was no mistaking that Candi was both upset and sincere. Baltes' short hair made a convincing statement that he was in the military. "I'm taking him right to the hospital," Candi said firmly.

"All right." The policeman stepped back from the window so the two could get on their way.

The doctor at Mounds Park Hospital thrust a wooden stick into Baltes' open mouth. "You have a red throat," he informed Baltes, saying he probably had a cold or the flu, then sent him home. Back home things did not improve. Baltes remained sick and was plagued by fever and chills.

"I can't handle this anymore," he told his family and Candi. "I'm booking a flight back to the Great Lakes Naval Hospital."

Before he left something wonderful happened. He got a surprise phone call from a little boy. "I found your wallet in the bathroom. All your money is still in it," the child excitedly told him, experiencing the joy that comes from helping another.

Baltes checked into the Great Lakes Naval Hospital with a 105-degree temperature. The hospital staff immediately started an IV and gave him alcohol baths. The narrative summary on the clinical record dated October 23, 1968, read: "He returned to the hospital and stated that for the past several days he had temperature spikes with chills. Evaluation was then served at the time with malaria smears and blood cultures. Chest x-ray, temperature spikes persisted. On October 2, 1968, blood smear was positive with Plasmodium vivax. At this time the patient was transferred to the medical service for treatment of malaria."

Baltes had cheated death once again. Upon his recovery he was reassigned to Edson Range at Camp Pendleton, where he was promoted to primary marksman instructor. In his new rank, Baltes was in charge of teaching an entire platoon of boot camp recruits how to shoot and qualify on the rifle range.

In Vietnam, U.S. servicemen continued to gallantly fight and die as more Americans became opposed to the war. Two weeks after the 1969 record-setting Moratorium Day antiwar demonstration, Baltes got an urgent long distance phone call from his mother. With a heavy heart she told her son, "Gerry, I have some bad news. Bobby's dead."

"Bobby Pruden?"

"Yes."

Bobby Pruden lived three doors down from the Baltes family. Bobby and Gerry had grown up together and went to the same schools. And, like Baltes, Bobby went into the military after graduating from high school to serve his country.

"Was he killed in Vietnam?" Baltes wanted to know.

"Yes!" choked his mother. "Can you come home?"

"Certainly."

Baltes arranged for emergency leave and flew back to St. Paul for Bobby's funeral. When one of the pallbearers could not get military leave, the Prudens asked Gerry to fill in. In uniform, Baltes put his childhood friend to rest with full military honors at Fort Snelling. Robert J. Pruden died in Vietnam on November 29, 1969, while serving with the army in G Company, 75th Infantry (Ranger), of the Americal Division. He died a hero and, for his actions in combat, was posthumously awarded America's highest medal, the Medal of Honor.

After the funeral, things were not the same on the street where Bobby and Gerry had once played as kids. As the neighbors returned to their snow-covered homes on Euclid Street, they could still hear the childish laughter of Bobby and Gerry playing outside together. Now the Pruden home stood out as a painful reminder of the war in Vietnam. People on the block could not help but wonder, *Who will be next? How many more young people will have to die?*

In spite of their opposing views about the Vietnam War, Baltes' and Candi's affections for each other grew. On February 15, 1971, Gerald Baltes and Candi Dupre were married. The war that divided a nation could not split them apart. Their love for each other was stronger than their opposing views about the war.

23

OPERATION
PIPESTONE CANYON

Mark Mulvihill knew if he rotated home that someone fresh out of training would take his place. The combat experience he acquired in 1968 was extensive. It would take a long time for a green replacement to learn what he already knew. An inexperienced new guy could get himself and others killed, and that thought bothered Mulvihill. When the time came to rotate back to the States, he volunteered to serve another six months.

By March 1969 Mulvihill was louder and more outspoken than ever. He enjoyed strutting around giving orders. His recent promotion to corporal often enabled him to call the shots. But it takes more than stripes to be a good leader. It takes more than rank to make Marines follow a superior into combat and perform to their fullest. To what extent Mulvihill had those leadership qualities remained to be seen.

Operation Pipestone Canyon started on May 26, 1969, with the objective of getting rid of the 36th NVA Regiment. One year earlier, the Marines had driven the enemy out of Dodge City and Go Noi Island in an operation called Allen Brook. But by 1969 the enemy forces had returned to terrorize the civilian populace into providing food and money for their cause. Small detachments of North Vietnamese and Viet Cong regulars were again attacking the Marine and ARVN bases with rockets and mortars. Mines and booby traps reappeared.

Operation Pipestone Canyon was designed to rid Dodge

City and Go Noi Island of enemy forces, once and for all. The combined operation involved American, South Vietnamese, and South Korean military units amounting to ten infantry battalions supported by large artillery, naval gunfire, armor force, and a provisional land-clearing company.

The operation got under way with 1st Battalion, 26th Marines, and 3rd Battalion, 5th Marines, attacking eastward. For the next five days they encountered increasing resistance the closer they came to Dodge City and Go Noi Island. Sixteen enemy soldiers were killed. Although the enemy soldiers were unable to kill any Marines in direct combat, they fought back using mines and booby traps that wounded one hundred Marines and killed ten. The two advancing U.S. Marine battalions reached predetermined points and stopped. They were not the main body of the American attack, as the enemy had been led to believe; they were a blocking force.

On the morning of May 31, the 1st and 2nd Battalions of the 1st Marines, along with the three battalions of the South Vietnamese Army, swept down from the north toward Dodge City. Marine artillery units and naval gunfire cleared the way for the advancing troops. At the same time, the 1st and 2nd Battalions of the Korean Marine Brigade sealed off areas to the west and south. The U.S. Marines and allied forces had successfully surrounded the enemy. The enemy sites used to attack the military installations along the coastal lowlands of Da Nang were about to be destroyed.

The Marine battalions positioned to the north swept down into Dodge City. The enemy troops wisely chose to flee their bunkers and tunnel complexes. After a week of scattered fighting, the first of many Marine elements began to emerge from the south side of Dodge City. The Ky Lam River was all that separated them from Go Noi Island. For three days the number of Marines poised along the north side of the river steadily increased, as more and more units exited Dodge City to arrive at the river. With the sweep of Dodge City complete, the noose around Go Noi Island was tight.

On June 10, sixteen days into Operation Pipestone Canyon, Mulvihill knew a lot was happening to the south by the number of fighter aircraft flying overhead. The high-altitude B-52 bombers passed overhead and out of sight, dropping their deadly payloads. Seconds later the ground under Mulvihill's feet shook violently and clouds of black smoke rose up on the horizon.

A telltale sign the operation was entering another phase was the sight of twenty-two transport helicopters spread across the sky. After passing overhead they fanned out in two directions toward different landing zones on the southeastern side of Go Noi Island. No one had to tell the enemy there were troops aboard the choppers. American and Korean Marines alighted from CH-46s and began to sweep northward. Squeezed between the blocking forces and the advancing Marines, the enemy's options were limited.

Mulvihill had not forgotten the previous year's island fight on the outskirts of Da Nang, when the NVA had chosen to be incinerated by napalm rather than surrender. Mulvihill fully expected that the enemy would again fight to the death.

Mulvihill's unit was operating from a forward command post in Quang Nam province. As the Marine units on the south side continued to press the enemy and tighten the stranglehold on Go Noi Island, an increasing number of amtracs carrying supplies and equipment to the forward positions came under attack. "Every time we go out, we get ambushed. An amtrac doesn't have any firepower. All it has is a thirty-caliber machine gun," Mulvihill complained to his superiors.

On June 13 something was done to improve their protection. In addition to a machine-gunner sticking out each vehicle's top hatch, the four amtracs going for supplies had a tank at the front of the column and another at the rear. The officer who was put in charge asked, "Who knows the area? Who knows what to look for? We need a volunteer to guide the armored column to Phu Loc to get supplies."

Mulvihill volunteered, for he knew the topography of the river and where to cross. Unlike amtracs, the two tanks in the column couldn't float; they had to have solid ground on which to travel. Mulvihill knew the exact place in the river that would be shallow enough for the tanks to cross over.

When the column reached the river, Mulvihill climbed on top of the lead tank. From there he had the best view of the river and could direct the driver where to go. Before starting across Mulvihill informed the officer in charge of the convoy, a first lieutenant from one of the infantry companies, "Right around the bend is where we got ambushed."

The first lieutenant called to the other officer with the convoy, a second lieutenant, who then walked over to where the convoy commander and Corporal Mulvihill were standing so they could confer together. What the three Marines didn't realize is that directly below where the second lieutenant was standing was a well-concealed land mine.

Apparently it was command detonated, set off from afar by the enemy, as none of them had done anything to set it off. The explosion totally disintegrated the second lieutenant and shredded the convoy commander beyond recognition before the three Marines had even gotten a chance to talk. The blast was so strong that it killed or wounded many of the infantrymen who were standing near the tank. Mulvihill took shrapnel in his back and arm, and both of his eardrums ruptured from the concussion.

A call for a medevac went out. The chopper arrived quickly but found more wounded than it could carry. Mulvihill's wounds were serious, but when they tried to evacuate him, he refused to go. "It's not that serious," he lied. Mulvihill knew how important his knowledge of the river was to the success of their mission.

"You should be checked out," the corpsman insisted.

"Hey! I can't go!" Mulvihill snapped. With bleeding shrapnel wounds and ears ringing, Mulvihill climbed back up on top of the lead tank, so he could direct the driver to a place on the river that was shallow enough for the tanks to cross over.

The lead tank started across the river with Mulvihill and the corpsman riding in exposed positions on top. The rest of the convoy followed behind. Halfway across Mulvihill noticed something unusual up ahead. Through the clear water he saw a sandbar. *That sandbar wasn't here yesterday!* Mulvihill thought. Then he realized what it was, made a fast grab for his flak vest, and yelled at the top of his lungs, "That thing is a bomb or a land mine! Doc, get off!"

It was too late. The tank was already rolling onto the sandbar. Mulvihill's reaction was to leap off the tank. Just as his legs began their upward spring, the 500-pound bomb went off. Mulvihill was thrown some thirty feet into the air. When he came down, his back, arm, and head hit the side of the tank before his body ricocheted off into the river and disappeared from view. With a new set of wounds that were worse than the first, Mulvihill sank into the depths of the river. No one knew if he was dead or alive.

Mulvihill felt himself being rushed through a shaft toward a bright light. The closer he got to the light, the brighter it became. At the end of the shaft he could see an opening with the figure of a person standing in it. When the figure reached his hand into the shaft, the light followed it. Just as Mulvihill started to reach out his hand to the welcoming figure, he looked back down the shaft and saw the top of his tank. He was lying on top of it and he was surrounded by the Marines who had just pulled him from the river. Looking back toward the light, he could see through the opening at the end of the shaft. On the other side there was a table with a bowl of fruit on the center of it. Three people were sitting at a table smiling at him. One looked like his grandfather and another looked like his uncle. Both had died many years earlier.

Mulvihill kept thinking how much his fellow Marines needed him. If they tried to cross in the wrong place, they would die. He knew his fellow Marines were depending on him to guide them safely across the river. With all his heart he wanted to complete his mission. As Mulvihill was about to enter into the light, he began screaming, "No! No! No!"

Suddenly Mulvihill woke up and he found himself lying on top of the tank, surrounded by the Marines who had pulled him from the river. He was right where he had seen himself lying only seconds earlier. Mulvihill tried to sit up.

"Take it easy. You've got a lot of injuries," one Marine told him.

Mulvihill's head throbbed with pain. He reached up with his hand and gently touched his head. Just touching it hurt. Then he felt something wet and tacky on his hand. When he brought his hand down, there was blood all over it.

"Can you feel that?" the corpsman asked Mulvihill as he poked along various places on Mulvihill's leg.

"No. I got no feeling on the side of my leg," Mulvihill answered. He tried to get up.

"Stay down. You need medical attention. We got a chopper coming," the corpsman told him.

"No! I'm not leaving," Mulvihill informed the corpsman. Then he asked, "Is everyone okay?"

"All five tank crewmen were wounded," the corpsman informed him.

"What about the lead tank?"

"It was totally destroyed by the blast."

Mulvihill refused further medical attention and got up with the same determination that had kept him eating at the diet tables in boot camp. He withstood his own pain and started to help with the other casualties. After the last wounded Marine was loaded on to the chopper, Mulvihill turned to the others and said, "We got a river to cross."

Mulvihill limped to the front of the convoy and climbed on top of what would become the lead vehicle. Inspired by what they saw, the other Marines spread the word, "We're moving out."

With multiple wounds and a head injury, Mulvihill valiantly guided the convoy safely across the river. Only after the Marines were safely on the other side and able to continue their mission without him did Mulvihill permit himself to be medevaced out. When Mulvihill was put aboard the chopper, he had no feeling in his left leg. After the chopper lifted off, the corpsman started cutting off Mulvihill's clothes. His bare body revealed multiple puncture wounds.

"I have no feeling below my waist now," Mulvihill said nervously.

"I'm concerned about that," the corpsman said as he wrapped the bandage around Mulvihill's head wound.

"It's the strangest sensation—like I'm paralyzed," Mulvihill's voice quivered fearfully.

The lone medevac chopper held a steady course for the Da Nang medical facility. Once Mulvihill got there, he was immediately treated for his numerous injures. The cause of his paralysis was a herniated disk in his back and a break in the L1 vertebra. For his actions on June 13, 1969, Mulvihill was awarded the Bronze Star.

PART THREE:
AFTER VIETNAM

24

POST-TRAUMATIC STRESS DISORDER

"Diane, both of them were shot and killed. The one on my left fell and his head landed right on my feet. I was just standing there and no one shot me. It's got to be those prayers, because I should not be alive."

Skip Schmidt told his sister Diane the whole story, knowing that she faithfully went to church to light the vigil candles and pray for his safe return. Diane was pleased to hear her brother acknowledge God, because when he left for Vietnam, he had never said anything to indicate he had any religious beliefs.

Skip hit the streets of Minneapolis wearing his uniform and expecting a hero's welcome. A few days later, Diane saw Skip wearing outdated civilian clothes. "Skip, why don't you wear your uniform?" she questioned.

"Because they ridicule me and make fun of me. They wanted to know how many people I shot. They wanted to know how many ears I brought home," Skip said bitterly.

Diane could see he was deeply hurt and questioned him further. "What else did they say to you?" she demanded to know.

"They tell me the war in Vietnam is wrong. They tell me I was foolish to go."

Diane became defensive. "Skip, I don't care what anybody

says. You have a lot to be proud of. You have served your country so well."

"Right," Skip answered skeptically. He was grateful for her support, but her voice was but a faint whisper in a roar of opposition.

On October 21, 1968, Skip was medically discharged from the Marines and got a job at the Edina Country Club. As 1968 drew to a close, young people from coast to coast protested the war in record numbers. Slowly, but surely, the increasing opposition to the war stripped Skip of his noble feelings. If the war in Vietnam was wrong, what was he to make of his photo "My first NVA"? What was he to make of 2/4's impressive body count?

In February 1969 Skip met Cynthia, a five-foot-four-inch-tall cheerleader with dark brown hair and bluish green eyes. [At her request, "Cynthia's" real name has not been used.] They spent their time going to movies and walking hand-in-hand around Lake Nokomis. They had much in common, and the two quickly fell in love.

Cynthia noticed Skip had trouble being around people his own age, many of whom were opposed to the war in Vietnam. He felt more comfortable taking her to visit his family and relatives. Cynthia knew little about Skip's military service. He never wanted to talk about it, and she was afraid to ask for fear of what she might find out. She did not even know how he had been wounded.

When a news brief came over the car radio about the Vietnam War, Cynthia said something about the "killing," and Skip suddenly became quiet and wouldn't talk. He just drove in silence for a long time. Another time at a drive-in movie, a guy took notice of Skip's Vietnam veteran car sticker. The stranger confronted Skip, saying that he didn't believe Skip was a Vietnam veteran. Skip just sat there in silence, until the guy finally walked away. Cynthia thought it was a strange way to react to the situation.

Skip's behavior continued to change. He unexpectedly quit his grass-mowing job at the country club. He tried several different jobs but didn't stay at any one of them for very long. He started having trouble getting along with people. By the end of 1969, he was often edgy and started fighting with Cynthia over the littlest things. Cynthia thought it was because Skip was having a hard time dealing with the divorce of his parents.

His relationship with Cynthia continued to deteriorate, but their ideas of a good time did not change. He and Cynthia often ended up at John and Diane's house for supper.

"By the way, when are you going to finish my car?" John asked lightheartedly. Skip had recently started to go to auto body school as part of his vocational rehabilitation for his service-connected disability. When John had gotten into a fender bender, Skip offered to fix his car for free. Skip drilled a bunch of holes in the car door to take out the dents. That's as far as he got; he never got around to finishing the repair. John didn't press the matter but sensed something was wrong. It was like Skip was sinking into a hole. There was something inside eating away at him. John noticed Skip was turning into a loner.

After John and Diane finished remodeling their basement, they threw a small party and invited Skip and a couple of John's friends, who were former sailors who had been to Vietnam. As they talked about their Vietnam experiences, Skip, who rarely drank alcohol, began having a few. That was about the only time he would talk about Vietnam.

As Skip talked about Vietnam, he became very nervous and excitable. The former sailors shot suspicious glances back and forth at each other as they listened to him. Before Skip could finish one sailor interrupted, "Oh come on! That didn't really happen. You're making it up."

In an angry outburst, Skip started shouting at the big sailor and threatening him with violence. John grabbed Skip and dragged him outside, where he tried to calm him down. "I understand what's going on," John said, trying to console Skip and share in his disappointment for not having been believed. "And you've had too much to drink."

Once outside with John, Skip just broke down and started to cry without saying why. John was one of the few people Skip could cry in front of. Later that evening, after everyone had left, John told Diane, "I know Skip's hurting terribly inside. It's like he crushed about something."

"What's happening to him?" Diane pressed her husband.

"To be quite honest with you, I don't know. He's not letting anything out. I have my ideas on what the real problem is."

"What? Tell me," Diane insisted.

"I think when he returned from Vietnam, he thought he was going to be a hero, and that people were really going to be proud of him. I think coming back from overseas and not getting the recognition that he thought he should was devastating," John told her.

Diane and John strongly believed Skip's problems were somehow service related. They noticed how hard it was for Skip to deal with people's attitudes about the war. When Skip returned from Vietnam, he was proud of his disfigured hand and actually showed it off. They noticed that now, when around people he didn't know, he would hide it from view by placing his good hand over the top of it. During this trying period, the bond between Skip and John grew stronger. Skip knew John would be there for him. "Diane, he did a lot of crying again. I told him that was okay. I told him it was okay to do that sort of thing," John told her.

It was difficult for Cynthia to understand how her boyfriend could go from being a fun-loving person to someone who was always arguing and fighting. But because of all the fun times they had had in the beginning, she hung in there.

It was very clear to everyone Skip was unhappy. He was suffering from something, and his family could see he was in need of more help than they could give him. Skip's family agreed the place to go for help was the Department of Veterans Affairs (VA).

On November 9, 1970, Skip was taken to the VA to be interviewed by the Day Hospital staff. The VA admitted Skip to the Day Hospital for a twenty-four-day evaluation and treatment period. The evaluating psychologist's diagnosis was "anxiety reaction in a paranoid personality."

The second clinical report, written on January 20, 1970, by the director of the Day Hospital stated:

> This twenty-one-year-old veteran was admitted to the Day Hospital on November 9, 1970. At this time the veteran stated he was experiencing difficulty in getting along with people. The veteran stated that prior to going in the service he did not have those kind of feelings. The patient has started the Day Hospital program. He participated in all of the prescribed activities during the first week. However, as the patient began to stay in the Day Hospital, it became apparent to the staff that the patient was not interested in following through with the suggestions as offered to him by the staff and other patients. He was sporadic in attendance. Patient, on his own, terminated his affiliation with the Day Hospital Program and was therefore discharged on January 20, 1971. Diagnosis—emotionally unstable personality.

The VA concluded that Skip's symptoms fit a well-defined mental illness that had nothing to do with his military service.

Skip tried to make use of his VA vocational schooling by getting a job at Teigen's Body Shop. He worked there as a body-and-fender man and limited his friendships. He often complained to Cynthia that he was having troubles at work and blamed his boss for them. He continued blowing up at people. The ups and downs of their relationship were starting to wear Cynthia down. Their future together did not look bright. She felt that she had to make a break and start a new life without him.

There was an unexpected knock at Diane's door. It was an old friend of Skip's who had served in the army. "Come on in," Diane invited.

"I'm here about Skip," he said awkwardly.

"What about Skip?"

"Do you realize what a hard time he is having?" Skip's friend inquired.

"We know he's not been himself for a while. We're all very concerned about him."

"Do you know about the dreams?"

"What dreams?" Diane questioned.

"A couple times, when I needed a place to stay, Skip put me up in his apartment and I stayed overnight."

"Yes," Diane responded.

"He has a terrible time at night! I mean, the *dreams* he is having! He wakes up in the middle of the night screaming his head off and reaching for a gun! And he's wringing wet! I thought somebody should know."

Equipped with this new information Diane questioned her brother about it. Skip opened up a little. "Yeah, I have dreams . . . no, nightmares. I can't sleep at night," he confessed.

"What are these dreams, these nightmares, about?" Diane wanted to know.

"Vietnam," Skip answered.

"How long has this be going on?" Diane persisted.

"For a while," Skip admitted.

"Why didn't you tell us?"

Skip shrugged; he didn't know why. Then he stated, "Diane, I shouldn't even be here. I shouldn't even be alive."

Diane cringed. It was the same thing Skip had said when he first got home, only this time he did not make it sound like he had beaten odds. "Skip, what are you talking about?" Diane demanded to know.

"All my friends died. Some died in my arms. They're all dead. Everybody died." Skip sounded distressed and depressed.

"Skip, that's not your fault. It's not your fault," she insisted. The sadness in his eyes told her that he didn't believe her.

Diane was sure she was right about the cause of Skip's problems and phoned her mother. "Mom, it's the hell he saw. It's the people he made friends with over there, and how everybody died—a lot of them died in his arms. He can't understand why he came out alive. He's still living in Vietnam. He's never really come home. I think that's his problem."

At the urging of his family Skip returned to the VA for more help. The VA reviewed Skip's symptoms. Could it be that Skip was suffering from something like "shell shock," "combat fatigue," or "combat exhaustion," which were well-documented forms of combat neurosis? The problem in making such a diagnosis was that the symptoms of combat neurosis develop rapidly after the traumatic event—not a year or two later.

A newly published book, *Massive Psychic Trauma,* was beginning to circulate within the scientific community. It was a comprehensive presentation of clinical findings by psychoanalysts and psychiatrists, who had extensive experience with the treatment of survivors of Nazi extermination camps and the atomic bombings of Japan. Of particular interest was the "survivor syndrome." Some of the common psychiatric conditions being noted among the survivors were a depressive mood, a tendency toward withdrawal, short-lived angry outbursts, feelings of helplessness, insomnia, nightmares, and fear of renewed persecution that often culminated in paranoid reactions.

Perhaps the most interesting aspect of these findings was the existence of a relatively symptom-free interval between the traumatic event and the onset of symptoms, which were sometimes months or years later. This symptom-free interval was characteristic particularly among victims who were the only or nearly only survivors. These survivors carried, in addition to the burden of their trauma, a second burden: ever-present feelings of guilt for having survived the calamity to which the others had succumbed. It was also noted that survivors would have crying spells, where they would just break down into tears when confronted with their past trauma.

One of the contributors to the book, Dr. Emanuel Tanny, M.D., a practicing psychiatrist and a clinical associate professor of psychiatry at Wayne State University in Detroit, Michigan, wrote in reference to the survivors of Nazi persecution:

> For the last eight years, I have been a consultant to the Veterans Administration Regional Office in Detroit. Over and over I was impressed with the fact that psychic traumatization is either not recognized, or is minimized even in the VA. The conventional approach to psychic trauma prevails and is characterized by the assumption that the patient is malingering, or at least exaggerating.

> The manifestations are expected to fall into the
> category of some well-known clinical entity.

In his summary statement Dr. Tanny warned, "If one does not pay close attention to all these pitfalls, the patient must defend himself by keeping the treatment infrequent, short-term, or quitting prematurely—against psychiatric advice."

In June 1969, President Richard M. Nixon fulfilled his campaign promise to bring the troops home. He announced the withdrawal of twenty-five thousand American troops from South Vietnam. By the end of 1971 American troop strength in Vietnam was down from 536,000 to only 140,000. On March 30, 1972, North Vietnam launched a major offensive across the DMZ into South Vietnam. A few weeks later, on May 1, the North Vietnamese captured the city of Quang Tri. Most Americans went about their business of turning a blind eye toward South Vietnam. But unlike most Americans, Skip was familiar with Quang Tri. Four years earlier to the day, Skip was ten miles north of Quang Tri, fighting the battle of Dai Do. To hear that the city had just fallen into communist hands made for a bitter reality. He wondered what his buddies had fought and died for.

Skip's problems continued. He looked like a civilian with his long hair and mustache, but Diane still suspected that behind the facade he was still very much a Marine and that his Vietnam experiences were still very much on his mind. "Are you still having trouble sleeping?" Diane asked.

"Yes," Skip admitted. He dreaded going to sleep, for with sleep came the night tremors.

"What's the VA doing to help you?" Diane asked her brother.

"They've got me on sleeping pills." Again, Skip brought

up a frightening subject. "Diane, I don't know why I am alive. Everyone I know is dead. I should not be alive."

"Skip, you shouldn't feel that way," Diane insisted.

Skip continued to isolate himself from others and became even more of a loner. The apartment Skip rented in Minneapolis turned out to be just one room in a boarding house. He shared a common bathroom and kitchen with the other residents.

On Halloween 1972 Diane's doorbell kept calling her to the front door. Every few minutes she opened the door to be greeted by little kids dressed up like spooks and goblins. "Trick or treat," the children giggled and yelled, holding up their bags. At one point, while Diane was dropping candy into their bags, the phone rang. She finished handing out the treats and hurried over to the phone.

"Hello," Diane said cheerfully. It was Skip.

"I'm looking for Mom. Is she there?" Skip asked.

"No, Skip, Mom's not here. Are you sleeping any better?" Diane wanted to know.

"Not really. Diane, it's not possible for anyone to live like this. This has been going on for too long." Skip sounded depressed. Then her doorbell rang; it was more kids wanting treats.

"Skip, I've got more kids at the door. Can you hold on?"

"I forgot it was Halloween. I'll let you go," Skip responded.

"Okay." Diane hung up and hurried to the front door. She spent the remainder of the evening handing out candy.

On November 15, 1972, Skip's oldest sister Colleen phoned Cynthia. "Cynthia, have you heard from Skip?" Colleen asked.

"Not for a couple days. We had another falling out. We broke up again," Cynthia answered honestly.

"We haven't heard from Skip, and we can't reach him by

phone. Could you go over and check on him?" Colleen asked. "See if his car is there, then call me back. I'm at work."

Cynthia hung up the phone. The last time she had seen Skip was two days earlier, when she had broken up with him. He had walked off crying and kept saying, "I can't take it anymore! I can't take it anymore! I can't take it anymore!"

Cynthia telephoned Skip. After a couple of rings, someone living in the boarding house answered the phone.

"Hello," a man answered.

"Is Skip Schmidt there?" Cynthia asked.

"I'll go see." A few minutes later the man returned to the phone and said, "I knocked on his door. There's no answer."

Cynthia hung up the phone. No matter how many times they fought and split up, Skip would usually call her the next day, but this time he hadn't.

Cynthia had a really bad feeling as she drove over to Skip's place. She saw his car parked out front as she went inside the boarding house to his room. Cynthia knocked on Skip's door. There was no answer. She tried opening the door, but it was locked. She went down downstairs and knocked on another door. An older man opened his door and Cynthia said, trying to remain composed, "There's been no answer. I'm very concerned about Skip because he's been sick."

The older man was able to secure a key and together they returned to Skip's room. The man opened the door a few inches and then pulled it closed. He turned to Cynthia and said, "You don't want to go in there!"

"Why?" Cynthia asked. Then she started to cry, because she already knew.

When the medical examiner entered the room, Skip was hanging from a closet door, with his feet touching the floor. A white cloth belt was tied to a doorknob and passed up and over the top of the door and around his neck. He was dressed in a shirt and blue jeans; his body was cold to the touch and was with full rigor. The room was neat and clean. No note was present. There was no evidence of any drug use.

The family felt Diane should be the one to call the priest, as she had been the one who lit the vigil candles and prayed for Skip's safe return from Vietnam. Diane phoned Father Robert Vashro. When she and John got married, he was the priest who performed the ceremony.

"Father Vashro, this is Diane Van Bergen. My brother Skip just died."

"I'm so sorry to hear that," consoled the priest.

"I'm calling to make arrangements for my brother's funeral, and we would like to have a mass said for him," Diane continued.

"How did he die?" questioned the priest.

"Suicide. He was a Vietnam veteran, and he saw a lot of heavy fighting over there. When he came back, he kept having horrible nightmares and couldn't sleep. He was being treated by the VA when he committed suicide," Diane told the priest.

"Diane, we cannot say a mass for him. Suicide is a mortal sin. A mortal sin is a very grievous sin. The commandment *thou shall not kill* applies to the taking of one's own life as well."

"But, Father! Skip couldn't sleep. He was sick."

"Exactly how did your brother die?"

"He hanged himself," Diane said, her voice starting to quiver.

"I'm sorry, Diane. Your brother deliberately and willfully took his own life," the priest said angrily.

"No, he didn't. No, he didn't," Diane sobbed.

Diane was devastated, because in the Catholic faith, if you die with a mortal sin on your soul you go to hell—not just temporarily, but for all eternity. It was bad enough to know she would never ever see Skip again. But to think that Skip was burning in hell, suffering in great agony and would be for all of eternity, was unbearable.

The Schmidts were able to take Skip's body into the church and have prayers said, but there would be no mass said for the sinner, Wallace R. "Skip" Schmidt.

The Schmidt family drew together and picked out 5 Matthew for the prayer card:

> Blessed are they that mourn, for they shall be comforted. My Jesus, have mercy on the soul of Wallace R. "Skip" Schmidt. Born November 18, 1948. Passed away November 15, 1972. O gentlest heart of Jesus ever present in the blessed Sacrament; ever consumed with burning love for the poor captive souls in Purgatory, have mercy on the soul of thy departed servant. Be not severe in thy judgment but let some drops of thy precious blood fall upon the devouring flames and do thou O merciful Savior send thy angels to conduct thy departed servant to a place of refreshment, light and peace. Amen.

After Skip's death, Diane wondered if Skip would have been better off without her prayers. What was the point of lighting all those vigil candles and praying for Skip's safe return only to have this happen?

For eight years after Skip's death, the Schmidt family tried to convince the authorities that the war had been a major factor in their son's death. When all was said and done, the doctors, the government, and even the church held to their original belief that Skip was a sinner and a flake. The closure the Schmidt family hoped for never came. The circumstances surrounding Skip's death left an open wound that would not heal.

Not a day went by that Eugene wasn't thinking about Skip. He was painfully aware that he knew very little about his son's combat duty and would probably never know. When the gnawing pain of guilt would bite at his heart, he would tell himself, *I should have been more of a hugging father instead of a Gunnery Sergeant Dad.*

Jackie was angry with her brother. She was mad that he had brought so much hurt to the family. *How could he do that to us?* she would think as tears filled eyes. Diane could not accept her brother's death and would think, *My brother did not commit a mortal sin. If anything, society did, for sending those guys over in the first place.*

Skip's suicide left them with many unanswered questions. Monica would sometimes say, "I sure wish we would hear from somebody who knew Skip in the service. I wonder if he was liked by the other Marines?"

Similarly, Diane would say, "I would like to talk to somebody who served with Skip in Vietnam, so we could find out what happened to him over there." The chance of that happening was unlikely, because most of the Marines who served with Skip never survived their tour of duty.

As more time passed, the number of Vietnam veterans committing suicide continued to grow. Concerned people started to investigate. In 1980 the third edition of the American Psychiatric Association's *DSM III: Diagnostic and Statistical Manual of Mental Disorders* gave Skip's illness a name. It was called post-traumatic stress disorder, or PTSD for short. The exact number of Vietnam veterans who committed suicide as a result of their military service will never be known, but there is much to suggest the numbers are huge. By 1985 the VA quietly opened 135 veteran centers across the country to help Vietnam veterans suffering from PTSD. More than two hundred thousand Vietnam veterans sought treatment. The number of veteran centers would ultimately total 206. Unfortunately, the Schmidt family never heard a word about any of this, because PTSD was not recognized by the VA at the time of Skip's death.

25

ANGUISH

On his first day back to Minnesota from Vietnam, Larry Jones walked into a bar on University Avenue and sat his shrapnel-filled body down on a barstool. His military haircut set him apart from the rest. After thirteen months in Vietnam, it felt good not having to worry about incoming rockets and ground attacks.

It was hard for him to hear exactly what was being said by the people around him, because an exploding mortar had damaged his eardrum. He could, however, hear one guy talking about the Vietnam War in unfavorable terms. To Jones, who had been away for more than a year, the man's negative words sounded radical and hard to stomach. He tried to ignore the man speaking out against the war. He thought, *Snap out of it! You're home now! You made it! You're out of that damn place! Don't let that loudmouth ruin everything.*

Finally, Jones could not take it anymore. He pushed himself away from the bar and walked over to confront the man bad-mouthing the U.S. presence in South Vietnam. "I am tired of listening to all your bullshit," Jones told the man.

The man smashed Jones in the face with a beer bottle. Jones fell to the floor and the assailant jumped on top of him. Somebody pulled the man off and Jones got back on his feet. The two men faced each other in silence. When Jones glanced around the bar, he saw everyone staring at him with contempt. He reached up with his hand and felt his upper lip; it was split open.

Jones had a hard time with the way people were looking at him. No one seemed to care that he was bleeding. No one was reprimanding the man who had attacked him. Instead, they all just stared coldly at him. Jones wondered, *Why? I didn't start the fight! I didn't throw the first punch! All I did was stand up for my country.*

To the patrons in the bar on University Avenue, Jones represented something unconscionable—the war in Vietnam. Their silence and icy expressions told Jones to leave. Holding his hand over his mouth, Jones headed for the door. No one followed or offered to help. The split lip was bad enough to require stitches, but Jones could not bring himself to seek medical help. To have to explain the situation to somebody would have been too painful. Instead, he drove around in his car for hours, trying to sort out his mind. Eventually the bleeding stopped, but his upper lip would be scarred. To cover the ugly reminder of his welcome home, Jones grew a mustache. From that night on, Jones had no desire, or intention, of ever talking about Vietnam again.

Larry Buske was honorably discharged in February 1970. After returning from Vietnam, his alcohol consumption started to become a problem. He stopped at the bar on Friday nights after work and did not return home until Sunday.

"Get him some counseling. There's something wrong with him!" Buske's father-in-law would say. That never happened, and his marriage lasted only six months. Buske later met Rhonda Hantge. Their dates often ended up in a bar where Buske would start to drink. When he drank he thought about the war and his true feelings came to the forefront. Thinking about Vietnam would make him become depressed. He kept his thoughts and feelings to himself and would sneak off to be alone.

After the two fell in love and got married, Buske would wake up during the night to go to the bathroom. Sometimes he would not return to bed. When he turned up missing, Rhonda would go out to look for him. One time she found him curled up on the ground sleeping in a nearby park. Another time she found him underneath their car.

Buske's parents and family were at a loss over what to do. He tended to be a bit unpredictable, and once even hit his brother without knowing why. At times he would become combative and spout off to people. It seemed like he was always looking for a fight. This was not the behavior that got Buske his military conduct marks of "excellent" and "outstanding." Buske told no one about the guilt he felt for having served in Vietnam.

Robert Gates was honorably discharged from the Marine Corps on March 23, 1970. One of the first things he did was hit the bottle pretty hard. It was no secret Gates liked to drink and have a good time. But this time things were different; he was bitter and felt slighted. While he was fighting in Vietnam, others his age were back home tossing beach balls. They seemed to have no idea about the sacrifices he and his fellow servicemen had made. What really tore him apart was that most people simply didn't seem to care.

Many of his friends who had not gone into the military were in their third year of college. When the subject of Vietnam came up, as it invariably did, someone would turn to Gates and make statements like "You volunteered for *that*!" or "Nobody took you by the hand" or "Oh, Vietnam! Who the hell cares? Let them fight their own war."

Gates kept his anger to himself. Many nights he would drive to his parents' cabin on Knife Lake, where he would drink alone and think, *Nobody gives a shit about what happened to us,* until he passed out.

Gates continued to get completely blitzed. Drinking was something he enjoyed, for it brought him comfort. Frequently, he went to the local taverns and bars to get drunk. He continued to go alone up to his parents' cabin and drink bottles of wine. In quiet seclusion he drank excessively. Glassy-eyed, he tried to figure out why everything had turned out so miserably. It was hard to make sense of it all. The majority of Americans were rising up and speaking out against the war. He felt hurt and betrayed. He found himself on the outside looking in. He felt alienated and distant from the peers he had left behind back in June 1967.

On May 6, 1970, less than two months after Gates returned home, more than one hundred colleges and universities shut down as thousands of students joined the nationwide campus protest against the war in Vietnam. Angered by the invasion of Cambodia (South Vietnamese and American forces had attacked communist sanctuaries in Cambodia) and the slaying of the four students by the National Guard at Kent State University on May 4, they boycotted classes on more than three hundred campuses across the country.

Governor Ronald Reagan closed the entire university and college system in the state of California in response to more than 280,000 students protesting against the war. Across the nation, similar protests took place. The feelings many young people had for those who did not oppose the war were of condemnation.

Gates continued to drink excessively. For a full week he remained drunk, without once regaining his sobriety. In the middle of the night he would stumble into the house half bombed. His parents were at a loss for what to do.

One morning Gates woke up on his parents' front lawn. On the ground next to him was an empty wine bottle. He noticed all his personal belongings had been thrown into the street. His first thought was that his parents were really pissed; he was right. His father came out of the house and informed him, "Until you can straighten out, get the hell out!"

Nothing his parents had said or done until then had worked to stop his excessive drinking. They loved him too much to sit by and do nothing. Maybe this would be the strong message their son needed to stop his self-destructive behavior.

In June 1971 Christy Sauro Jr. fulfilled his four-year enlistment, returned home, and rented a small apartment. His mother and younger brother, Mike, lived in a mobile home nearby. Mike was only fourteen years old when Sauro had gone into the Marines. During the four years his brother was gone, he became quite the ladies' man. His mother joked about how the girls were always phoning and chasing after Mike.

Sauro hoped to cash in on his younger brother's popularity with the girls. He wondered what Mike had told his friends about him. One afternoon Sauro went to his mother's place for a visit. When no one answered the door, he used the spare key to let himself in. While he was waiting for someone to return, the doorbell rang. He went to the door and opened it. Standing outside were two good-looking girls.

"Is Mike home?" they asked. Both had long, straight hair and wore tight-fitting hip-huggers with flared bell bottoms. Their brightly colored tops left more exposed than covered. One was barefoot and the other wore sandals. Both looked great.

"Mike's not home," Sauro answered with a welcoming smile.

"Who are you?" they asked.

"I'm Mike's brother," Sauro answered.

The two girls looked at each other with puzzled

expressions, and then laughed. One said skeptically, "Come on! Who are you?"

"Really, I am Mike's brother," Sauro repeated. After being discharged from service, he had let his hair grow long. Maybe that's why they weren't able to make the connection.

"Come on! We've known Mike for years. He'd have told us if he had a brother. Who are you, really?" persisted the one girl.

"If you're Mike's brother, how come we've never seen or heard of you before?" the other girl jumped in to show she could not be easily fooled.

"I've been in the Marine Corps for four years," Sauro answered.

Both girls looked a bit taken back. Then their outgoing friendly manner faded, and one asked rather coldly, "When will Mike be back?"

"I don't know when he'll be back. Can I give him a message?"

"No, we'll see him later." With that the girls turned and abruptly left.

Sauro went over and stared blankly out the window. What had just happened? What did it mean? He tried to keep from reading too much into it. Still, he could not help wondering if his younger brother had been reluctant to tell his friends he had an older brother in the Marines. Maybe the two years stationed in California had made him too paranoid. Maybe he was making something out of nothing. But why didn't four years of military service and having fought for their country prompt one word of friendly conversation?

Sauro went into the living room, where he sat down and turned on the TV. He turned the channel past a few game shows to the noon news. The local newsman looked like he was about to report a disaster. Looking straight into the camera, and with the kind of sensitivity that had kept him on the air for years, he solemnly announced, "According to a recent survey, 51 percent of Americans believe the Vietnam War is morally wrong. Polls show that 71 percent of Americans believe the war has been a mistake."

Sauro turned off the TV. He sat back down on the couch and stared at the empty TV screen. There was a pit in his stomach; emotions long suppressed pounded to come out. He remained seated feeling drained and weak. He had faced crisis overseas without a flinch, like the time when 2/4 had sustained heavy casualties, and he had stood on the hangar deck with body bags stacked up around him like cordwood. The deaths of all those Marines were extremely distressing, yet there was no unbearable pain and no tears. Nature was doing its job. But today something was different. The emotional insulation that had served him so well in Vietnam was noticeably absent. Today, for the first time, he felt real pain—like someone had just kicked him in the chest.

He thought about the military operations and campaigns he had participated in, and how they were responsible for an overwhelming number of deaths. He did not know the actual death toll other than it was substantial. His mind raced: if the Vietnam War was wrong, what did that make *him*? The emerging picture was not pretty. The conclusion seemed inescapable. He had contributed to the wrongful deaths of hundreds of thousands of people. To say he was not somehow responsible was out of the question. He had volunteered for the Marines! He could have fled to Canada, or gone to jail, rather than fight in the war. The choice was his to make. Sauro lowered his head and whispered, "Oh, my God! What have I done?"

The guilt Sauro felt for having served in Vietnam kept eating away at him. A few days later, things came to a head. It was around ten o'clock in the evening. He was at home with his mother and brother. All day long Christy had been a bit testy, but no one gave it much thought. Then, his brother Mike said something too minor and insignificant for anyone to remember, but how Sauro exploded remained in memory. To the shock of his mother, he grabbed his eighteen-year-old brother by the shirt. In a fit of rage he slammed his brother up against the wall with such force that the glass in the nearby window shattered into pieces and fell to the floor. Not knowing what else to do his mother cried out, "Stop it! Please stop it! Leave him alone!"

Sauro looked at his mother. She was visibly shaken and had tears in her eyes, which stopped him cold. His mother was not the crying type. Sauro let go of his younger brother and stepped back. He felt terrible. During the entire episode, Mike never raised a hand to his older brother. Whatever thoughts he had he kept to himself. Sauro looked at his brother, who was glaring back contemptuously. He had seen the expression on Mike's face many times before, when he was stationed in California. It was the same look young people, his peers, who were opposed to the war gave him because he was in the military. It was a look of loathing and disgust. A look that said, *Please leave! Go on! Get out of here!*

Without a word, Sauro grabbed his winter coat and left. He got in his car and drove away into the night. Since his return from Vietnam in January 1969, the war had kept closing in on him like a vice. Vietnam was like living a nightmare from which there was no awakening and no escape. Every time there was something new to suggest that the U.S. military involvement in the Vietnam War had been wrong, the vice tightened. The crushing conclusion was that Americans were the bad guys. Like other Vietnam veterans, he was left holding the bag for the hundreds of thousands of North Vietnamese patriots who were killed fighting off the invading army of Americans. Inside,

Sauro felt like he was being torn apart. The Vietnam War was wrong. He had made the wrong decision. Serving in Vietnam cut at his heart like a knife. As he drove east on Interstate 94 toward St. Paul, he could not help thinking about something he had been taught as a child: *Thou shall not kill*! The wording of the commandment was painfully clear. There were no exceptions. It did not say, "Thou shall not kill except when fighting for freedom and democracy." The wrongful taking of one human life seemed unforgivable. Once a life is taken it can never be returned.

Participating in the wrongful killing of just one person would have been bad enough, but Sauro knew the number of lives involved was staggeringly higher. The Vietnam War was another Holocaust. He imagined that the American soldiers who fought in Vietnam would go down in history and be hated like the Nazi soldiers he had grown up despising.

Sauro drove the streets under the cover of darkness for hours, trying to sort things out in his head. He thought, *The day will come when I'll have to answer for what I did—not in some court of law but before some higher power*. To be standing in judgment surrounded by the Vietnamese killed in the war was not a pleasing thought; nor was the idea of going to hell.

After a little more driving around Sauro came up with a better scenario. He thought, *Religion is just a bunch of hocus pocus. There is no such thing as God. I have never seen any proof*. For someone who rarely went to church before going to Vietnam, and not at all after, these thoughts made it easier to justify his new view. He thought, *The world is so screwed up, how could there possibly be a God!* Not believing in God meant he no longer had to worry about being eternally damned. By the end of the night, Sauro felt better but the guilt remained.

Sauro's adjustment to civilian life was typical of many other Vietnam veterans. He kept quiet about his military service and took advantage of the GI Bill. In 1973 he graduated from the University of Minnesota with a Bachelor of Arts degree. He was hired by Mutual Service Insurance, a local insurer that went by the abbreviation MSI, before it later became a part of a larger insurer known as Country Insurance & Financial Services. In addition to pursuing his new career as an insurance agent, he continued his education and earned a Bachelor of Technology degree from Northwest Missouri State University in 1975.

Bruce Sommer completed his thirteen-month tour of duty in Vietnam and voluntarily extended it. One time he was supposed to have been on a plane that crashed and his name was on the manifest. Back at his section, when they announced the casualties from the crash, Sommer got to a phone and called his captain to let him know that he was still alive. The incident stuck in his mind and months afterwards he thought, *Maybe I am being saved for something. Maybe I am supposed to affect somebody someplace or have somebody affect me—teach me something—or I am to teach them.* Ten months into his extension, his tour of duty came to a surprising end. For some time Bruce had been troubled by the loss of life on both sides. He worked in avionics as a systems technician. There were times when he monitored hidden listening devices that were used to detect the enemy moving at night under the cover of darkness. Bruce helped pinpoint where the enemy was. After the air strikes were called in, what Bruce heard was silence. And it bothered him to think, *Someone's father just died. Someone's brother just got killed.*

Things came to a head one rainy night when Bruce was out guarding fuel supplies. He turned to the Marine next to him and said, "I can't do this anymore!"

The Marine looked totally shocked and then asked Bruce, "How long have you been here?"

"Twenty-two months," Bruce answered. The next day Bruce was sent home. He finished up his enlistment stateside and was honorably discharged in 1971 as a sergeant E-5. He returned to Minnesota and moved into the basement of his mother's house. For the next three months, he stayed in the basement working on a sketch that represented the anguish he felt for having served in Vietnam. For him, working on the drawing was therapy. After Bruce finished the drawing, it bothered him to look at it. He didn't like it and threw it out. Unknown to him, his brother Paul saw it and retrieved it from the trash.

On January 27, 1973, the United States, South Vietnam, North Vietnam, and the Viet Cong signed formal ceasefire agreements in Paris. The agreements required, among other things, the withdrawal of all the American troops from Vietnam within sixty days. On March 29 the last U.S. ground forces left Vietnam. Although the peace talks later broke down and the war resumed, Congress opposed the return of any American troops to Vietnam. By midyear Congress sharply reduced the military aid to South Vietnam. For all practical purposes, the longest war in America's history was finally over. The prevailing mood was not one of joyous celebration. To hear the elected officials say the United States had achieved "peace with honor" rang hollow.

All Vietnam veterans could do was to try and remain detached from the events taking place. ARVN was one million strong, but no match for the NVA, and the entire I Corps area fell to North Vietnam. The ground that the U.S. servicemen had fought so hard to defend was lost. For the people of South Vietnam, the fight for democracy had come to a tragic end. More than one million panic-stricken South Vietnamese fled their homes in advance of the approaching communist soldiers. Fifty thousand South Vietnamese civilians died trying to flee their own country. The United States did little as South Vietnam fell to the communists, and, instead, carried out the will of the majority, who wanted the people of South Vietnam to fight their own war. On April 30, 1975, South Vietnam surrendered to North Vietnam.

Approximately three hundred sixty-five thousand American soldiers had been wounded in Vietnam and about fifty-eight thousand had been killed in action. Additionally, more than ten thousand died from sickness or accidents. Almost four million American soldiers had served in Indochina since 1964. The troubling question, for which no one had an answer was, *For what*?

26

ONE NATION UNDER GOD

February 1978 marked the tenth anniversary of the Tet Offensive of 1968. The major U.S. military victory went uncelebrated. Vietnam veterans tended to keep quiet about their military past. Just how often they thought about the war would have surprised most people. Some thought about Vietnam a few times a month, while others thought about it a few times a week, and still others thought about it daily. This was a secret they shared with no one, not even with each other. There were no words of comfort, no advice for the thousands of Vietnam veterans across the country who were sinking deeper into despair. America had yet to recognize that some eight hundred thousand Vietnam veterans were suffering serious social and emotional problems due to their involvement in the war.

Sauro's parents moved from the city of St. Paul to rural Woodbury, Minnesota, when Chris was eight years old. Three years later, when he was eleven, Chris got himself a job working on the farm of Jacob and Patricia Jordan. For twenty-five cents a week, he did the daily chores, which included milking two cows by hand, and all sorts of other farm labor. It was obvious to everyone that the job was just a pretense so the youthful horse enthusiast could be around some real horses. But it was the Morgan stallion "Coco" that really caught Sauro's eye. Whenever Jake, a member of the Ramsey County Mounted

Sheriff Patrol, saddled Coco up it was a sight to see. The chocolate-colored Morgan appeared in parades and patrolled the fences at one of the state's largest attractions, the Minnesota State Fair. When the spirited Morgan went prancing by people would stop, look, and point. A few years later Sauro's parents divorced and he moved with his mother and brother to North St. Paul, taking with him his dream of one day owning a Morgan horse.

In 1976 Sauro and his wife, JoAnn, purchased a modest rambler on eight acres in Stacy, Minnesota. In 1979, in his spare time, he started to build a pole barn from scratch in anticipation of buying a Morgan horse. But on January 24, 1979, a tragic event caused him to put his hammer down. Although it was unrelated to the war, it would in time become very emotionally relevant for Sauro. Nine-year-old John Frenning, son of Robert Frenning—like Sauro, an insurance agent for MSI (Mutual Service Insurance)—was walking home when he was hit by a car. For a split second, the approaching driver's view of John crossing the street had been blocked by a turning school bus. At fifty pounds, his small body was no match. The boy never saw the car that struck and killed him.

Robert Frenning was a well-established agent. Perhaps if such a tragedy had befallen someone else, the number of lives touched would not have been so great. Word of little John Frenning's death spread quickly. People came from all over for the visitation.

Sauro arrived at the funeral home toward the end of the evening. In spite of the late hour, the large number of visitors had not dwindled. It was easy to find Frenning. The flow of people led directly to him. The strain of the ordeal had taken its toll on Frenning, who looked frail, drained, and weary.

"Bob, I'm so sorry!" Sauro said, as the two came face to face.

"I know," Frenning acknowledged weakly. He put his hand on the younger agent's shoulder and gave a squeeze of appreciation for his attendance. The line of people waiting to see Frenning never seemed to shorten as more arrived to pay their respects. Sauro made his condolences brief and stepped away. He noticed people gathered around a small object on display at the funeral home. "What's going on over there?" Sauro asked.

"It's the Bible the boy was carrying when he got hit by the car! You should see it!" a woman said, her voice rising with excitement as she pointed toward the object of curiosity. Sauro joined the crowd gathered around the item. He could hear people saying to one another, "Look at this. See how it opens along the crease to the same page and passage every time!"

What was on that page that was so interesting? Sauro wondered. Having not read the Bible, he had no idea what to expect. When his turn came, he inspected the damaged Bible and saw how it had been creased in the accident to open to the same page every time. The passage on the opened page read: "For I am now ready to be offered, and the time of my departure is at hand. I have fought a good fight, I have finished my course, I have kept the faith: Henceforth there is laid up for me a crown of righteousness, which the Lord, the righteous judge, shall give me at that day: and not to me only, but unto all them also that love his appearing."

Sauro was unaware of how difficult it would have been to find a more fitting chapter and verse than 2 Timothy, Chapter 4, Verses 6–8, anywhere else in the Bible. He thought it was nothing more than a matter of chance, but it did seem to bring the grieving family some comfort.

On the way out of the funeral home Sauro had to pass by Bob. "I saw your son's Bible. That's really something," Sauro said, trying to make Bob feel better.

"It's consoling for me to know that John had the Bible with him when he died. I know he's in heaven. Still, it's hard to deal with," Frenning told Sauro as he looked over at his wife and four young children who stood nearby. Then Frenning said something to Sauro that, at the time, meant very little, but would remain in his memory: "It's very interesting how the Lord works. He sends us little messages from time to time. But you have to be watching for them, or you'll miss them."

Sauro never told anyone about the recurring funeral scene that he began to imagine after the embarkation officer he served with was killed in action on October 11, 1968. At the time Sauro had only eighty-six days left in-country, but thoughts of going home were not on his mind. Instead he imagined a funeral scene, where the fallen officer's family watched as the officer's casket was being lowered into the ground. That image was followed by another, where one of the officer's loved ones was sitting in a chair staring out a window, too overwhelmed and grief stricken to do anything else. Those scenes persisted, day after day, week after week, month after month, and year after year, until the birth of a very special horse in 1982, just a couple of years after Sauro's dream of owning a Morgan horse came to pass. A Morgan mare that he owned gave birth to a colt. And to the surprise of his wife, and everyone else, he named the colt "Lieutenant Schryver." It was a bolt from the blue because he never talked about his military service. Who this military figure was and why Sauro named the colt after this man appeared in the North Central Morgan Horse Association's bimonthly newsletter that circulates throughout the Midwest to Morgan horse breeders, trainers, riders, and other interested parties. The stallion issue of February 1983, in the farm news section, provided some insights into the colt's naming.

We hope our bay colt, born March 5, 1982, will grow to be worthy of a special honor bestowed upon him. In 1968, while serving in Vietnam, Marine helicopter pilot, First Lieutenant P. E. Schryver, was killed in action. The Sauro Farm has commemorated this exceptional man by naming its first-born colt in his honor. The primary purpose of this colt will be to promote the memory of this brave man who fought hard for peace and freedom. Our intention is to show the parents, and other survivors, of Lieutenant Schryver, that their son, and the great sacrifice he made for his country, has not been forgotten.

In spite of naming a colt after a fellow Marine, Sauro still did not talk about Vietnam or his military service. He continued to keep his experiences to himself. He made no attempt to seek out other veterans or join any veterans' organizations. From the way he conducted himself, no one would have guessed he had been in the service, much less that he routinely thought about Vietnam. And that's how it was with the other members of the Twins Platoon.

On June 1, 1983, a few months after the article was published, Sauro wrote a letter to the Marine Corps to ask for help in locating the officer's parents. The Department of the Navy responded by forwarding his letter to the officer's next of kin. The last known address was fourteen years old and no longer correct; the officer's next of kin had moved from New Jersey to Florida. Still, the letter reached its proper destination. Three weeks later there was a return letter.

Dear Mr. Sauro:

We recently received a letter from the Department of the Navy that had been sent to our old address and was forwarded by a friend. The letter contained an inquiry by you to the Navy Department asking for the address of First Lieutenant P. E. Schryver's parents. We are naturally curious and wonder why, after 15 years, this request is made. If you care to pursue this further you can write to us at the address below and it will be forwarded to us.

Sincerely,
A. E. Schryver

Sauro wrote back, relating how their son was a great leader and a strong influence in his decision to go to college. He told them about the circumstances surrounding their son's death, about how their son's helicopter had gone down and that he had been killed in action. He wrote, "Looking around the room, I could see each Marine trying to choke back the tears. Not even knowing what time it was, I asked if I could go to lunch. Lieutenant McCarthy said yes and dismissed me. I went out behind a supply tent and cried."

Sauro wrote about how he had named the first-born colt "Lieutenant Schryver," in honor of their son, and that every time the colt entered the show ring, it was a living tribute to him.

On September 18, 1983, Sauro received another letter from the officer's next of kin.

Dear Mr. Sauro,
Please forgive me for taking so long to answer your letters. It did bring back some very sad memories. From

the tone of your letter you must have thought a great deal of Peter and still do. The naming of your first colt after him is a wonderful way to perpetuate his memory and I know he would be real proud, just as we are.

When he left for Vietnam I had all confidence in his safe return. We weren't prepared for that night when two Marines stood at our door bearing tragic news.

Perhaps if Peter had lived a full active life he would have accomplished many wonderful things here on earth and his reward would have lasted only as long as someone remembered. I'm only writing this to tell you that through his death he accomplished something that will last through eternity. It was as his mother and I reached out in desperation for strength, along with some miracle that took place, that we found ourselves on our knees speaking to God. From that time until now we have put our lives in the Lord's hands and trust in the shed blood at the cross for our eternal security.

Although Peter's life on earth was cut short as we see life, in God's eyes Peter made the supreme sacrifice for his fellow man and in so doing was also responsible for two souls being eternally secure.

You see Peter accepted Christ as his Savior while still living in New Jersey. We will see him again not as parents and son, but as brothers and sister in Christ.

I hope that I haven't offended you in any way. You see the Bible says that everything happens for the good of those involved. As humans we find it hard to understand this, but God in his infinite wisdom allows all things to take place and we have to trust him as little children. Peter's mother and I do.

We wish all success in whatever you do. Our home is now in Plant City, Florida, about forty-five minutes from

Tampa Airport. If you are ever in the vicinity we would be glad to meet with you.

Sincerely,
A. E. Schryver

After reading the letter, Sauro went out to the corral and looked at the young stallion. With all his heart he wanted the colt to become a champion show horse. But it was an unlikely scenario. He was a novice trying to train his own horse; it was strictly trial and error. The colt's confirmation was less than perfect and his frequent misbehavior in the show ring further diminished his chances of winning. In sharp contrast to Lieutenant's arrival in a rented-by-the-day horse trailer pulled behind a car were the arrivals of some of the top competition in air-conditioned semi trucks with the horses inside off-loaded by an entourage of handlers and professional trainers. Such mismatches were striking. So, when the 1983 show season ended without Lieutenant Schryver having won a single championship, no one was surprised, including his novice trainer. The elusive first-place ribbon and trophy were not Sauro's only burden. There was still the unresolved problem of his Vietnam service. He was still unable to come to grips with his guilt for having served in a war that the majority of Americans believed was immoral and unjust.

From time to time things happen that are most unlikely. Real-life events occur in strange ways, filled with odd twists and improbabilities that turn the seemingly impossible into a reality. And so it was on July 29 at the 1984 District Four Morgan Horse Show, when a dark bay colt rose to the occasion and performed surprisingly well. Afterward, the public address system clicked on and it was announced, "The winner of the two-year-old stallion halter class is Lieutenant Schryver."

Later, at home that night, Sauro held the first-place blue ribbon and the impressive walnut plaque that went with it. The inscription on the plaque read, "1984 District 4 Morgan Horse Show." Every time Sauro looked admiringly at the ribbon and plaque, the word *champion* came to mind. He could hardly wait to write and tell the Schryvers that the colt named after their son was now a champion.

In his mind he pictured them opening the package and lifting out the contents. Upon seeing the ribbon and the plaque they would know right away the colt named in memory of their son had grown up to be worthy of the special honor bestowed upon him. There was one glitch, though. Sauro suspected the Schryvers would feel uncomfortable keeping the ribbon and plaque if they thought they were depriving him of the joy of the trophies. It was a long shot, but Sauro contacted the show secretary to see if a duplicate set could somehow be obtained. He was told that one of the classes had been cut, leaving the show committee with one extra set, which he could have. Sauro and the Schryvers were both able to have a winning plaque and ribbon!

As Sauro was typing the letter to the officer's parents, something interesting happened. When he got to the part in his letter that called for the word *champion,* he could not think of how to spell it! For someone who had used the GI Bill to obtain two college degrees, it was very frustrating, and most unusual, for him not to be able to spell the simple word *champion*! No matter how hard he tried, he could not remember the correct spelling!

Finally, he gave up and got out the dictionary. With the definition of the word under his nose he began to read it. It was no surprise to read that a champion is "one who holds first place or wins a prize in a contest." But the definition did not end there. The definition continued, "A champion is one who fights for, defends, or supports the cause of another."

After reading that part of the definition, Sauro thought, *That's why I joined the Marines. That's why the Twins Platoon stood so proudly before the fans at Met Center. That's why Lieutenant Schryver was flying the helicopter when it went down. They were all trying to help the South Vietnamese people fight for freedom and democracy.* According to the dictionary definition, they were all *champions.* Never before had he heard Vietnam veterans being referred to as champions, but the definition really fit.

Sauro closed the book, recalling something that happened five years earlier, when nine-year-old John Frenning was struck and killed by a car. The words of the boy's father, Bob Frenning, came to mind: "It's interesting how the Lord works. He sends us little messages from time to time. But you have to be watching for them, or you'll miss them." It seemed like he had gotten a message.

When the October issue of the *NCMA* Morgan horse newsletter arrived in the mail, he felt he received another. Sauro was casually paging through the magazine when he saw in bold letters at the top of page twenty-five, "6th Annual District 4 Morgan show, July 29, 1984, Jordan, Minnesota."

The headline jumped out at him—that couldn't be the right date, could it? Was that the show in which Lieutenant Schryver had become a champion? Sauro read down the page to double-check, and, sure enough, Lieutenant Schryver was listed as the winner of the two-year-old colt class. It was the right show, but was it the right date? Sauro went over and checked the calendar, which confirmed the date was not a mistake.

Reading the headline, he realized for the first time that the day Lieutenant Schryver became a champion was his own birthday. It had never occurred to him before because his birthday had been celebrated much earlier in the month with his brother Mike, daughter Angela, brother-in-law Keith, and mother-in-law Donna. Because they all had July birthdays, they got together early in the month and celebrated all the birthdays at one time to make things easier. By the day of the horse show, his birthday was far from everyone's mind. Once again Frenning's words came to his mind.

What he discovered touched his heart in a most personal way. Until now, he thought no one else knew how much he really had wanted the colt to become a champion. Until now, he thought no one else knew how difficult it was to try and sort things out about Vietnam. Until now, he thought no one else knew all his closely guarded secrets. What he read at the top of the page twenty-five changed all of that.

The championship win on Sauro's birthday was a message from heaven that restored his faith in the Lord. The champion plaque that has hung on his wall to this very day reminds him that God knows why he went to Vietnam.

27

TEARS OF BLOOD

There are times when answers to decade-old questions
remain a mystery, when silence and honor are quiet partners,
when old wounds are slow to heal.
—Cliff Buchan, News Editor, "Remembering One Fine
Marine" (an article about Skip Schmidt), July 3, 1997,
Forest Lake (Minnesota) Times

In 1990 Skip Schmidt was high on the list of people who Sauro wanted to see. They had shared many interesting experiences in boot camp and, for two months, had been no more than an arm's length away from one another. While Sauro was stationed in Vietnam, he saw Schmidt twice. The last time Sauro saw Skip it was in May 1968 aboard the USS *Iwo Jima*, shortly after Skip had been wounded in action. Sauro never forgot the shape that Skip was in or the things that he had told him.

On October 27, 1996, Sauro's search for Skip came to an end. He met Skip's family, including Diane, who had remarried, her last name changing from Van Bergen to Finnemann. He learned they had been waiting all these years to hear from someone who had served with Skip in the Marines. He shared with them what he knew about Skip the Marine. It was when the Schmidt family talked to Sauro about Skip that he learned of their ordeal. In Diane's house he saw a photo of Skip in his Marine Corps uniform superimposed in a family photo taken years after his death. He saw and listened to a family in mourning as all of them tearfully told him of Skip's last two years on earth.

What happened over the next six months was truly amazing. Every vital piece of information about Skip's experiences in Vietnam came to light in a variety of ways. When Sauro researched Skip's military and medical records, he discovered Skip was suffering from PTSD. In 1972 it was an illness that had not yet made its way into the diagnostic manuals. If it had, Skip would have been a textbook example of someone suffering from the disorder.

The records also contained a handwritten letter by Skip that detailed his combat experiences. The fighting he described was brutal and horrific. In his letter Skip referred to all the casualties by name. The final lines of his eleven-page letter are compelling: "I was in pretty bad shape that night too. The next day I was OK and I led E Company into another bloody massacre. And H Company the day after that. I can't begin to really explain what it was like seeing your friends die, the bleeding and the smell of burning flesh—no, burning friends."

The information in Skip's letter was verifiable and all of it did check out with amazing accuracy.

A special remembrance ceremony for Skip Schmidt was held at the Fort Snelling National Cemetery in southwest St. Paul on Sunday, June 22, 1997. The Schmidt family met Baltes, Barnes, Buske, Carter, Cirkl, Cusick, Ehn, Gates, Jones, Marlowe, Rice, Ries, Sauro, and Seldon. It was the first time the members of the Minnesota Twins Platoon had come together since boot camp.

Some of the surviving members of 2/4 attended, such as Gunny Brandon, Skip's company gunnery sergeant, and Mike

Summers, a fellow grunt who served in the trenches with Skip; both of them flew in from Oregon. Skip's battalion commander during the battle of Dai Do, William Weise, who had retired from the Marine Corps as a brigadier general, flew in from Alexandria, Virginia, to personally present Skip's medals to the family.

For the Schmidts the years of waiting to meet someone who had served with Skip in the Marines was over. The June 22 program was a solemn but uplifting celebration. Following the ceremony everyone was invited to Diane's house to celebrate the coming together of the Minnesota Twins Platoon. On behalf of the family, Diane handed each member of the Twins Platoon a scroll tied by a ribbon. The document she had penned was worth more to them than silver and gold.

"The Silent Heroes"

It has always been said that war is hell; calling it a
    conflict does not make it better.
When young men die in the line of duty; calling it a
    mistake does not make it all right.
Those who left our country in protest of the Vietnam
    War received a Presidential Pardon and were
    allowed to come home....Forgiven.
Those who stepped forward to fulfill their duty by
    serving our country, never received the celebration
    or the respect they deserved.
Instead, Vietnam veterans came home from an unpopular
    war and quickly learned to be silent.
They did their best to silently cope with the loss of
    their friends and justify why so many young men
    had to die.

They did their best to get on with their life and try to put
the war behind them. A painful silence.
Today you have broke your silence to come pay your
respect to a fellow Marine.
Today we want to honor you. You are the proud: you
are the brave; you are the reason we live in a country
that is free.
Thank you for risking your life for freedom.

Sincerely,
The family of PFC Wallace R. Schmidt
By Diane Finnemann

Before the get-together was over, two World War II Marine
fighter planes appeared overhead. They swept down and passed
over Diane's home three times at tree-top level to honor Skip.

In 1968 Gunny Brandon had put Skip in for the Silver Star
medal for his heroic actions against North Vietnamese Army
forces at Lam Xuam (East) on March 12, 1968. The medal is
so prestigious that it must be approved at the highest levels, by
the commandant of the Marine Corps and the Secretary of the
Navy. Gunny's original requested was lost in the system, but
adequate records remained to put it back on track in 1997.

On February 8, 1998, a second ceremony took place at
the state capitol building in the eloquence of the rotunda. In
Minnesota's Hall of Heroes, Private First Class Wallace R.
Schmidt, U.S. Marine Corp, was posthumously awarded the
Silver Star. More than one hundred people turned out for
the special event, which included three more members of the
Minnesota Twins Platoon: Mulvihill, Paulseth, and Sather.
General Weise, Gunny Brandon, and Mike Summers also

attended, along with Colonel Gavlick, Skip's company commander in Vietnam.

Colonel Gavlick, one of the principal authors of the citation, made the formal reading.

> The president of the United States takes pride in presenting the Silver Star medal posthumously to Private First Class Wallace R. Schmidt, United States Marine Corps, for service as set forth in the following citation:
>
> For conspicuous gallantry in action against North Vietnamese Army forces at Lam Xuam East, Gio Linh Province, Republic of Vietnam on 12 March 1968. As his company was engaged in brutal, close-quarters combat, Private First Class Schmidt remained at the forefront, typically just a few yards from well-positioned and heavily armed enemy soldiers. With both sides fighting savagely throughout the day, Private First Class Schmidt repeatedly fought and crawled through withering enemy fire to first rescue a severely wounded fire team leader, then a squad leader with multiple wounds, and later a combat photographer with ultimately fatal wounds to relative safety.
>
> As Marines and corpsmen continued to fall from enemy fire, and despite sustaining a wound himself, Private First Class Schmidt assumed control of the immediate situation, reorganized the few able-bodied Marines who remained around him, and fearlessly led them in, doggedly dragging other wounded Marines to safety. Private First Class Schmidt's courageous actions,

perseverance, and selfless devotion to duty reflected great credit upon himself and were keeping with the highest traditions of the Marine Corps and the United States Naval Service.

For the President
John H. Dalton
Secretary of the Navy

In a most remarkable way, Skip's family learned the truth about his illness and what a hero he was. Finally, they understood why he took his own life. The time had come for their wounds to heal. At the family's request, a number of Skip's fellow Marines were asked to speak at the Silver Star ceremony. Sauro finished by saying:

Now, after nearly thirty years, Skip is recognized for the hero that he was. And his family knows the truth about his illness, his post-traumatic stress. Why is that? As I think back on the events that have taken place, I don't think they would have been possible without some help from above. I am inclined to think the answer to why this is happening is printed right on Skip's prayer card, which was given out at the time of his death. At the very top of his prayer card is a bible verse that says, "Blessed are they that mourn, for they shall be comforted." I think the promise made in that Bible verse is being fulfilled. I believe the medal Skip's family will get today reflects the recognition Skip got a long time ago in a place called heaven.

General Weise believed, and he stated at both ceremonies, that Wallace Schmidt was as much a casualty of the enemy action in the Vietnam War as were the men who dropped and died on the battlefield from enemy bullets. He believed Skip died from service in Vietnam.

In Washington, D.C., the National Vietnam Veterans Memorial stands, with two adjoining black granite walls inscribed with the names of all Americans who died in the Vietnam War, as well as those who were still listed as missing in action when it was being built. Missing from the wall are names such as Wallace R. Schmidt. The Wall starts at ground level on both sides and ascends upward with its highest point in the middle. Perhaps not intentionally, but most appropriately, its design resembles the tip of an iceberg. Hidden from view is the specter of an even greater number of casualties, those who may have died by suicide as a result of their service in Vietnam.

Bruce Sommer appeared in good health when he returned from Vietnam. A few years after being discharged, he was diagnosed as having Type II diabetes. Because there was no history of the illness in his family, the news was shocking.

In the fall of 2002, Bruce received a phone call from Sauro, who said, "I hear you're not doing so well." When attending a funeral, Sauro had bumped into Sommer's boss who had filled him in on Bruce's condition.

"My mortality has shortened," Bruce said, with a chuckle.

"How disabled are you?" Sauro asked.

"I go for kidney dialysis three days a week. I am losing my sight. My hands constantly tingle, making it hard to pick things up and hold on to them. I eat like a baby and I have to use a walker to get around," Bruce summarized.

The last time the two had seen each other was eleven years

earlier, when Bruce exercised the last guaranteed insurability option on a life insurance policy that Sauro had sold him when he first started working as an insurance agent.

"Bruce, the life insurance policies you purchased have waiver of premium. I'll stop by and help you apply for those benefits," Sauro told him.

Later, when they were face to face, Bruce told Sauro, "I heard my diabetes might be due to Agent Orange, so I phoned the VA and asked them about that. They're sending somebody out and they want all of my medical records." Bruce had something else to tell Sauro. "I have something kind of strange to tell you. Do you remember when you called to tell me about the ceremonies for Skip Schmidt, and that I was invited?"

"Yes, I remember. Why?" Sauro answered.

"Both times, after you called to tell me that there was going to be a ceremony for Skip and that I was invited, I cried tears of blood."

As soon as Sauro returned home, he phoned Diane and told her how Bruce had cried tears of blood after being invited to her brother's ceremonies.

"I would like to meet him. I have something to give him. Would you see if he would be willing to meet with me," Diane asked.

Sauro called Sommer and asked, "Bruce, do you like surprises?"

"No, not at all. What did you have in mind?" Bruce wanted to know.

"When I bring out your insurance papers, I want to bring along someone who would like to meet you," Sauro told him.

"Who?" Bruce questioned.

"Diane Schmidt," Sauro answered.

There was a few seconds of silence followed by, "Yes. I would like that. I have always wanted to meet her."

The best days to meet were Tuesday or Thursday, because

on Monday, Wednesday, and Friday, Bruce went to the clinic for five hours of kidney dialysis, which left him too drained for company.

On August 15, 2002, the two went for their visit at Bruce's home. Diane presented Bruce with his copy of the "The Silent Heroes." Like the others, the scroll came as a pleasant surprise and was the well-deserved "thank you" he had never received for serving in Vietnam.

"Diane, there is something I would like to show you," Bruce said reluctantly. "I have wrestled with this for some time. I have wondered all week if I should show it to you or not. I hesitate because I don't know if it will be helpful or hurtful. I don't want to do anything that would hurt you or your family," Bruce said, trying to find the right words.

"What would you like to show me?" Diane encouraged.

"It's a sketch I drew after I returned home from Vietnam. I don't show it to people. I don't like it. But it may help you understand what your brother was going through. It might help you understand what would cause him to take his life," Bruce explained.

"I'd be honored to see it," Diane reassured Bruce.

Bruce told Sauro where he could find the sketch. A few minutes later Sauro returned from the garage carrying a large black garbage bag.

"Take it into the other room and uncover it. You should see it from a distance first and then from up close," Bruce instructed.

The sketch was an awesome depiction of how many Vietnam veterans felt about their military service. From a distance, the sketch was of a man's head tipped back in anguish. Closer up, it was a mosaic of tiny doodles showing what the returning veteran came home to. Looking at it was like reading a novel and was as personal as a journal.

"I am so glad that you showed this to me. It definitely helps me understand what my brother was going through. What you have done is incredible," Diane told Bruce.

"Chris told me that both times, when you were invited to my brother's ceremony, you cried tears of blood. Is that because of your diabetes?" Diane asked, having not heard of that happening to anyone.

"I think it can be. But it's never happened to me before or since," Bruce answered.

Diane arranged another visit so her sisters could see the sketch. She thought the sketch should be introduced into the art world. Bruce was happy to show it to them but was not willing to let other people see it.

When Sauro returned for another visit, Bruce told him, "I keep thinking of the odd sequence of events that got you here with Diane. How bizarre is that! You're at a funeral. You happen to run into my employer. You happen to have a conversation with him and find out that I am disabled. And being the kind of insurance guy you are, you remember there is this clause in my policy. And that is okay. Had you just shown up and did some business, you would have never seen the sketch, because I don't show it to people. I have never shown it to you before. And I have never shown it to anybody. But because you were bringing Diane . . ." Bruce didn't finish what he was trying to say. He didn't have to. They both knew something special was happening.

In September 2002, the VA notified Bruce that he was eligible for disability benefits. They determined that his disability was service related and his diabetes was presumed to be due to his exposure to the herbicide Agent Orange.

Diane was able to persuade Bruce to let her clean up his sketch and have it framed. She got him to agree to have it made into a print and have it introduced into the art world. Its value was quickly recognized, and in March 2003, the National Vietnam Veterans Art Museum in Chicago, Illinois, acquired Bruce's original sketch. It went on display on the main wall facing the memorial honoring those who lost their lives in the war. This location allowed ample space for visitors to examine and appreciate the detail of his work.

Bruce's health continued to deteriorate and both his legs had to be amputated below the knee. Humorously, he called them "Shorty" and "Longfellow" because one was shorter than the other. He spent his last year in and out of the hospital and nursing homes, where he helped pass the time by taking good memories and enhancing them. "That watermelon that I ate was a little sweeter than it actually was. In that race I didn't come across the finish line in fifth place, I came across in first place," Bruce would explain with a lighthearted chuckle. His failing health reached the point where his doctor asked him if he would like to discontinue his dialysis. After giving it some thought Bruce's answer was no. He explained his decision by saying, "It must be the Marine in me. I can never surrender or give up."

In the early morning hours of September 27, 2004, Bruce Sommer awoke sensing something was seriously wrong. From his hospital bed he pushed the button that summoned the nurse. She took one look at Bruce and hurried off to get the doctor. In the few moments she was gone Bruce peacefully passed away. Prior to his death he had been able to witness the growing popularity of his sketch. In the last year of his life he received an abundance of feedback on how it was teaching others about the Vietnam War. Bruce Sommer's sketch continues to help thousands of people understand the feelings of anguish that so many Vietnam veterans experienced when they returned home from the war.

BIBLIOGRAPHY

BOOKS

American Psychiatric Association. *Diagnostic and Statistical Manual of Mental Disorders IV Edition*, 1980.

Aronson, Elliot. *The Social Animal.* San Francisco: W. H. Freeman and Company, 1972.

Blackman, Raymond V.B. (editor), *Jane's Fighting Ships 1968–69*, London, Sampson Low, Marston & Co., n.d.

Brandon, P. E. *Gunny.* Oregon: Bennett and Miller, 1995.

Burke, Tracey and Mimi Gleason. *The TET Offensive January–April, 1968.* New York: Gallery Books, W. H. Smith Publishers Inc., 1988.

Bowman, John (Editor). *The Vietnam War: An Almanac.* New York: A Bison Book, 1985.

Chinnery, Phil. *Air War in Vietnam.* New York: A Bison Book, 1987.

Dean, Chuck. *Nam Vet.* Oregon: Multnomah Press, 1988.

Ezell, Edward. *The Illustrated History of Personal Firepower. The Vietnam War.* New York: Bantam Books, 1988.

Fails, William R., *Marines and Helicopters 1962–1973.* Washington D.C.: History and Museums Division, Headquarters U.S. Marine Corps, 1978.

Giap, General Vo Nguyen. *How We Won the War.* Pennsylvania: Recon Publications, 1976.

Hammel, Eric. *Khe Sanh: Siege in the Clouds.* New York: Crown, 1989.

Helms, Michael. *The Proud Bastards.* New York: Zebra Books, Kensington Publishing Corp., 1990.

Karnow, Stanley. *Vietnam, a History.* New York: The Viking Press, 1983.

Krystal, Henry. *Massive Psychic Trauma.* New York: International Universities Press Inc., 1968.

Lavigne, Lieutenant J. A., (Editor). *The Ugly Angels: Vietnam 1968 (Cruise Book).* Missouri: Walsworth, 1968.

McCoy, J. W. *Secrets of the Viet Cong.* New York: Hippocrene Books, 1992.

Morrison, Wilbur. *The Elephant and the Tiger.* New York: Hippocrene Books, 1990.

Murphy, Edward. *Vietnam Medal of Honor Heroes.* New York: Ballantine Books, 1987.

Naval History Center, Dept. of the Navy, *Dictionary of American Naval Fighting Ships Vol. III 1968*, series 1959–1981.

Nolan, Keith. *Battle for Hue TET 1968.* New York: Dell Publishing, 1983.

Nolan, Keith. *The Magnificent Bastards.* New York: Dell Publishing, 1994.

Olson, James. *Dictionary of the Vietnam War.* New York: Peter Bedrick Books, 1987.

Owen, Major General J. I. H., Editor. *Brassey's Infantry Weapons of the World.* New York: Bonanza Books, 1979.

Quaytman, Ph.D. Wilfred. *The Vietnam Veteran. Studies in Post-Traumatic Shock Disorders.* New York: Human Sciences Press, Inc., 1987.

Rosen, Ephraim and Ian Gregory. *Abnormal Psychology.* Philadelphia and London, W. B. Saunders & Company, 1965.

Shay, M.D., Ph.D., Jonathan. *Achilles in Vietnam*. New York: Touchstone, 1994.

Shulimson, Jack, Lieutenant Colonel Leonard Blasiol, et al. *U.S. Marines in Vietnam: The Defining Year, 1968*. Washington D.C.: History and Museums Division, Headquarters U.S. Marine Corps, 1997.

Smith, Charles R., *U.S. Marines in Vietnam: High Mobility and Standdown, 1969*. Washington D.C.: History and Museums Division, Headquarters U.S. Marine Corps, 1988.

Smith, Donald (Editor). *Marine Corps Recruit Depot 1967 San Diego, California*. California: Jostens Military Publications, 1967.

Telfer, Major Gary,Lieutenant Colonel Lane Rogers, and Keith Fleming. *U.S. Marines in Vietnam: Fighting the North Vietnamese, 1967*. Washington D.C.: History and Museums Division, Headquarters U.S. Marine Corps, 1984.

Time-Life Books, Editors of. *This Fabulous Century 1940–1950*, Volume V. New York: Time-Life Books, 1969–70.

Time-Life Books, Editors of. *This Fabulous Century 1950–1960*, Volume VI. New York: Time-Life Books, 1969–70.

Tolson, Lieutenant General John. *Vietnam Studies: Airmobility 1961–1971*. Washington, D.C.: Department of the Army, 1973.

U.S. Marine Corps, History and Museums Division Headquarters. *The Marines in Vietnam 1954–1973*. Washington D.C.: Headquarters U.S. Marine Corps, 1974.

U.S. Marine Corps Association. *Guidebook for Marines*. Virginia: Marine Corps Association, 1988.

U.S. Navy Department. *American Naval Fighting Ships Vol. III 1968*. Washington D.C.: Naval History Division, n.d.

Vietnam Veterans Memorial Fund. *Vietnam Veterans Memorial of Names*. Washington D.C.: Vietnam Veterans Memorial Fund, 1982.

Westmoreland, General William. *A Soldier Reports*. New York: Doubleday & Company, Inc., 1976.

PERIODICALS

Greenberg, Lawrence. "With Her 16-Inch Guns, the USS *New Jersey* Was the Only Battleship on the Gun Line in Vietnam." *Vietnam*, February 1990, 16.

Greenberg, Lawrence. "'Spooky': Dragon in the Sky." *Vietnam*, April 1990, 22.

Harkins, Michael. "Magnificent Pressure Exerted." *Vietnam*, Summer 1989, 42–49.

Isby, David. "There Was Nothing 'Guerrilla War' About North Vietnam's Heavy Artillery. It Was King of the Battlefield." *Vietnam*, December 1989, 10.

Morgan Horse, News of the North Central Morgan Association, February, 1983.

National Review. "Eighty-eight Got Away." 1969, 60.

Newsweek. "The Dusty Agony of Khe Sanh." March 18, 1968, cover and 28–36.

Schultz, William. "The Truck That Fled Cuba." *Readers Digest*, July 1969, 98–103.

Scruggs, Jan. "Building the Vietnam Memorial." *Vietnam*, April 1992, 26–32.

Weise, Brigadier General William. "Memories of Dai Do." *Marine Corps Gazette*, September 1987, 42–55.

NEWSPAPERS

Buchan, Cliff. *The Forrestville (Minnesota) Times.* "Col. James Noll will speak at 3rd District memorial program on May 17th." May 7, 1998.

Goethel, Arno. *St. Paul Pioneer Press.* "Boswell Hurls Twins to 3–2 Triumph." June 29, 1967, 20.

Horning, Dick. *St. Paul Dispatch.* "He died protesting! For his country." February 11, 1968, 4.

Hutchinson Leader. "Pfc. Thomas Healy is 3rd area victim of Vietnam War. 1967."

Hutchinson Leader. "Lost in Time" (poem). 1967.

St. Paul Dispatch. "Fifty-Eight men enlist in services." July 11,1967, 14.

Star Tribune. Associated Press. "Increased cancer rate found among Marines who served in Vietnam." September 4, 1987, 1A and 13A.

Swegles, Fred. *The Register.* "Chapman college has 'el toro campus'." August 16, 1969, E10.

The Stewart (Minnesota) Tribune. Editor. "Dear Mr. President." February 8, 1968.

VIDEOTAPES

CBS Video Library, produced by CBS News. New York, *The Vietnam War with Walter Cronkite — The TET Offensive*, 1985.

United States Department of Defense. *The Battle of Khe Sanh*, Spinnaker Software.

PERSONAL INTERVIEWS BY THE AUTHOR (all recorded)

Bain, James
Baltes (Dupre), Candi
Baltes, Gerald
Barrette, Robert
Barnes, Jeffery
Borreson, Bradley
Brandon, Gunny P.E.
Buske, Larry
Carter, Robert
Cirkl, Edward
Cusick, Robert
Cynthia (not her real name)
Ehn, Gary
Finnemann, Diane
Gates, Robert
Goodman, Mary
Gregor, John
Groeschel, Gene
Holzinger, Rudy
Jones, Larry
Knutson, David
Leach, Monica
Marlowe, Terry
Mulvihill, Mark
Page (Schmidt), Colleen
Paulseth, David
Rademacher, Larry
Rice, Charles
Rienke (Schmidt), Jacqule
Ries, Michael
Sather, Timothy
Schmidt, Eugene
Schmidt, Shannon
Seldon, David
Sipe, Robert
Sommer, Bruce
Summers, Michael
Thorkelson, Steve
Tittle (McGraw), Eileen
Van Bergen, John

AUTHOR'S COMMUNICATIONS
Verbal and/or Written

Doble, Tim
DuBois, Thomas
Frenning, Robert
Gavlick, Lieutenant Colonel Michael, USMC
James, Mike
Olson, Mary Kay
Peterson, Calvin

Schryver, Ed
Schryver, Marion
Weise, Brigadier General William
   USMC

MILITARY RECORDS
Baltes, Gerald
Barnes, Jeffery
Barrette, Robert
Buske, Larry
Carter, Robert
Cirkl, Edward
Cusick, Robert
Ehn, Gary
Gates, Robert
Goodman, Kenneth
Holzinger, Rudy
Jones, Larry
Knutson, David
Paulseth, David
Rademacher, Larry
Rice, Charles
Sather, Timothy
Sauro, Christy Jr.
Schmidt, Wallace
Seldon, David
Thorkelson, Steve

MILITARY MEDICAL RECORDS
Baltes, Gerald
Buske, Larry
Cirkl, Edward
Cusick, Robert
Goodman, Kenneth
Holzinger, Rudy
Jones, Larry
Knutson, David
Paulseth, David
Rademacher, Larry
Sauro, Christy Jr.
Schmidt, Wallace

MISCELLANEOUS DOCUMENTATION
Copies of the twelve citations awarded
   to the various units Minnesota
   Twins Platoon members were
assigned to and for which they are
   eligible. They consist of the
   Presidential Unit Citations, Navy
   Unit Commendations and
   Meritorious Unit Commendations.
Copy of the Republic of Vietnam
   Cross of Gallantry and Republic of
   Vietnam Meritorious Unit Citation
   Civil Actions honors, with
   unit time periods for the awards
   and a listing of eligible units.
   Various units the Minnesota Twins
   Platoon members were assigned to
   are eligible.
Command Chronology for HMM-362,
   1 April to 15 April 1968.
Command Chronology for HMM-362,
   15 April to 30 April 1968.
Command Chronology for HMM-362,
   1 October to 31 October 1968.
Numerous personal letters written to
   and by members of the Minnesota
   Twins Platoon while on active duty.
Numerous pieces of correspondence
   between the families of deceased
   Twins Platoon members and
   various agencies as detailed in the
   text and appropriately noted.
In support of the text members
   of the Minnesota Twins Platoon,
   their fellow Marines, and family
   members provided hundreds
   of photos.